When the Final Buzzer Sounds

NHL Greats Share Their Stories of Hardship and Triumph

An Anthology
Including Works by
Charles Wilkins
and
Colleen and Gordie Howe

TRIUMPH
B O O K S
CHICAGO

After the Applause by Gordie and Colleen Howe and Charles Wilkins and *Breakaway* by Charles Wilkins used by permission of McClelland & Steward, Inc., *The Canadian Publishers*.

Library of Congress Cataloging-in-Publication Data

Howe, Coleen.
 When the final buzzer sounds / by Colleen and Gordie Howe and Charles Wilkens.
  p. cm.
 ISBN 1-57243-392-2
  1. Hockey players—Canada—Biography. 2. Career changes—United States—Case studies. 3. Career changes—Canada—Case studies. I. Howe, Gordie, 1928- II. Wilkens, Charles (Charles Everett) III. Title.

 GV848.5A1 H68 2000
 796.962'092—dc21
 [B]
                                                                    00-057759

This book is available in quantity at special discounts for your group or organization. For further information, contact:

Triumph Books
601 South LaSalle Street
Suite 500
Chicago, Illinois 60605
(312) 939-3330
Fax (312) 663-3557

Printed in the United States.

ISBN 1-57243-392-2

Book design by Patricia Frey

For Ralph Currie
who first took me to Maple Leaf Gardens
and for the Grandview Penguins of 1997,
my all-time favorite hockey team.
—C. W.

TABLE OF
Contents

Introduction

When the Final Buzzer Sounds

One of the great NHL defensemen of the 1950s and '60s, Hall of Famer Bill Gadsby, once said to me, "Everything would be fine if the good Lord had given guys like me the capability to play hockey until we were sixty-five. Then we wouldn't have to start life over at forty."

Unfortunately, the Creator was neither a good career strategist nor a perfect general manager, meaning that, for many professional hockey players—the stars as well as the margin-dwellers—life tends to hit a Great Divide somewhere between the ages of thirty and forty.

Some players bridge the divide more easily than others. Contemporary players have often made enough money to compensate for almost any career upheaval that might append their retirements. Others have educated themselves or have an inclination for business or hockey management that makes retirement a relatively natural progression.

But all too many over the years have been unable to make the crucial psychological adjustments that are necessary when they are deprived, often against their wishes, of the camaraderie, adrenaline highs, and intense sense of purpose that has focused their lives as players.

In the pages that follow, stars such as Bobby Hull, Stan Mikita, Yvan Cournoyer, and Phil Esposito describe the strong sense of frustration that gripped them as they cast about for new fulfillment during the years that followed their playing days. Even Gordie Howe and Rocket Richard, whose inspired and inspiring careers might have been taken for the stuff of dreams, suffered disappointment and humiliation upon retirement, even at the hands of the franchises to which they had all but given their lives.

Some players, such as Eric Nesterenko, turned to alcohol and drugs upon retirement. (Reggie Leach jokes that, whereas most players play sober and drink when they retire, he drank heavily as a player and sobered up later.)

Some ex-pros turn away from the game entirely—sometimes to other sports, with mixed results. Yvan Cournoyer turned with limited success to the contemporary sport of roller hockey, as did players such as Ralph Backstrom and Tiger Williams. For Stan Mikita, the transition into the world of pro golf turned out to be the retirement transition from hell.

"Society has such exaggerated expectations of these players that the guys figure they have to put on a successful front no matter what," says Donna Esposito, who was married to Phil Esposito through much of his career. "But a lot of these guys are just lost. And of course most of them are too proud to ask for help. They'll walk into a restaurant, and the manager will say, 'Oh, come on in, great to see you!' They're treated like celebrities, and they're ashamed to admit they're hurting. Their dignity is on the line."

Certainly, the franchises themselves could have done more for the players of the fifties, sixties, and seventies. To this day, many pros of the era have nothing but contempt for those who ran the game. Eric Nesterenko characterizes owners past and present as "really nasty, vicious, greedy, self-serving people." Reg Leach says, "The players are nothing but cattle to the owners. You can give everything to an organization for years, and they'll still dump on you and toss you out the door without giving it a thought."

"The sad truth," according to Colleen Howe, "is that the league is far more concerned that its corporate sponsors be taken care of than it is about the players who have made the game what it is."

When the Final Buzzer Sounds contains the life stories of nine of the finest and most fascinating hockey players of hockey's golden years, the years of the six-team league and early expansion, which many students of hockey consider the historic high ground of the professional game.

In writing the profiles, I have attempted to station myself somewhere between the lionizing mythology that surrounds and even traps our professional athletes and the seldom-witnessed realities of their lives. My subjects were remarkably forthcoming. In some cases, they took me into their confidence with an almost painful honesty. The book, as a result, is as much about vulnerability and survival as about the game of hockey. More simply, it is about well-known hockey players, now retired, speaking with honesty and clarity about who they are, where they've been, and what they've seen and felt. In most cases, the profiles also encompass the players' wives, who for the most part are unknown to fans but who perhaps possess a clearer perspective than anyone else on life behind the scenes and beyond the glory years.

Because the profiles were written not as a single group, but over a period of time, they are collected here with brief epilogues that convey a sense of what each player has been up to since the piece was completed.

It hardly needs saying that book-length manuscripts do not come together without the advice and assistance of many people. This one is no exception. For their help along the way, I would like to thank, among others, my friend Dan Diamond for his assistance and advice; my agent Jennifer Barclay for her goodwill and encouragement; my publisher, Mitch Rogatz, for his hard work and suggestions; as well as James Duplacey and Phil Pritchard, two of hockey's most knowledgeable students, for their generous suggestions and advice.

I would also like to thank my family for their loving patience and tolerance, and Gordie and Colleen Howe for their organizational help, which was instrumental in getting parts of the book written, and for their generosity and friendship over the years.

As always, the process of book-building has been both exciting and instructive, and I trust the chapters that follow will be as engaging to read as they have been to research and write.

Charles Wilkins
Autumn, 2000

Yvan Cournoyer

A Simple Man at Heart

When eight-year-old Kurtis Cournoyer asks his dad for a bedtime story, he knows pretty much what to expect. "Yvan sits down beside him," says Evelyn Cournoyer, "and, without exception, the first words out of Yvan's mouth are, 'Once upon a time, there was a little boy who had a dream.' . . . And Kurtis and I say to ourselves, Oh, no, not the Dream again!"

The little boy, according to the tale, lived in a small town in rural Quebec and wanted nothing more in life than to play hockey for the Montreal Canadiens.

Because he was smaller than most boys his age, he was prepared to work extremely hard to make his dream come true. And every day, all winter, he spent every possible moment either on the town rink or on the tiny sheet of ice in his backyard. In summer, he fired hundreds of shots a day against the wall of his parents' garage.

Eventually, he moved with his family to Montreal, where, as a teenager, he continued to pour every ounce of his energy into improving his hockey skills.

And, sure enough, one day when he was nineteen years old, his hard work bore fruit, and he was summoned by the great coach Toe Blake to suit up with Les Glorieux, the Canadiens, the mythic standard bearers of the pride of French Canada.

He could not have been prouder as he pulled on the Canadiens sweater for his first game. And he could not have been more excited as he lined up for his first shift beside two of the heroes of his boyhood, Henri Richard and Jean Beliveau.

And he could not have been more daunted as he glanced across the face-off circle at perhaps the greatest hockey player of all time, Gordie Howe.

The Little Dreamer scored his first NHL goal that night, and the following season had his name inscribed on the glistening flanks of the Stanley Cup.

"That's where the story always ends," smiles Evelyn, "with the boy winning the Stanley Cup. Then it's lights out."

Were it not for Kurtis's sleep requirements, Yvan could easily extend the triumphal little roman à clef into the wee hours of the morning. He certainly has a storyteller's capital in his nearly five hundred big-time goals, his four All-Star team selections, and his ten Stanley Cups. He could add heroic subplots from the most remarkable hockey series ever, between the Canadians and Soviets, in 1972, or from the 1973 playoffs, when he led all combatants with fifteen goals and won the Conn Smythe Trophy as that year's premier playoff performer.

If he decided to darken the narrative, or take it into the shadows of the campfire, he could introduce his numerous debilitating injuries: to knees, back, head, shoulder, Achilles tendon, ankle; or his thirteen trips to the operating room; or the intense psychological pressures of being a marquee player in one of the fastest and most dangerous sports on earth.

He could bring in the goblins he encountered in the early autumn of 1979 when it struck him with the finality of a death sentence that the resonant dream of his boyhood was over. "I'd missed most of the previous season with a back injury," he explains, "but I'd come to training camp in September and had scored a few goals, and I thought I was going to be okay. If everything went well, I hoped to play another couple of years."

But when he awoke the morning after a preseason game against the Philadelphia Flyers, he was unable to walk, let alone skate, "and I knew that was it," he says.

> **"It took me five years to accept that I was really retired!"**

The intervening years have brought Yvan enviable domestic and professional success. But any discussion of the eighteen months that followed his retirement from the Canadiens still brings a perceptible strain to his normally beatific face.

"It took me five years to accept that I was really retired!" he exclaims. "You play hockey all winter from the time you're five years old; you have the excitement, the camaraderie, the schedule to follow, and then, boom, it's over, and there's a very large hole in your life. In order to fill it, you do this, you do that, you go to work, probably at a job you don't understand, and every time you see a game, you have to convince yourself again that you're no longer a part of what's happening on the ice. Although deep down you still believe you are. You still think maybe you could play."

"Even now, looking at pictures from back then, I can see how drawn he was with the stress," says his wife, Evelyn. "We've been together more than twenty years, and in all that time, it's the only rough period he's had."

Evelyn submits that part of Yvan's postretirement agony was his lack of any choice concerning the termination of his career. "If he'd been able to say to himself, okay, I'll play this season, or the next one, and that'll be it, he'd have had at least some sense of control, as well as the time to prepare himself mentally."

What made the separation even harder for Yvan was his extraordinary emotional attachment to the Canadiens franchise, to its personnel and players, and even to its historic building. "You've got to remember," he says, "I played my entire career, from bantam to the end, in Montreal, and that from the time I started with the Junior Canadiens, at seventeen, I played at the Forum."

Not surprisingly, his evocations of those years are liberally sprinkled with the vocabulary of blood connection. Toe Blake, he says, was "like a father," his teammates "like brothers," the whole organization "one *grande famille*." To the players, the Forum was known affectionately as "*la maison*." "It wasn't my second home," says Yvan, "it was my first."

In the months that followed his abrupt departure from the game, he and Evelyn cast about futilely for a manageable approach to the future. As a distraction and a means of staying fit, they took up skiing, one of the few sports Yvan could handle with a bad back and reconstructed knees.

"One day," brightens Evelyn, "Yvan hit on the idea of a brasserie. He and I had always enjoyed restaurants, and with his popularity—well?"

A short time later, as they drove along Thirty-second Avenue in Lachine, a working-class suburb in west Montreal, where Yvan had lived as a boy, Yvan noticed a large open lot near the busy intersection of highways 13 and 20, not far from Dorval Airport. "It was a perfect spot for a restaurant," he says, and within days he was negotiating its purchase from Canadian National Railways. Within weeks, he was dickering with architects over plans for the capacious restaurant and bar that would eventually stand on the site. "Yvan always thinks big—no half measures," says Evelyn. Indeed, Brasserie 12—so named for Yvan's sweater number—was to be a six-hundred-seat showplace, a monument not just to eating and drinking but to the life and accomplishments of its famous founder. (Coincidentally, it would stand directly across the street from La Bibliotheque Municipale Saul Bellow, a monument to Lachine's other widely celebrated son, who was born in the town in 1915 and won the Nobel Prize for Literature in 1976.) Moreover, the brasserie was to be a model of proprietary accountability. "I didn't just want to own it, I wanted to run it," declares Yvan, "to be there, to meet the people, sign autographs—if they were coming to my brasserie, they weren't going to go away disappointed."

So concerned was Yvan about his personal role in the development of the place that, before construction began, he took the unusual step of naming himself official project contractor, defying local building ordinances to a degree that cost him thousands of dollars in fines. But the price of his misdemeanors was insignificant compared to the value and satisfaction he got from unfettered management of everything from the pouring of the concrete foundations to the erection of the walls and the installation of the plumbing and wiring.

The fascination with trades and with manual productivity was by no means new for the novice restaurateur. As a teenager in Lachine, he had spent countless hours in his father's machine shop on Remembrance Street and had taken four years of machine-shop training at technical school. "If I hadn't been a hockey player," he says, "I'd have been a machinist like my dad." In fact, he once wedded his passions for hockey and for machining by cutting a dozen solid steel pucks on the lathe in his father's shop. "They weighed two or three pounds each," he smiles. "I'd go downstairs at home and shoot them at the basement wall, to build up my strength." When the foundations of the house began disintegrating from the pounding, Yvan's parents ordered him outside, where he fired his pucks into bales of hay against the family garage.

When Brasserie 12 opened to the public in late 1981, the food was as good as promised—the house specialty was what Evelyn refers to as "top-quality roast beef"—and a veritable rapides of beer flowed out through the taps, across the bar, and down the patrons' throats. In no time, the place was one of Molson Brewery's largest accounts in the province. And for the next dozen years, Yvan and Evelyn poured as much energy and time into the ambitious watering hole as Yvan had ever poured into hockey. The two routinely showed up three hours before the restaurant's 11:00 A.M. opening time to receive deliveries of meat and vegetables, to work with the chef, and generally to prepare for the day. "Yvan was always up to his elbows in something," says Evelyn. "He'd help in the kitchen or deal with the suppliers or staff. At the noon hour, of course, he'd be behind the taps, right there in the middle of things, where the people could see him."

More importantly, he was positioned where the brasserie's thousands of patrons could approach him, greet him, make the (albeit fleeting) acquaintance of the five-feet-seven-inch bullet who was at one time the fastest man on skates. Hour after hour, day after day, Yvan smiled his wide, unassuming smile for the customers' cameras, and dispensed autographs on four-by-eight-inch postcards bearing effulgent likenesses of himself, plus the logos of the brasserie and of its preferred intoxicant, Molson Export Ale. "Yvan is really very shy," says Evelyn. "He's not one to initiate any sort of social interaction, so the set-up was perfect. He'd just be there, and the customers would come up to him, or he'd walk among the tables and people would stop him as he passed. If, say, a ball team or a hockey team was coming in late, they'd phone ahead, and Yvan would wait and meet them. In the beginning, we were both there all the time, twelve hours a day, easy. Kurt spent the first few years of his life there! He'd be under the tables, or, when he got a little older, helping stack glasses or doing other little jobs."

Evelyn makes it clear that she and Yvan did not merely serve their customers but entertained them, provided a sybaritic parade of Christmas parties, Halloween parties, Western parties, lobster parties, and oyster parties. She produces a stack of corroborative photos, showing revelers in various states of merriment, wearing cowboy outfits, goblin suits, softball uniforms, invariably snuggled up to her and Yvan—or just to Yvan—and, for the most part, to one or more pitchers of freshly tapped suds. "We knew these people!" she enthuses. "That's what made it fun! The place would be packed to the doors every Thursday, Friday, Saturday night. If you were a nonsmoker, forget it."

Fast-forward a decade to a recent Sunday afternoon in June, a day on which most of Quebec is celebrating the first long weekend of the summer. But the celebrations have by no means penetrated Brasserie 12, which, although open, is as silent as the Pharaoh's tomb. In a corner of the glass-enclosed terrace, three rather wide-angled men, the only occupants of the cavernous establishment, are loading up noiselessly on omelettes and Texas-style fries. They are sharing a pitcher of draft beer which, for all the pleasure it is giving them, might just as well be vinegar.

More than a year has passed since Yvan and Evelyn relinquished ownership of their once-cherished brasserie. And yet even in his absence, Yvan's spirit pervades the place in much the way a vapor extends to every nook and niche of its container. It's in the panoply of Habs memorabilia on the walls, in the framed photos and the ubiquitous numeral 12 that appears on the menu and placemats and outdoor signs; it's in the phone number: 637-1212.

Perhaps most poignantly, it resides in the memories of the customers—a significantly reduced crowd these days—for whom the place will never be anything less than the house that Yvan built. "I ate a lot of meals in there over the years," says Lachine resident Guy Sabourin. "I never knew Yvan well, but I used to like to see him behind the bar. It was nice to go in there and see him."

"He still comes in once in a while," says a brasserie waitress. "But not very much anymore."

*   *   *   *

On a morning in late August, Evelyn Cournoyer sits in the living room of their home on the northern outskirts of Montreal, speaking circumspectly about their departure from the restaurant trade, which had apparently supported them well for nearly a dozen years. While she is reluctant to say much, she makes it clear that their move was influenced both by economics and demographics. "A lot of things changed between 1981 when we opened and the mid-nineties when we sold," she says. "Certainly the recession made things harder for us. I mean, it was hard everywhere, but Lachine, in particular, tends to be industrial, and during the late eighties and early nineties a lot of local factories and warehouses went out of business. There just wasn't as much money around, or as many people."

In addition, by 1990 customers had a far broader choice of local bars and restaurants in which to spend their money than a decade earlier. Barbecue St. Hubert, the corporate chicken shack that has become Quebec's preeminent chain of restaurants, capitalized directly on the locus of activity created by the brasserie by putting up a large outlet immediately next door.

"People were also drinking less by the early nineties," observes one brasserie bartender. "And the laws against drinking and driving had gotten stricter. Today's average drinker has two or three beers and says, 'That's enough,' whereas in the old days a table of guys would come in and plough through five or six pitchers!" He points unenthusiastically at the self-operated breathalyzer machine, the Alcotest, that stands just outside the brasserie's washrooms. "Until recently," he says, "you didn't see many of those."

In addition to the economic and sociological pressures that were impinging on their operation, Evelyn and Yvan had quite simply grown tired of the quotidian demands of food ordering, menu preparation, staff scheduling, the endless cash-outs, the payroll, and accounting responsibilities, not to mention the necessity of being on the premises day in, day out, month after month, year after year. "You don't notice your weariness as much when things are going well," says Evelyn, "but with the recession we had to work harder and harder, and of course we weren't getting the same rewards."

During the couple's last year at the brasserie, they found themselves attempting daily miracles both in the kitchen and on the balance sheet. "We were determined not to compromise our standards," says Evelyn. "We always used the best meat and vegetables, for example. But at the same time, we were cutting our prices to the point where we were putting out daily specials, full-course meals, for under three dollars. The long and short of it is, we'd given all we could to the restaurant business. We miss the customers and staff—we had a lot of friends at the brasserie—but we were ready to do something else."

Part of the *something else* that followed the sale of the brasserie was a move from urban Laval to the semideveloped farmlands around Blainville, a saturnine village off Route 640, some twenty-five kilometers north of Montreal. The elegant grey-brick home into which the Cournoyers moved is part of an upscale subdivision built by Yvan's friend Mario Grilli, a Montreal developer for whom Yvan was doing publicity work when he first laid eyes on the place. "Yvan called me and said, 'You've gotta come see this house,' and as soon as I saw it I knew we were destined to live here," says Evelyn, who was attracted not only by the structure but by its seductive view across field and forest to the distant skyscrapers of downtown Montreal. In the months since taking possession, she and Yvan have turned the surrounding acreage into an arboretum of conifers and hardwoods scattered with birdbaths and feeders that attract a summer population of finches, warblers, and hummingbirds.

Inside, despite its rather lean decor and lines, the place invites both relaxation and play. Indeed, just to the left of the front door, where a visitor might expect to see a dining or sitting room, stands a full-sized billiard table, surrounded by choice remnants of Yvan's career in hockey. Draped casually on a chair are three hockey sweaters of different vintages and repair. The oldest, Yvan's first as a Canadien, is of knitted wool, decidedly faded, and suggests an era far dimmer to the memory than the early sixties, when it was worn. By comparison, the newest of the three sweaters, Yvan's last as a Hab, seems, in its shapeless dimensions and bright, uninspired acrylics, to embody some zipless season inhospitable both to comfort and to the spirit of the man who wore it. The two sweaters are fitting symbolic parentheses to a career that began in a parochial six-team league whose teams traveled by train (and whose players began their careers at $10,000 a season), and ended in a financially free-wheeling twenty-one-team league that spanned four time zones and included teams in subtropical climates.

But it is the third of the three sweaters, a yellowed and tattered relic, that most stirs the imagination and curiosity—partly because it was worn by Yvan in the epochal Soviet-Canada series of 1972, but more so because of its comically crude hand-customization. Six inches, at least, have been snipped off the bottom, and the resulting edge bound with awkward hand-applied stitches. The sleeves have been likewise chopped and hemmed, while the neck has been expanded two or three inches, by way of a hand-ripped vent through the neckline and down the front of the sweater. The impression, understandably, is that the garment—neck excluded—was initially too big for Yvan (in his red uniform, the short but sturdy Montreal captain was once compared to a mailbox). And yet looking at it now, it is difficult to see how even the smallest of NHL players could have compressed himself into such a tiny piece of apparel. "I don't think he could get into it today, even without shoulder pads," jokes Evelyn.

Which isn't to say that Yvan, at fifty-one, is in anything less than top-notch shape. While not exactly thin, he is certainly trim and muscular, and, although his blondy-grey hair has pretty much retreated from the foredeck of his scalp, his face is that of a slightly prankish cherub and is all but free of wrinkles.

Yvan was born in 1943 in Drummondville, Quebec, a town of some forty thousand inhabitants, a hundred kilometers east of Montreal. Like many boys from provincial Quebec, he served mass at the local parish church. He allows, in fact, that he knew his catechism better than his school lessons, which he detested. "I was always happy to be in church," he grins, "because when I was there it meant I wasn't in school."

But more than any place on earth, he loved the local outdoor rink, which he shoveled for small pay, and where he embraced organized hockey with such fanaticism that, as a peewee, he played goal because he couldn't bear the thought of coming off the ice, as forwards and defensemen occasionally had to do. His father worked in a machine shop in Montreal and saw his wife and children only on weekends. "Then when I was thirteen," says Yvan, "he bought the shop, and we moved into Lachine."

> **"From the time I was fourteen, I had a very strong belief that I was good enough to make it in pro hockey."**

There in west Montreal, Yvan's hockey career began in earnest, although not without encumbrances. At the time, he explains, Lachine was "quite English," and the first hockey team he joined was exclusively anglophile. Unable to speak anything but French, he was forced to use hand gestures to make himself understood to his coaches and teammates. "I was shy anyway," he says, "and I'd get so nervous about not speaking the language that I'd probably have quit and gone home if I hadn't loved hockey so much."

In order to improve his English, Yvan eventually signed on with the Lachine Lakers, a largely English-speaking football team, whose season overlapped with the hockey season. "I played linebacker and ran back kicks," he says. By late winter, however, he was so exhausted by the efforts of autumn that he could barely finish his hockey schedule.

If the pro scouts were concerned about his apparent lack of stamina, Yvan was not. "By this time," he says, "nothing was going to stop me. From the time I was fourteen, I had a very strong belief that I was good enough to make it in pro hockey."

The Montreal Canadiens, who owned Yvan's professional rights, had much the same feeling and, throughout Yvan's teenage years, watched the young prodigy with possessive anticipation. When he was seventeen, they assigned him to the Montreal Junior Canadiens, a team for which he scored a remarkable fifty-four goals during his final year of junior eligibility. But it was not just his scoring that impressed the Montreal management; it was his astonishing speed. "From the time I was a kid," he acknowledges, "I was always the fastest guy on the ice."

But speed and offensive skills were initially not enough to earn him a regular shift with the Canadiens after joining the club full-time in 1964. Wary of what he perceived as a weakness in Yvan's defensive game, and concerned by his lack of stature, coach Toe Blake used him almost exclusively on power plays. Not one to brood, Yvan did what he had always done: applied himself to the chore at hand, becoming in the process so proficient in his specialized role that, during the 1966–67 season, playing at best part-time, he scored twenty-five goals, no fewer than twenty of them when the team had a manpower advantage. "This was at a time," he notes, "when twenty goals was still a very respectable season in the NHL."

Yvan's emergence as an all-around star coincided roughly with Blake's retirement in 1968. Blake's successor, Claude Ruel, decided that the young winger's speed and savvy were far too valuable to leave cooling on the bench. What's more, he had proven that he was perfectly capable of handling the prodigious physical battering that pro hockey inflicts even on a player as elusive as Yvan.

Off the ice, Yvan's life was moving at a pace to rival his speed at the rink. Shortly after joining the Canadiens, he married his teenage sweetheart—"my first girlfriend," he confides—and by 1974 was the father of three children.

"Looking back," he says, "I know I made a mistake getting married too young. But at the time I was naive. I didn't know. I just stuck with it."

From the point of view of some players on the team, Yvan was something of an enigma. "He was a private person," says teammate Gump Worsley, whose observations are echoed by fellow Hab John Ferguson. "He didn't say much, didn't socialize much—I never felt I knew him very well. Except on the ice. I knew him as a player."

"I was shy, not private," insists Yvan. "You have to understand that the NHL is mostly an English-speaking league, and the sports media and players are mostly English. And even after five years with the Canadiens, I still wasn't confident enough to express myself comfortably in English." If Yvan needed a cross-cultural coming out, he got one in 1972 when he was chosen to represent Canada against the best hockey players from the Soviet Union, many of whom, it turned out, were among the best in the world. For most fans and sportswriters, the series was a kind of ideological dust-up between the individualized gamesmanship of the West and the bloodless functionality of state-controlled sport. But initially it was governed less by ideology than by conditioning. The Canadians significantly underestimated the strength and skill of the Soviets and, after a summer of inactivity, spent much of the first four games—the Canadian leg of the series—struggling to catch their breath. But by the time they reached Moscow, their endurance was at game level, and ideology had indeed become a factor. It was never more significant than in the fabled final game, when the Canadians played on the fiercest of competitive instincts against the daunting but inflexible mechanics of the Soviet system. In the clinching moments, none other than Yvan Cournoyer, who minutes earlier had scored the game-tying goal, made a play no Soviet of that era would have dreamed of, let alone perpetrated, placing a Westernized instinct for chance above any measure of form and, in the process, deciding the outcome of the series.

"Let me tell you what happened," says Yvan, whose detailed recollections of the play might suggest that it had been enacted that morning, not twenty-three years before. "The puck was in the Russian zone, and my left winger and centerman both went off the ice. I went to go off, but in the middle of the ice I suddenly changed my mind; I thought, I'm going to give it one last try, and I went back on my wing. The Russian defenseman must have thought I'd gone to the bench, because he threw the puck blindly around the boards to clear the zone. And there I was," says an animated Yvan, whose boyhood compulsion for staying on the ice beyond his time was not only alive but was about to spark the most heralded play in the history of Canadian hockey. "I intercepted the puck, and saw that Phil and Paul [Esposito and Henderson] had come from the bench. I tried to give it to Paul, but it shot ahead of him and went into the corner. Phil picked it up. Paul fell, got up, came in front of the net. Out came the puck, and he put it in!"

Yvan's face broadens in a smile. "And it all went back to my changing my mind about going off. If I hadn't stayed on, there wouldn't have been a goal, because there wouldn't have been anybody to intercept the puck."

Appropriately enough, Yvan figures prominently (albeit seen from the back) in Frank Lennon's famous photograph of the celebration that followed the goal—a shot often referred to as a photo "of Paul Henderson."

That Yvan is seldom, if ever, identified as a figure in the famous depiction hardly seems to register with him. "When I see it," he shrugs, "I know what I did. I don't have to read my name or see my face. I had a good series, but I give Paul all the credit for scoring. He scored winning goals in each of the last three games."

Yvan's success in Moscow carried over into that year's NHL season, bringing him his sixth Stanley Cup and the Conn Smythe Trophy for a remarkable playoff performance that featured fifteen goals and ten assists in seventeen games.

In 1975, he succeeded Henri Richard as captain of the Canadiens. But his successes with the team were not reflected in his private life, where

> **"If I hadn't stayed on, there wouldn't have been a goal, because there wouldn't have been anybody to intercept the puck."**

his marriage was sinking slowly into emotional receivership. "Then it was over," he says, "and I was back on my own."

Yvan's emotional life, however, would soon take a dramatic turnabout. "One day in, I guess, 1977," he says, "I was passing through Dorval Airport with the team—we were going to a game in Chicago—and I noticed a very pretty young woman in an Air Canada uniform." The two exchanged glances and Yvan subsequently left a note with the young woman's coworkers, asking if she would meet him for a drink upon his return the following Monday.

"We met," says Evelyn, "and what can I say?—it was love at first sight. I always say it was his eyes that caught my attention; he says it was my smile that caught his."

Physical attractions notwithstanding, the pair's personalities have been ideal complements through eighteen years of courtship, marriage, and business. Where he is taciturn, she chats; where he is retiring, she is social, drawing him out, encouraging him to expand his range of self-expression—"but in a good way," stresses Yvan. "Evelyn is very sincere, very loving, very considerate."

"Yvan is certainly more outgoing than he was," submits Evelyn. "It used to be, he'd hardly even smile for a photo."

Evelyn has given Yvan a refined command of English, and he has taught her French. "When we met, we could hardly speak the other's language," she says. "Now Yvan speaks English so much, I have to encourage him and Kurtis to keep up their French."

One thing that has not changed for the couple is their obvious sensual compatibility. When they speak of one another their voices take on a perceptibly elevated charge, and each of them remembers vividly the intense chemistry that united them when they met nearly two decades ago.

"Evelyn is beautiful," Yvan says unselfconsciously.

"It still gives me a thrill," says Evelyn, "when we pass one another and he gives me that special little look that he gave me that day in the airport."

On a morning in late June, Yvan sits ten rows up in the Montreal Forum, watching the Chicago Cheetahs, a professional roller-hockey team, during their game-day workout. He is nattily attired in a white shirt, navy blue dress slacks, and tasselled loafers. His black socks are of the sheerest silk. The Stanley Cup ring on his left hand and the Hall of Fame ring on his right are each as big as King Solomon's seal and resplendent with commemorative diamonds.

In quiet, confident English, Yvan describes how, when he left the brasserie, he made a business move that brought him not only into the brave new world of roller hockey, where for a couple of seasons he was coach and manager of the Montreal Roadrunners, but happily back to "*la maison*," the home he had known for sixteen years as a junior and professional hockey player.

"I first saw roller hockey in 1992," he says. "And one of the first things I noticed about it was that the players were having such a good time, and so were the fans; they just loved it, and this impressed me. In a lot of sports, the players and fans just don't seem to enjoy themselves much anymore."

Six months later, the owners of the Montreal franchise approached Yvan about running the team that they were about to found. "I thought about it for three or four months," says Yvan, "and, based on what I'd seen of the league and the game, I decided to take a chance and go with it."

The job, for Yvan, meant an intense commitment of time between early May, when the team began coming together, and the Labor Day weekend, by which point the league's twenty-four-game schedule and playoff tournament were over. "The other eight months were much less demanding," says Yvan. "Some promotion, some meetings, player signings, some planning for the future."

Yvan modeled the Roadrunners after the firewagon teams for which he played; indeed, they were named after the speedy desert bird that provided his own nickname during his years as an NHL dervish.

"The whole thing was just terrific for him," says Evelyn. "And for me too. We were always talking about it, discussing the coaching, thinking about promotions. Yvan's a competitive sort of person, and it was really exciting for him to have that sort of challenge back in his life."

Evelyn is a slim, attractive woman, with long blond hair and an exuberant smile. At Roadrunners' games, she sat directly behind the Montreal bench, about ten rows up, and put every ounce of her ample enthusiasm for life not only into support for the team but into a kind of psychic endorsement of her husband's efforts behind the bench.

"When you play for the Canadiens, you develop a real fear of losing," says Jocelyn Guevremont, who played for several NHL teams and has since worked at developing roller hockey in Quebec. "Yvan brought that to the Roadrunners. He was very fiery as a coach, very intense."

Roller hockey is at best a distant cousin to the version of the sport on which Yvan made his mark as a player. Yet, it is easy to see why he and numerous other ice-hockey stars—Mark Messier, Bernie Federko, Ralph Backstrom, Garry Unger, Doug Wilson, Rick Kehoe, Dennis Maruk, Terry Harper, Tiger Williams, among others—have been attracted to it as owners, managers, or coaches. Because there is no way to stop quickly on roller blades, for example, the game is an ongoing exercise in loops and long turns, balletic perpetual motion. And inasmuch as there are only four skaters per side, and no bluelines to restrict play, there is plenty of open space, allowing for a stylistic anarchy unknown to the more traditional game. Play features extraordinarily long passes and (mostly) unobstructed free-wheeling for the better players. It is a sport that favors speed and maneuverability, but not size, and at which Yvan in his salad days would have excelled.

It is equally easy to see why the game is reported (albeit by its own touts) to be the fastest-growing sport in North America. For beyond its aesthetics and openness, and its apparent appeal to investors, it carries none of the hoary old cultural baggage, evinces none of the traditional partisanship, that burdens the hopes and expectations of NHL fans, not to mention the players' and coaches' hopes for themselves. It is actually possible to go to a game and enjoy it no matter who wins, a feat seemingly unachievable for the average NHL fan.

What's more, the game is manifestly less ponderous about its image than are more established sports. Aimed largely at families, and particularly at children and teenagers, it is replete with brightly costumed mascots and cheerleaders. The players in their high-tech skates and gear look like road warriors, and the souped-up team names—Sacramento River Rats, Florida Hammerheads, St. Louis Vipers—would not be out of place among the preposterous plastic action figures that infest contemporary toystore shelves and have an undeniable lock on the imaginations of six- and seven-year-old boys. Those same names, it might be pointed out, are all but interchangeable with those of the post-punk grunge bands that pretty much define the poetics of late-twentieth-century teenagers. All of which is far from coincidental; the marketing is shrewd, although transparent enough that it maintains a kind of pleasingly funky innocence. Games in some cities are accompanied by barbecues, rock concerts, and displays of indoor fireworks.

The sport, in brief, is more "fun" than ice hockey. Yet establishing it in Montreal was what Yvan refers to as "a major challenge" that required "a lot of patience and a lot of hard work." The press in particular were resistant.

"The good thing," says Evelyn, "was that the kids got into it—you still see Roadrunners T-shirts all over Montreal. And people always came out of the Forum saying, 'Wow, that was great!'"

But Yvan's short, happy life with the Montreal Roadrunners came to an abrupt and unexpected conclusion in October of 1995.

Not that Yvan wasn't happy with the team, or they with him. He had guided the Roadrunners to the Roller Hockey International finals just a month earlier, narrowly losing the league championship (on the Forum floor) to the San Jose Rhinos.

But in the world of Yvan's past—specifically, the National Hockey League—events were unfolding that would have a profound effect on the former star's future. At the Montreal Forum, Yvan's alma mater, the

Canadiens, were going nowhere. Fast. When, after four games, the state of the team's ineptitude had become obvious, coach Jacques Demers and general manager Serge Savard were summarily fired, having won the Stanley Cup with the Canadiens just two seasons earlier.

> **"We did our best. We had a lot of injuries those years."**

For two days, media and fans speculated aggressively over who would take control of the team.

There were raised eyebrows on the morning of the second day when the Canadiens announced that the manager's job had gone to Rejean Houle, who had never managed, and that the new head coach was Mario Tremblay, who had never coached.

In fact, the only member of the new coaching staff who had any experience at all was the erstwhile coach of the Montreal Roadrunners, Yvan Cournoyer, who had been unable to resist the invitation to ditch his new love and return to his old.

Hope ran high in Montreal that Houle, Tremblay, and Cournoyer, who represented tradition and energy if not experience, would produce the same successes now that they had all known as players.

For Yvan, the move represented the very real possibility that he would one day coach in the NHL, perhaps even with the Canadiens.

But that possibility would be predicated on the success of his tenure. Question was: Would the legendary assistant who had guided his roller hockey franchise to the top of its sport have a chance to make his influence and instincts felt in this new situation?

Unfortunately, Tremblay's irascible personality, which had served him well as a player, turned out to be poorly suited to contemporary coaching. He was stubborn and inflexible, and quarreled quickly and fatally with the team's one indisputable asset, goaltender Patrick Roy, who was traded to the Colorado Avalanche, a team that promptly won the Stanley Cup.

After two years of cartoonish unsuccess, Tremblay was fired—and with him Yvan, who had never had a chance to show what he could do.

"As an assistant," he said recently with a shrug, "you say what you think, but it doesn't always make any difference. We did our best. We had a lot of injuries those years. I'll tell you one thing—we worked hard, seven, eight months a year. But if you're going to coach, you have to be ready to move on."

Unsubstantiated rumors suggested that the players lacked respect for Yvan, but if it was true it was almost certainly a function of the team's decidedly negative response to Tremblay. According to one source close to the team, "The players just stopped playing for Tremblay. It was a question of respect. He had to go."

Whatever the case, Yvan was again out of hockey. And if there was a small silver lining to the cloud that enveloped him, it was that, for a while at least, he was able to return to doing more of the things he loved. "He just never stops," says Evelyn. "If he's not involved with sport, or on some other business, he's gardening or cutting grass, or he's doing something with Kurtis, or working with his tools around the house."

Or, occasionally, taking a little time off. In fact, if Yvan and Evelyn's years together could be captured in a metaphor, it might well be found in the magnificent retreat they have built for themselves in the Laurentian Mountains, a ninety-minute drive north of Montreal. Although they refer to the place modestly as "the chalet," it is in fact a prepossessing vacation home that features an expansive interior of cedar and pine, soaring vertical spaces, and a vast stone fireplace. Yvan has done much of the work on the place himself, inside and out. "He's got a shed full of tools and equipment up there you wouldn't believe," says Evelyn. "Every sort of implement you can imagine, some of them made years ago by his dad in the machine shop. He just loves working with his hands." She disappears into the recesses of the house in Blainville, reappearing presently with a photo album gorged with pictures of the cherished mountain residence, and of Yvan at work—here on a ladder tending to the eaves, here chopping wood, sawing lumber, mixing cement, yukking it up with Evelyn and friends. Here are the two of them placing stones in an extensive outdoor retaining wall. "Eventually, we'll retire there," she says. "As it is, we go up year-round—for Thanksgiving, for Christmas, for skiing. In winter, we build a bobsled rim down the hill beside the house, right out onto the lake."

Back home, Yvan exercises his love of manual chores in a myriad of ways that includes ironing, washing dishes, and household repairs. He recently installed hardwood trim on the kitchen counter and built a wine cellar in the basement to house the wine he has begun to make and bottle. He acknowledges having something close to a fetish for hand tools and admits to "going crazy" in the tool departments of stores. "I'm a simple man at heart," he says. "I like a project." He does not like reading and says so with the certainty of a man who knows and accepts himself and is not about to explain or apologize. "I watch TV instead," he says. "I could watch CNN all day."

"He doesn't even read about himself!" says Evelyn. "On the rare occasion that he does pick up a book, he turns to the last page first—I guess from all those years of picking up newspapers and turning to the sports pages at the back."

Yvan himself has not played hockey for many years—at least not in public. "My knees are too bad," he says. "People expect you to play like they remember you in your prime, and I can't. And I don't want to disappoint anybody." He admits to a fondness for good food, but whatever calories he adds he sheds just as quickly on the fitness equipment in the basement at home, where he works out for an hour or more a day, mostly on the treadmill. "He's too shy to workout in public or at a club," confides Evelyn.

He is not so shy, however, that he is reticent to express an opinion, or reluctant to speak out if he feels an injustice has been perpetrated. He is scornful, for instance, of the NHL's all-but-criminal insensitivity in failing to provide an adequate pension plan for the players of his era. "You'd think they'd have been bright enough to establish a decent plan," he says, "but they weren't. And we're paying for it now. I get the pension, but you can't go far on eight or nine thousand a year. Some of the guys'll have to work till they drop."

Yvan will not. "I've done well," he admits. "I had good contracts in hockey; I've had great jobs since. I've fulfilled my dreams. If you can get up in the morning and look forward to going to work, and don't just see it as so many hours on the job, you can't complain. I can't complain."

Nor can Yvan complain about his place in Quebec's cultural pantheon, where he enjoys an almost iconic status. His relationship with his public is uncomplicated. They are adoring; he is appreciative—and singularly unassuming about his fame and accomplishments. "I just don't see myself as special," he says. "Hockey was my profession, my job. A great job, yes, but still a job. When you need a plumber, send for this guy, a carpenter this guy.

"When you need a hockey player, send for Yvan. He'll try to get the job done."

*   *   *   *

Epilogue

While Yvan's departure from the Canadiens left him without full-time work, it did not leave him without prospects or income. Like so many former Canadiens, he has for years been a part-time public relations representative for Molson Brewery, attending golf and hockey tournaments on the brewery's behalf and playing exhibition softball on their team of former Canadiens. And, for several years, he and Evelyn have operated an agency through which Yvan can be hired as a promotional front man by any company or endeavor that might need fronting and that the couple deems worthy of their services. "And he's an inventor!" smiles Evelyn, who explains that a one-piece suit of hockey underwear designed by Yvan was marketed briefly by Winnwell sporting goods, who paid Yvan a royalty on every set of longjohns they sold.

For a while during the late 1990s, he was also a celebrity front man for Robin's Donuts, not to mention a rumored franchisee as the chain expanded into Quebec.

Like many former stars, he is also a frequent participant in events that allow fans to schmooze with the heroes of the past. Last summer, Yvan and Evelyn were featured guests on Norwegian Cruise Line's celebrity hockey cruise in the Caribbean. And just months ago, Yvan took time away from the family and chalet to be part of a hockey "fantasy camp," at which five winners of a beer-sponsored contest were treated to a week's training with a number of aging Habs stars, including Jean Beliveau, Henri Richard, and Frank Mahovlich.

Asked recently if he would return to the precarious world of coaching if the chance were to arise, Yvan said, "I'd never say no to coaching. I don't love the stress, but it'd be a nice way to stay in the game, maybe even win another Stanley Cup. Hey," he laughed, "I've lived with risks all my life. I never wore a helmet! I've been in the restaurant business."

Yvan also battled the Russians during the height of the Cold War. "After that," he shrugged, "coaching in the NHL is no risk at all."

CHAPTER

2

Phil Esposito

In the Capital of the World

(Editor's note: The following profile was written somewhat earlier than others in the book. It is included here, updated only by its epilogue, because it covers its subject's career and transition into retirement with such intensity, detail, and focus—and from a perspective that would have been impossible to achieve at any time since.)

It was a mild afternoon in mid-March, 1989, nearly seventy days before the fall of the axe—before the *New York Daily News* would run the unforgiving headline: ESPO'S A GONER. Yet even then, ten weeks before the fact, Phil Esposito had an uncanny suspicion that his marriage to the Rangers was unlikely to last. And he didn't hesitate to say so as I sat with him in his office on the fourth floor of Madison Square Garden.

At one point, as he delivered a particularly dark assessment of the nature of his work, he stopped mid-sentence and said, "Ya know something? I don't think I'm gonna last around here. I'll probably be outta here by October—I'm almost sure I will." A journalist's dream: the liberated subject who can, and will, say what he wants with impunity.

The only thing Phil didn't foresee that day was the harsh means of his departure after three years as general manager of the New York Rangers. "I imagine when it happens I'll just walk away from it," he said, "pack up and leave."

But not all aspects of Phil's perspective were entirely in sync that afternoon. Within ten minutes of revealing his doubts about his future, he declared that he would one day lead the Rangers to the Stanley Cup. "I have no doubt about it," he said. "That's what's going to happen."

When I arrived at Phil's office that day, he was in the middle of a dramatic long-distance telephone conversation, objecting passionately to a *Toronto Globe and Mail* article that had depicted him as "a typical New Yorker—loud, cocky, and insensitive." As his objections gained momentum so did the volume of his voice, until he was all but shouting into the phone that New Yorkers were not the insensitive animals they were assumed to be; that New Yorkers were not to be mistaken for the armies of rude New York taxi drivers, most of whom came from elsewhere anyway; that New Yorkers, contrary to their press image, are as sensitive and decent and humane as anybody anywhere, and that the next time such-and-such a writer badmouths New Yorkers and Phil Esposito he'd better be prepared to do it to Phil's face and not gutlessly behind his back, and . . . well . . . yes . . . Phil was upset.

But having vented his anger, he set down the phone, becalmed, hospitable, and, indeed, quite unlike a rude New York taxidriver, who probably came from somewhere else anyway.

Phil himself came from somewhere else: Sault Sainte Marie, Ontario, a smallish northern city on the far eastern spur of Lake Superior, a place light years from the bustle and grime of Manhattan. And although he has not lived in the Soo for more than thirty years, he has far from outgrown the small-town viewpoint and habits with which he grew up. "It was funny when we started going to the theater in New York," he smiled. "I'm so big I'd always be worrying about whether or not the guy behind me could see. Here was this forty-year-old kid from the Soo slouched way down in his seat so as not to block the view. I'd come out of the theater all hunched over. My wife is a Bostonian; she'd say, 'Sit up, Phil! Don't worry about it! They'll see around you!' But I could never shake this uncomfortable feeling that I was spoiling it for somebody else. That's my small-town background. And I hate standing in line. In the Soo, ten people was a big line-up; if I saw that big a crowd, I'd walk away, do something else. My father used to pack a lunch if he was going for a twenty-minute drive! Now, I drive two hours a day just to get to work and back. My father's rolling in his grave watching me."

On this particular afternoon, Phil looked very New Yorkish in fine Italian cap-toed shoes, black-and-white striped shirt with plain white collar, flowered silk tie, and an elegant black suit, double-breasted and impeccably tailored of wool and silk. His office, too, was a study in New Yorkish good taste: immense Sheraton desk, plush carpet, built-in bar and television, chesterfield, easy chairs, subtly recessed lighting. On a side table sat a small lamp, the base of which was a scaled-down replica of the Stanley Cup, with a shade bearing the logo of the New York Rangers.

> ## "I feel a hundred times more vulnerable as a GM than I ever did as a player."

The comfortable trappings notwithstanding, it was apparent that all was not well at Thirty-third and Seventh Avenues. Phil was upset—deeply disturbed. The job was getting to him; the coach was getting to him; the players were getting to him; his bosses were getting to him. One facet of his office, more than any other, hinted at his life within the Ranger organization in those latter days—a life slowly closing around him. It was (almost too obviously) that the place had no windows. "I have absolutely no outlets for my stress on this job," he admitted quietly at one point. "As a player I was able to release the pressures through the hockey itself. Here, all I do is absorb, absorb, absorb. Sometimes I don't know how I survive it. I should be getting some recreation, but I haven't got time. It should help me to get out to our home in the country, but as soon as I get there the phone starts ringing! I know one thing: I've got to find a vent. I keep thinking that if I get through this year I'll be all right. Then I figure I'll never make it through this year, that I'd just as soon pack it in. I mean hockey is such a precarious business, and I feel a hundred times more vulnerable as a GM than I ever did as a player. Every time we lose, I start to get doubts. Right now I'm thinking, Holy cripes, we've lost six out of our last seven games, we've been terrible, we're in a prolonged slump, our power play is horrendous, and I start imagining that I can help this power play. But I'm frustrated because I don't really know how to go about it—to help my coach, Michel Bergeron, without interfering, without sounding as if I'm trying to do his job for him. I respect him too much as a coach to force myself on him. And it's frustrating me. It's eating my guts out. The only way to get in there would be to fire Michel, and I don't want to do that. As a GM, you're supposed to be able to separate yourself from your coach, but for me that's impossible. I'm a second guesser by nature."

Phil was particularly bothered that afternoon by the way in which the pressures of his work were beginning to impinge on his life at home. He said, "The other day for the first time in a very long time, I allowed my frustrations to affect my relationship with my wife. And that's not fair, getting impatient with her over what's going on here. I was sorry about it. I sent her flowers. I even get impatient with my three-year-old daughter. The other night I called home, and when she answered the phone and wanted to talk, I said, 'Get Mommy!' And she said, 'Why?' I said, 'Just get her.' Then, of course, I felt guilty. I should have had time to talk to her. I feel guilty about what I do at work sometimes, too. In spite of my reputation for trading—and I'll admit I've made a lot of trades; what did the paper say, forty-two?—I don't like trading guys; it upsets their lives something awful. I feel badly about it. But if I say that, I'm accused of being a phony, of grandstanding. One thing I've learned about this business, you really don't make a lot of friends."

Listening to Phil describe a typical day in his life as a GM—the mere nuts and bolts of the job, minus the larger emotional pressures—was, in itself, daunting: "Start out with an hour's freeway driving," he said. "Then maybe three or four meetings with various people—my boss, my coach, an agent, p.r. people. This morning I spent a very tough two hours with an agent, hammering out a contract. I might spend six or seven hours on the phone in a given day. Sometimes more. On a game day, I don't get home till about midnight, at which point I'll often turn on the TV and watch more hockey. Then maybe I'll be on the phone with somebody from the West—Rogie Vachon in L.A., Pat Quinn in Vancouver, Glen Sather in Edmonton. It's often 3:00 A.M. before I get to bed."

The previous night (not a game night), Phil had watched parts of four NHL games on television and fielded a dozen or more work-related phone calls, two of them lasting an hour or more. "I don't even like the telephone," he grimaced, "but I'm on it all the time! I can't get off it! It's part of the job! I've even got one in my car! In the summer, I take a portable with me to the golf course! In fact, I was on the golf course last year when I got a call from Czechoslovakia, telling me that this Czech player, Horova, was coming over. He wanted to know what I was willing to pay him! On the golf course! I've had calls from agents at two in the morning!"

Phil estimated that, between the phone and the television, he was being robbed of perhaps 80 percent of the time that he might otherwise spend happily with his wife and daughter. "Last weekend, my little girl said to me, 'Daddy, do we have to watch hockey again?' And the answer is yes, it's part of being a GM. I have to know the league inside out if I'm going to trade successfully. It's a twenty-four-hour-a-day job. Seven days a week."

* * * *

Phil's life in New York began when he was traded from the Boston Bruins to the New York Rangers in 1975. He had been perhaps the greatest forward in the history of the Bruin franchise. During nine years with the team, he won five scoring championships, two Stanley Cups, and two Hart Trophies as the league's most valuable player. He was named to eight All-Star teams and, in 1970–71, scored a then-inconceivable seventy-six goals (152 points). "The thing about Phil," said a former teammate, "was that he wasn't a pretty skater like Orr or Hull. He kind of lumbered along, and for that reason he never got quite the acclaim he deserved. But once he was near the net, nobody was better. If you could get the puck to him, he was strong enough not just to control it but to muscle free and get a shot. A lot of fancy little forwards can dazzle the fans, but when it comes to doing what a forward is supposed to do, which is putting the puck behind the goalie, they can't do it. Phil could do it."

He could do it so well, in fact, that he had every reason to believe he'd be a Bruin forever. The story is told that when he got the news of his trade he sat on the bed in a Vancouver hotel room and wept. "If you tell me I'm traded to New York," he told his coach, Don Cherry, "I'll jump out that window."

According to Phil, it took him two years following the trade to accept that he was no longer a Bruin. "I'd look in the mirror with the New York sweater on, and I'd say, Hey, wait a minute—where's the Boston crest? When finally I did accept that I was alive and well and living in New York, my first thought was, How on earth am I going to cope with all this traffic?"

His real acceptance of the Big Apple came when he and his wife Donna moved from the house they'd bought on Long Island to an apartment at Fifty-ninth Street and Second Avenue. "From that point on we loved this city," he smiled. "Loved the restaurants, loved the theater—I'd never attended the theater. I got to like the musicals. I saw *Cats* twice— saw *They're Playing Our Song* three or four times. I went to numerous openings of Neil Simon plays because I got to know Neil through his producer, Manny Eisenberg. One night I invited Neil and his wife Marsha Mason to a hockey game. They came, and they liked it. Donna and I went out for dinner with them afterwards."

One morning in the middle of winter, 1981, Phil woke up with a feeling he had never experienced before: he was fed up with playing hockey. "I was supposed to go to practice that morning," he recalled, "and I said to Donna, 'Ya know, this is a drag.' She'd had no advance warning. I just didn't feel like it anymore. I'd always promised myself that if I stopped enjoying what I was doing I'd get out of it. And I'd stopped enjoying it. That was it."

Donna contends that, well before his retirement, Phil had shown a distinct inclination toward front-office work. "I wouldn't exactly call it a vision of the future," she says, "but he used to say he'd like to be a general manager some day."

The first step to that goal came quickly when a few days after calling it quits, Phil was invited to become the Rangers' assistant general manager under GM Craig Patrick. "That lasted three weeks," said Phil with unbridled disgust. "I didn't like it at all. I wanted to be involved, but I didn't do anything." Phil's relationship with his boss hit bottom one night when, during a game, he was yelling at a referee and was told by Patrick to keep quiet. "I turned to him, and I said, 'Whaddaya mean?' He said, 'We yell too much at them.' I said, 'It's part of the game, for cryin' out loud! I'm not swearing at him!' All I'd said was, 'Shake your head, your eyes are stuck! Get in the game!' Craig didn't ask me not to yell, he told me."

Following the game, Phil explained to Patrick that he didn't think their relationship was going to work. "I said, 'I like you very much, Craig, but unless I leave now I'm going to start second guessing you, and I don't want to do that.' And I also knew that I had a broadcasting job if I wanted it. Some time before, I'd been asked by Sonny Werblin, the head man here at Gulf Sports—they own the Rangers—if I'd be interested in broadcasting Ranger games when I finished playing. So the following season I started that."

During five years as a broadcaster, Phil also cast his net in several other occupational directions, one of which was restaurant ownership. "We called

"I really don't have a whole lot to sell except Phil Esposito."

the place 'Sticks,'" he said. "It was on Seventy-ninth Street, and, as far as the food and atmosphere went, it was a good place—we had line-ups outside. But after about a year I found out that my partner—a guy to whom I'd given my trust and who was running the day-to-day operation—was robbing the place blind. Suddenly, he took off, just vanished, and we had to close down. I paid off my part of the loan that we'd taken out to finance the place, and now I'm stuck paying his part too, because I'm Phil Esposito; I have a reputation to protect. The bank can't find this guy. Sticks was a nice place and all that, but I'm not the type of guy to hang around a restaurant—I'm not a big partier; I'm a married man. To really watch what was going on I'd have had to be there all the time. Live and learn. That was a very expensive lesson. I lost a lot of money."

Phil also lost money, at least initially, on his investment in the Sault Sainte Marie Greyhounds, a Junior hockey team, one of whose founders was Phil's father. Although he and his partners recently sold the team at a reported profit, they endured several years of heavy losses, including a one-year deficit in excess of one hundred thousand dollars.

Phil got involved as well in a designer clothing operation called Colors and was on the verge of introducing a range of big-and-tall clothes called "the Espo line" when the company was sold and Phil was dropped from its plans. He said, "I didn't have money in that one, just my name. When you get down to it, I really don't have a whole lot to sell except Phil Esposito. My name is good, and I owe that to hockey— I know that. And I protect my name and image. For instance, if Donna and I go to a party and there are drugs around, we get outta there."

As their various business ventures were raveling and unraveling during the early and mid-1980s, Phil and Donna put a prodigious amount of time and effort into the creation of the Phil Esposito Foundation, set up to help former players who were down on their luck. "We worked day and night to get it going," says Donna. "And it wasn't that we got paid, either. In fact, it cost us money. Phil simply decided that he wanted to give something back to the game. We completely devoted ourselves to it. I worked behind the scenes, bookkeeping, letter-writing, and so on. Phil took care of the public end. It was wonderful. It worked. I mean, there are a lot of ex-players who are lost—they don't have the ambition that a guy like Phil has. And certainly no one's knocking at their door saying, 'What would you like to do with your life?—Let us help you.' A lot of them turn to drinking or drugs. They've lost something that is very important to them. Suddenly they're not a part of this big family of players, with everything scheduled and organized for them. And of course most of them are too proud to ask for help. They walk into restaurants, and the manager says, 'Oh, come on in! Great to see you!' They're treated like celebrities, and they're ashamed to admit they're hurting. Their dignity is on the line. The foundation helped them. It allowed them to keep their troubles within the family, get turned around, and go out to face the world without anybody knowing what was happening. We put on hockey games and tournaments to raise money. And we got a lot of generous donations."

Phil said, "I never called the games old-timers' games. I called the guys Masters of Hockey. I thought it was asinine to call Bobby Orr an old-timer. And I didn't feel like an old-timer myself. We rented the Garden for $65,000 one time—that's what it cost to rent the place for one game—and we ended up making $60,000. Then we went to Maple Leaf Gardens and made $80,000. In the end, we got eighty guys jobs and gave financial help to a lot of others, including a number of guys who were sick and unable to work. Once, we flew a fella's family to him because he needed a blood transfusion, and only they could supply the blood."

Eventually, Phil approached the National Hockey League and attempted to get it involved with the foundation. "We needed a broader base for operating the thing," he said. But the league would have nothing to do with it. "And it seemed they were fighting it just because it was me," said Phil. "They seemed to imply that the only reason I was doing this was for my own glorification, or to make a dollar, or something, which was completely untrue and which of course made Donna and me feel terrible after all the work we'd put in. I said, 'Call it the National Hockey League Foundation, I don't care.' The only reason I called it the Phil Esposito Foundation in the first place was so that people would associate it with a name they recognized and would be more likely to support it. One time I went to meet with [NHL president] John Ziegler, and he said, 'Well, Phil, we do have a retirement fund; we call it a crisis fund. It helps guys out a little if they're in trouble, pays for funerals, that sort of thing.' I said, 'John, why is that news to me? How come I've never heard of this fund; I've been in the league twenty-five years! Why is it such a secret?' He said, 'Well, we don't like to toot our own horn about it.'

In the end, Phil and Donna allowed the foundation to lapse. "Without help," Phil said, "we just couldn't keep it going. The good thing that came of it is that every NHL team has now started an alumni association; they put on games and try to take care of their own people. Some of the owners pitch in, too."

In February of 1986, Phil was approached by the Rangers' owners, who asked quietly whether he'd be interested in becoming the team's general manager. Craig Patrick still held the post but would be fired within months. When the job was offered formally to Phil in June, he took it. Although he asked for a five-year contract he was permitted only three years. He said, "My thinking was that it would take five years to turn the team around, to make it what I wanted it to be. One thing I was able to get in the contract was that I had the complete right to hire and fire coaches, scouts, players, whoever. They didn't like it, but they put it in there." Phil noted, however, that he never actually had that freedom. "And that bothered me," he said. "I felt I needed it to do a proper job."

It also bothered Phil that the media hounded him at times over his penchant for making trades. He said, "I told them at a press conference the day I took the job, 'Hold onto your hats, folks. I'm going to do a lot of things here, and I'm going to do them quickly. You're going to think I'm insane, but I have a purpose. We're going to win here.' I explained this all to them, but then the minute I began making trades they started howling, Esposito has no rhyme or reason! He's going off in all directions! It was only when the team started moving up in the standings that they started talking differently. Since as far back as I can remember, I've always had to prove myself, no matter what I've done. I scored seventy-six goals in 1971, and yet nobody thought I was a great player until after the '72 series with the Russians. The question was, How good will he

be without Bobby Orr?—Bobby was hurt for the series. I did just fine
. . . I had to prove myself again during my first year as a broadcaster. I
had people saying, I can't believe the way he talks on the air! He can't
talk that way on the air! I used to talk exactly the way I talk in day-to-
day life—right off the cuff. Honest commentary. My producer used to
get livid! He didn't like that style. Then they all realized that it was working, that people liked it.

"Now I'm being doubted as a GM. Nothing comes easy to me—it's all
hard work."

Asked about the effects of the New York environment on his personality, Phil conceded that it had altered, perhaps toughened him. "Although
I think becoming a general manager has changed me more than the city
has," he said. "It's made me into a totally obsessive workaholic. New York
itself is often misunderstood. When people think of it they think only of
the muggings and murders and so on. But most of New York is beautiful—it's gorgeous! And the surrounding area is beautiful. Our area, up
around Bedford Village, is fantastic! We've got over four acres of land. I
was up at 5:30 this morning, and there were three deer in my backyard.
Don't get me wrong—New York will eat you up and spit you out if you're
not tough. Mentally tough. That's what you've got to be. But no matter
where you are, or what you do, you've got to be strong mentally to suc-
ceed. There's more pressure in New York for one reason only—the pace
of the city. Everything is fast here. Everything has to be fast here, because
it's the capital of the world, at least as far as I'm concerned. Economically,
for sure. New York runs the world. If you're not quick, you're going to
get gobbled up. Three hours after I spoke to Phil that afternoon, the
Rangers faced off against the Winnipeg Jets a few hundred feet from Phil's
office. They were gobbled up, losing decisively to a team that they should
have handled with ease. It was their seventh loss in eight games. A strong
season thus far was beginning to crumble.

In the aftermath of the game, the Ranger dressing room was like the
Seventh Salon of "The Masque of the Red Death." A half-dozen reporters
tiptoed around, daring not ask their questions too loudly for fear of vio-
lating the solemnity. Even in the corridor outside there was a festering,
viral gloom in the air. Team officials and functionaries, their faces a foot
long, padded gravely about, while Phil met in an anteroom with his
coaches and several senior players. The only people seemingly

unaffected were a few of the younger Rangers, who emerged from the dressing room chirping among themselves, two or three of them exchanging jocular pleasantries with members of the Jets, who were filing from their own room down the hall.

Presently, Phil emerged from his private tete-a-tete, showing the strain of a long day but nonetheless polite to those around him. He stopped briefly at a reception for goaltender Ed Giacomin, whose number had been retired in a pregame ceremony, and ten minutes later was at the wheel of his compact Lincoln, peeling north out of Manhattan.

It is an hour's drive from the Garden to Phil and Donna's home in Upper Westchester County, and for the first few miles of the drive Phil said little. But as he hit the south Bronx his frustration over the evening's carnage began to vent itself. "A game like that just upsets me so much," he said. "I feel angry at the effort my players put out, and at the fact that they weren't properly prepared mentally. We didn't have one guy out here tonight who was into the game. Not one guy. That's the coach's fault. It's his job to get these guys ready. And I'm angry at him for not going in there after the second period and blasting them. He should have been in there losing his marbles, throwing things at the wall. Sometimes players respond to that. I kept saying to myself, Why isn't he doing this? I know he wasn't because I was down in the dressing room. I wanted to do it myself, but it's not my place. So what do I do? I call Donna. She says, 'You sound tense—are you losing?' She doesn't watch it on TV; she's not a hockey fan at all. She used to come to the games when I was playing, but she's never cared that much. And I prefer it that way. She's always been there for me when I needed her, but it's best for our marriage that she doesn't become part of this hockey scene. Then the pressure would be double for me. She'd come to the games, and I'd worry about her. We'd be driving home, and she'd be talking hockey—I'd go crazy. She'd point things out about the game— maybe bad things, so-and-so played awful, and she'd be right. I don't need that. I need somebody just to sit and listen."

Phil paused for a moment and, as if uttering a perfectly sequential thought, blurted, "You just can't blow games to vastly inferior teams!"

As we hit the I-684 at Yonkers, Phil began to relax, eventually asking me if I had my tape recorder handy. He said, "We might as well put a few things down." The night was mild, and he reached up and opened the roof vent.

Expressing himself boldly and genuinely, for better or worse, has always been the mark of the man. And as we proceeded north into Westchester County, his conversation broadened until, before long, he was moving fluently, indiscriminately, from one subject to another, apparently enjoying the psychological release of random chatter. Here is a sampling of the night's thoughts and revelations:

ON THE 1972 SERIES WITH THE SOVIETS: "The experience wasn't as pleasant for me as it was for a lot of the guys. I thought the Russians were pigs—on the ice, I mean. Imagine them kicking our players with their skates! It was war for me. I've said this before, and I'm not very proud of it because I've never even killed an animal—I don't know how people can kill in a war—but there's no doubt in my mind that I'd have killed to win that series. It scares me, but it's true. And we did win. Our problem was that we only trained for ten days before the first game. We used to train for six weeks for NHL games! We weren't in shape until we got to Russia for the final four games. We could have played ten more games in Russia, and we would have won them all. We not only got into condition, we became a team, a team possessed, a team that refused to lose. I'd never reached that kind of emotional high before and have never reached it again."

ON PHYSICAL CONDITIONING: "During my playing days, I never did anything when it came to exercise off the ice. In training camp when they used to run, I'd hide in the bushes and throw water on my face to look as if I'd been sweating. And that stupid stationary bicycle—I hated that thing. What a waste of time! I did my training on the ice. I'd come into camp maybe ten pounds too heavy, and by the end of camp I'd be at my playing weight, 210–212.

"My cardiovascular system is great. I had a test in Russia, and they couldn't believe how good my heart was. Two years ago I had another one—I've got the cardiovascular system of a twenty-five-year-old. It's hereditary. And I say that even though my dad died of a heart attack at sixty-three. He ate himself to death. He was only 5'11", and he weighed 260. He ate sausages and salamis until they came out his eyeballs. I eat junk but not the really bad kind—I eat popcorn."

ON RELAXATION: "The only relaxation I get anymore is golf, and that can be pretty intense in itself. But I like it. And yet I can't play it unless it's for money! I don't care if it's only a buck—I'll go for it. But if it's just for fun, I can take it or leave it."

ON HOCKEY STARDOM:

"Sometimes I'm not sure there's all that much difference in talent between the

> **"I figure, if you've gotta go, go first class or don't go at all."**

stars and the lesser lights. But the guys with the most pride in what they do—with the most intensity and guts—come out on top. Take a guy like Gordie Howe—he's a very proud guy. No matter what he does, he takes pride in it. And that's done an awful lot for his career, both on and off the ice. I myself take a lot of pride in what I do. That's why I suffer so much over my work. I have full-scale anxiety attacks when things go wrong."

ON LUXURIOUS LIVING: "I need a good job because I like the good life, and I'm not ashamed to admit it. I love spending money. I figure, if you've gotta go, go first class or don't go at all. I'm not just talking about airplanes, but for nineteen years as a player I sat in economy, and I'm so big that in those skinny little seats, with people beside me, I couldn't even lift my arm to eat. I used to promise myself that when it was all over I'd ride up front in comfort. Same with hotels—the teams used to stay in dives. We didn't have the best, believe me. I remember staying in a hotel in Washington that was absolutely the worst joint I've ever seen. It was freezing cold! And dirty! So I always take a good hotel when I travel. A Marriott or a Holiday Inn is just a room to me—I want a hotel to be like home. In New York, Donna and I like the Pierre— Donna took me there on my fortieth birthday; we had a suite. And we've stayed at the Plaza and at the Helmsley Palace—that was nice. . . . When I was broadcasting, one of the things I negotiated into my contract was that I always flew first class. They didn't want to give it to me, so I said, 'Okay, I'm not going to be a broadcaster then.' So they gave it to me."

*   *   *   *

Upper Westchester County is an area of narrow winding roads, of towns with shiplap houses, of cemeteries as old as the American Revolution. Its farms and villages, once a day's travel by stagecoach from Manhattan, over muddy roads, are now bedroom communities for the well-healed slaves of New York. Mercedes-Benzes and BMWs sit in the lanes; pricey restaurants and fashion boutiques are the jewels of local commerce. This is not to suggest that twentieth-century gentrification has been unkind to the area: there are still neatly painted bandshells in the small-town parks, old wooden churches with perfect spires on the main streets, unpainted sheds in the backyards. The grassy hills and dense stands of maple and oak are largely unmolested by civilization.

Although Phil and Donna's address is Mount Kisco, the town nearest their home is Bedford Village, a snoozy, anachronistic little place with backwater charm and no discernible industry. "I grew up in Swampscott, Massachusetts, just a short walk from the Atlantic," said Donna, on the day of my visit with her, "but even though there's no water here, this place has always reminded me of home. It's very New England—the houses, the white clapboard church with its steeple. When we built, I felt very comfortable up here."

The Espositos' house, designed by Donna, is an elegant structure built of grey-brown stone, with a large swimming pool out back and a scattering of exotic saplings on the hillside lawn in front. Except for that lawn and a rectangular clearing of perhaps two acres behind the house, the predominant surroundings are hardwood forest, heavily veined with horse trails. "Before we moved out here, I used to come out this way every day to ride," Donna said. "I still ride every morning. My horse, Sneakers, boards about a mile and a half from here. She and I compete; we're in what they call the Hunter division. We go around a course doing jumps, just small ones."

Donna, who appears to be in her mid-thirties, is a slim, pretty woman with longish blonde hair. She speaks in a gentle Bostonian accent and when asked about her background did not mention that she is a triplet. She is in many ways an ideal match for Phil—quiet, private, introspective, tending to bring forth a gentle side of him that many people do not get to see. The two met in California in 1977, while Donna was working for Aetna Life and Casualty in San Francisco. "We'd been introduced years earlier in Boston," she said, "but I didn't remember it very well; Phil says he did. When we met again in California I thought his name sounded familiar, but maybe that was just because I was from Boston, and I would have heard it by chance on radio or television. I wasn't a hockey fan at all, and I'm still not, although I do appreciate the players' talents and the movement and excitement of the game.

Donna volunteered that she was attracted to Phil because of his "many-faceted" personality. "I realized right away," she said, "that he wasn't the sort of guy who was locked into one career or one frame of mind. He's a real individual—very outgoing, very confident. And very honorable and generous, too. Phil has a very good heart. All of these things impressed me."

Donna submitted that the same attributes enabled Phil to survive the transition out of active hockey without major disruptions. "The more you have going, the better off you are," she said. "If Phil ever left hockey completely, I'd have no worries about him. He goes into things so wholeheartedly, I'm sure he'd be a success at whatever he took up.

When the question was raised as to what he might take up if he left hockey completely, Phil reflected for a few seconds and said, "I'd probably do something in the public relations line. Right now I have a part-time p.r. job with the Sands Hotel and casino in Atlantic City, and I enjoy that. I drive over there from time to time—maybe once a month in summer, not so often in winter—and I meet the big players, do a little golfing. Sometimes I'll travel to Toronto or Montreal, wherever, and go to a party or a dinner put on by the Sands."

Confronted with the notion that his link to a major gambling establishment was somewhat out of whack with his concern for his public image, Phil was vociferous in explaining that the Sands is owned "not by mobsters" but by the reputable Pratt Corporation, owners of an international chain of hotels. "Why do people always think that gambling has to be tied in with drugs and so on?" he protested. "People who work for the Sands—or for any gambling outfit in New Jersey—have to get a license. And I'll tell you, these employees are scrutinized before they get it. In my own case, the authorities went right through my records, and if I'd had one little bleep or blemish, I wouldn't have got a job. And the gamblers themselves aren't criminals! Most of them are wealthy lawyers or businessmen or brokers. Sure, there's the odd so-called shady character, but you get as many of them in Madison Square Garden as you do in Atlantic City. If I suspect somebody, I'll ask my bosses, and they might say, 'Yeah, stay away from him.' I mean, I don't even go around the gambling tables. I walk through, say hi, and I'm gone. I stay up at the restaurant and the bar. Most of the time I'm in bed by midnight. But look at all this another way—do you know who the biggest promoters of gambling are? The government, that's who! They run more lotteries and gambling games than Atlantic City and Las Vegas put together!"

Defenses and arguments aside, Phil's true vision of the future that day seemed closer to his family and to Bedford Village than to the gambling tables of Atlantic City. "What's important is right here," he said earnestly. "We've got our lives all tied up with this house and this community. We love the area. Donna's really enjoying it, and Cherise is at a great school. I was just over there to pick her up, and I watched her in the playground. It was fun! I never did that with my two daughters by my first wife—they're twenty-one and twenty-three now. As I was watching Cherise, I said to myself, I've gotta do whatever it takes to keep this going till I'm fifty-five [Phil is forty-eight now]. By that time, I figure I'll be ready to let the work go, sell everything, do exactly what we want for the rest of our lives. On the other hand, if I feel I'm going to get sick, I'll cut out sooner. Worry is hard on me. When I get sick, it's generally because I'm worried. I'm not a big worrier—I don't worry about money, for instance. I always tell Donna, I can get money, because I'm not afraid to work. If we need something, I'll get it somehow. But sometimes I've got more than money on my mind."

*   *   *   *

Phil had more than money on his mind when, a month after my visit with him, he fired his coach, Michel Bergeron, starting a chain of events that would ultimately bring about his downfall as general manager of the New York Rangers. He himself took over as coach, leading the team through the final few games of the '88–'89 season and into the Patrick Division playoffs against the Pittsburgh Penguins, a team with which the Rangers should have been evenly matched. As it turned out, they were not. They failed to win even a single game in the best-of-seven series and were the first team eliminated from the NHL playoffs. The common thinking was that, regardless of the Rangers' late-season slide in the standings, Phil had made a strategic error in firing his coach with the playoffs so near at hand; the upheaval had hurt the team's prospects. Apologists, however, say the Rangers would have done no better under Bergeron, given that the team's chances were already reduced by injuries to several key players.

On May 24, Phil's boss, Jack Diller, the executive vice president of the Madison Square Garden Sports Group, entered Phil's office and announced that changes were being made and that Phil, too, was being fired. "I told him, 'Fine,'" said Phil. "He said, 'You don't seem that upset.' I said, 'I'm not. Whatever you think you have to do, you have to do. I did what I had to

> **"Whatever you think you have to do, you have to do. I did what I had to do when I fired Michel."**

do when I fired Michel.' Then I said, 'Am I going to get paid?' He said, 'No problem.' See, I still had fifteen months to go in my contract."

On the day following the firing, the *Toronto Globe and Mail* speculated that Phil's contract was worth some $300,000 a year to him. The newspaper also speculated—and Phil agreed—that he had been fired not over his dismissal of Michel Bergeron but because Ranger executives felt he did not present the "corporate image" they considered appropriate to the general manager's role: too flamboyant, too outspoken, too much his own man. In a closing note, the story said that Phil and Donna were about to put their house up for sale.

*   *   *   *

Nearly five weeks passed before I spoke to Phil by phone. I had been reluctant to call, to disturb what I imagined was probably something of a wake in Bedford Village.

I could not have been more in error. Or more surprised to find Phil hale and chipper and bubbly with optimism about the future. "I've formed a new company," he announced. "Espac Associates. Contracting management."

Phil explained enthusiastically that Espac is a partnership linking him to the Scabia Construction Company of New York and Defeo Brothers Demolition of Boston. He said, "My job is to initiate business for these guys—construction, demolition, whatever people want. I guess you could say I'm a kind of agency. I've already contracted the construction of two new buildings. Having a great time. Great money, too. And of course I'm still getting paid by the Rangers."

Phil expressed no resentment toward his former employers, although he did admit to frustration that he had not been given the five years he felt he needed to put together a winner. "Other than that, I have no negative feelings about it," he said. "The stress is gone! I'm relaxed for a change. People come up to me and say, 'Phil, you look terrific!' I feel terrific."

The tough part, Phil allowed, would come in September, when for the first time in forty-three years he would not be revving up for a new hockey season. "I know I'm going to miss it terribly," he said. "And the further the winter goes along, the worse it's going to get. I just hope I can take it."

Was the house up for sale?

"Who said that?"

"The *Globe and Mail* said you said it."

"What I said was that if another job in hockey came along, and it involved a move, then we'd put the house up for sale." Without skipping a beat, Phil revealed that if he didn't get back into hockey, he and Donna were thinking of buying a small farm somewhere. "Don't get me wrong," he said. "We love our place here. But it's way too big for the three of us. We'd like a place where we can have some animals for Cherise and where Donna can keep her horse. We've been thinking about Florida, maybe even California. Could be anywhere, though."

Never one to think small, Phil disclosed that, if the dream of a farm came to pass, he hoped to construct a five hundred–yard golf fairway on the property. "I'd have a green at each end, and nine tees at various points along the sides. You could play to either green from each tee, giving you eighteen different approaches. But, as I said, this is only if I don't get back into hockey."

And what were the chances of getting back into hockey?

"We'll just have to wait and see," said Phil.

In the meantime, was there anything he wanted to add to the story I was about to construct?

He thought for a moment, chuckled, and said, "Just tell the readers that if anybody needs a building put up, or needs one demolished, to let me know. I'll be happy to take care of it.

"Otherwise, that's about it."

*   *   *   *

Epilogue

Phil didn't stay long in the demolition business. When, in 1991, power-brokers and city officials in Tampa Bay, Florida, decided they wanted an NHL hockey franchise, they believed that of all people Phil was best suited to help them secure that franchise, and hired him to do so. They also believed Phil could best promote the idea of hockey in central Florida and could best manage an NHL team once it existed.

And in part they were right. Phil did help secure the franchise. And by shaking enough hands and making enough speeches in the Tampa Bay area, he was able to invent a narrow but optimistic niche for hockey in the Sunshine State.

However, in six years as General Manager of the Tampa Bay Lightning (1992–98), he was never quite able to do what his bosses most wanted done—create a winner on the ice. With Phil's brother Tony as director of player development and scouting, and Phil's old friend Don Murdoch as head scout, the Lightning wallowed through several mediocre seasons, narrowly making the playoffs just once, in 1996.

Ownership changed, and changed again—the second time bringing owner Art Williams into the picture and a new level of ineptitude at the top. Intolerance toward Phil grew. But in fairness to the one-time star, his superiors were meddling and tight-fisted . . . to the point where Phil was several times obliged to trade away good talent for bad. "All [team president] Steve Oto did was bitch about money," Espo said in a recent conversation. "He was always telling me which players had to go because their contracts were too big. I still laugh at people who ask me, 'How could you let so-and-so go?' It was because I wasn't given the money to pay these guys!"

When Tampa Bay's sparkling new Ice Palace was opened in 1997, Oto did not so much as provide a seat for Phil—this in an arena Phil had helped bring into being.

Art Williams stuck with Phil until the player contracts had been signed for the '98–'99 season, and then fired him after the second game. When the All-Star game was held at the Ice Palace later that season, Phil's name was not mentioned in connection either with the team or with the development of major league hockey in the area.

In the meantime, Phil's private life had been no smoother than his life in hockey. He had barely arrived in Florida when his marriage to Donna ended in estrangement and divorce.

But his love of Tampa Bay has survived. Perhaps surprisingly, so has his affection for the franchise he built. "I'm frustrated that I never got the chance to build a winner," he said recently. "But I still consider this team my baby. I follow them regularly on TV, and I hope this year, or next year, or the year after, they turn this league upside down."

Phil still lives in Tampa, where in the near future he plans to open a mortgage banking business. For the moment, however, he is committed to Fox Television, with whom he has a contract as a hockey analyst. The job takes him regularly to California for studio work, and last season he broadcast twenty Boston Bruins games on the road. "What I regret way more than losing my job with the Lightning," he said recently, "was giving up my job in broadcasting to become GM of the Rangers in 1986. That was the biggest mistake I ever made. In broadcasting you get to be around the game, but you don't have the stress. You don't have to worry about wins and losses."

Free of that stress, Phil plays golf daily, has lost thirty pounds, and, as he puts it, has "never slept better" in his life.

CHAPTER
3

John Ferguson

Ballet and Murder

Early in his career with the Montreal Canadiens, John Ferguson announced his desire to be the meanest, rottenest, most despicably miserable cuss ever to skate in the NHL. Which, as hockey desires go, was extravagant but not extraordinary. Long before Conn Smythe prophesied that if you couldn't beat 'em in the alley, you couldn't beat 'em on the ice. NHL aspirants realized that success in pro hockey had almost as much to do with belligerence as with beauty (poet Al Purdy called the game "a combination of ballet and murder").

The difference between Ferguson's desires and those of the young terror-mongers who might have shared them was that Ferguson had the power—a remarkable combination of physical strength and competitive malfeasance—to actually be the meanest, rottenest, most despicably miserable cuss ever to score a knockout (or a goal) in the dramatic burlesque that is Canada's national game.

Only twelve seconds had elapsed in Fergy's first NHL engagement, in 1963, when he took on "Terrible Ted" Green, the Boston Bruins' house vigilante, "going right over top of him," as Ferguson describes it, and placing a big red floribunda on his kisser.

Ferguson and students of his career are dutiful in pointing out that he also scored two goals that night, and a few days later he was named

NHL Player of the Week—the point being, of course, that he had not learned his hockey in a boxing ring and that he was far more than a headknocker. And he was! But it was not the news of his goal scoring that put the rest of the league on nervous alert over the arrival of the young left winger. What caught their attention was the impressive report that he had dusted off Terrible Ted, had done so with gusto, and just might be the meanest, rottenest, et cetera, ever to arrive in the NHL.

In fact, during the eight years that followed, Ferguson was exactly that, a free-ranging locus of vehemence and ill will, a kind of anti-Franciscan, sowing despair where there was hope, darkness where there was light, a broken nose and five loose teeth where, once, there was facial integrity.

It is one of those anomalies understood best by bag ladies and poets that, away from hockey, Ferguson has always been a paragon of discretion, a shy and considerate man, as avuncular as Wiggily, as obliging as Pooh. He was once referred to as "a real sweetie" by no less a witness than Nancy Bower, wife of Johnny Bower, the fabled Maple Leaf goaltender who knew Fergy's wrath as well as anyone during the years of their combatantcy. Which isn't to say that Ferguson has never betrayed social or personal raw edges, or that he has ever been taken for Casper Milquetoast, even in a dark room (Casper doesn't smoke cigars). But, away from the rink, he does indeed possess an unassuming mien, an innocence and sensitivity that, over the years, has revealed only traces of the professional animosity on which he founded his reputation as a player.

Discretion has figured so significantly in the composite of Ferguson's off-ice personality that, when it came time to write his autobiography in 1986, there were aspects of his life—thoughts, reminiscences, reflections on people and events—that he simply did not feel comfortable committing to print, for fear that some person or organization might somehow, somewhere, be offended.

"There are things you just can't put in a book," says Joan Ferguson, John's wife of thirty-seven years.

"Like what?" she and John are asked as they sit at the dining table of their home in Amherstburg, Ontario, on a mild mid-winter day.

"Well," John says circumspectly, and within seconds he has begun to explain how, for example, it has always been assumed that his retirement from hockey in 1971 was predicated strictly on the lure of opportunities in the knitwear and restaurant trades and at Blue Bonnet Raceway in Montreal. (He doesn't mention that that assumption has been perpetuated by the book itself.) "What I didn't discuss in the book," he continues, "what I've never discussed publicly, is that at a point during my second-to-last season, I felt . . . well . . . I guess you

> **"During that time, not one member of the Canadiens' ownership or management or coaching staff came to visit me, or even sent flowers or a card."**

could say betrayed by the Canadiens, an organization to which I'd given everything possible, and then some, for seven seasons."

At the root of John's comments is an injury he received just before Christmas 1969 when, in a game against the Minnesota North Stars in Minneapolis, a puck struck him so violently in the face that it detached the retina of his right eye and crushed the occipital bone beneath the eyeball. "I had emergency surgery in Minneapolis to correct the detached retina," he says, "but I didn't want to stay in the hospital there, so the next day I checked myself out and went to the airport to get a flight to Chicago. But before I could get one, the pain in my face worsened to where it was as if my whole head was being torn off. And my eye had begun to drop in its socket. At that point, it was all I could do to get back to the hospital in Minneapolis."

A day or two later, Ferguson reached Montreal and again entered the hospital, this time to have the damaged bone beneath his eye replaced with a plastic implant. "For six days over the Christmas holidays, I lay there in the Montreal General, either freezing to death in the hallway, waiting for the operation, or in excruciating pain after the drugs wore off. And during that time, not one member of the Canadiens' ownership or management or coaching staff came to visit me, or even sent flowers or a card. In fact, only one of them even phoned—Toe Blake. Once. And I'll tell ya, it soured me, lying there, realizing that apparently none of them cared. It was probably nothing personal, but it told me something, and while I was in hospital I promised that if I ever ran a hockey club I'd never ever let such a thing happen to one of my players. And I didn't. When I was general manager of the Rangers, then the Jets, we did everything we could for injured players—visited them, sent flowers, helped their families, anything to make them more comfortable."

It is typical of his personality, and of his commitment to team stability, that John has never mentioned his resentment towards the Canadiens. Yet he is adamant that it led directly to his retirement in 1970. "I did make a comeback for half a season in '71," he says, "and Sam Pollock offered me the captaincy if I'd stay on longer, but even that didn't sway me."

If John needed added incentive to convert his blades into ploughshares, he got it in spades from business partners with whom he'd gone into knitwear manufacturing earlier in the year, and who now managed to persuade him that he was about make his fortune in the trade. And initially their prediction seemed sound. "Within a year or two of my getting there we went from sixty employees to twelve hundred," says John. "We were going twenty-four hours a day, turning out every-thing from sweaters to dresses to pants."

While the knitting machines were turning yarn into golf shirts and profit projections, John's primary job was to get the company dub, Butternut Enterprises, through the doors of department stores such as Eaton's and the Bay. "But I was also an investor, a buyer, a designer," he says. "I'd go to Florida and California and bring back sample items, whatever was hot, and we'd do knock-offs and fire 'em out the door."

At the same time, the company opened "Fergy's" restaurant on Decarie Street beneath the garment factory. "I'd start the day at the factory," says John, "then I'd go down to the restaurant, check things out, keep things moving." In early afternoon, with a pickle and a smoked-meat sandwich behind his belt buckle, he would leave the restaurant and head to Blue Bonnet Raceway, where for years he'd been indulging the longest-stand-ing love of his life, horse racing, and where a short time hence he would be named assistant director of racing.

The impression is created, both in talking to John and in his book, that retirement at this point was one great swirl of productive activity, and that hockey, by comparison, was a rather bleary memory seen through the reducing end of a peepscope.

Joan Ferguson is considerably less idealistic in her view of the period, although painstaking in her determination not to tarnish the off-ice accomplishments of the man she loves. "I guess I'm a realist," she smiles, "and it seems to me, looking back, that John's business partners had an agenda that wasn't always conceived in John's best interests. They persuaded him, for example, that the Canadiens weren't giving him the money or respect he deserved, even though he was working himself to the bone for them. Of course, they wanted him full-time, to represent the company. His popularity in Montreal was a real benefit to them. At the same time, they more or less used his knowledge of horses to get into the racing business themselves. He worked with them for five or six years—we had money in the business—and only later, in thinking back, did he realize that he never did get a salary from them, even though he was president of the company."

Asked what John did get from the business, Joan responds bluntly, "Being busy. He was extremely busy. When it was over and the business sold, he certainly didn't come out of it with anything to speak of. And yet, being the man he is, he wouldn't breathe a word against these guys! Even after twenty years! I guess you could say he felt the same way about them that he felt about Mr. Selke [long-time general manager of the Canadiens], whose first contract with John was a handshake and a little piece of torn-off paper that said, 'I will pay you $7,500 for the season— F. J. Selke.' John carried it around in his wallet.

"If somebody is willing to shake hands with John, he feels they'll be as honest as he is about their agreement. . . . Really, I don't want to say too much more about the clothing business, except that I think we got out of it lucky, with ourselves intact and our family still functioning very well." Now Joan is laughing. "We had John's past lives analyzed one night for fun, and, as I figured, he's on his first life. He can be so trusting and naive. And yet he's so shrewd in other ways—with his horses and hockey, for instance."

It was John's shrewdness as a hockey man that, a year after his retirement from the Canadiens, led to what he calls his "greatest thrill in sport," surpassing five Stanley Cup victories and a handful of Executive of the Year awards won during his term as general manager of the Winnipeg Jets. For Canadians, the story of the Soviet-Canada hockey summit in 1972 has taken on biblical dimensions, dwarfing even the heroic victories of Canadians during the First and Second World Wars. And there are few parts of this seminal national story that are not well known even to casual fans of the game. However, one detail that has generally escaped codification is that if Harry Sinden, the team's general manager, had had his way, the Canadian contingent of left wingers—an iconographic cast featuring the likes of Frank Mahovlich and Paul Henderson—would have included the perhaps unlikely name of John Byway Ferguson. "He asked me to play, and the only reason I didn't," says Fergy, "was that there'd already been an ugly drawn-out debate over the exclusion of Bobby Hull from the team, because he'd left the NHL, and I felt my participation as a player, after more than a year of retirement, would probably have opened up another controversy that would have detracted from the focus on the series."

Fergy went on to take a proud and significant role in the selection, coaching, and management of the team and has never regretted his decision not to participate as a player. What does bother him are the infrequent but lingering questions—"they still come up"—concerning what a player such as he might have contributed to the Canadian effort should he have decided to put on a uniform. "People always saw me merely as a fighter," he laments. "They don't realize that I was All-Star in junior, an All-Star in the American League, that one year I led the Canadiens in goal scoring—twenty-nine goals in 1968–69—that twice I was the Canadiens' top-scoring left winger. What's a guy have to do? Everybody seemed to suggest that World War Three was going to break out if I played in that series. As a player I had other things to offer as well as toughness. And I knew that."

And Harry Sinden knew it; and so did Toe Blake, Frank Selke, and Sam Pollock—and a slew of rival coaches and players, not to mention anyone who ever played alongside John. "When I became coach of the Bruins," Harry Sinden once said, "I would have taken Ferguson over anybody else in the league. Anybody. He had the kind of aggressiveness that could lift an entire team and keep it hitting and fighting, long after it had passed the point of exhaustion."

It is hardly a coincidence that after his arrival in Montreal in 1963, the Canadiens, who had not won a championship in three years, went on to win Stanley Cups in four of the next six years, three times in the absence of their grand potentate, Jean Beliveau, who missed the finals because of injuries. Nor is it a coincidence that in some fifteen years of junior and professional hockey, John was never traded (who in possession of such a weapon would put it in the arsenal of a rival army?).

"It's a kind of chicken-and-egg thing," says Joan. "John was never traded because of his attitude, and his attitude was partly a result of him never having been traded. If he'd bounced around from one team to another like so many players do, he'd probably have gotten cynical, and his commitment would have wavered."

The annals of the era shiver with tales of his intensity and dedication: how once as a minor-leaguer he fired a puck at the head of a teammate who was kibitzing with a rival player during the warm-up for a game ("I missed," he says matter-of-factly). How he once stormed out of George's restaurant in Toronto, leaving an untouched steak on the table, because his teammate Dick Duff struck up a conversation with John's arch rival, Eddie Shack, who happened to come in ("I couldn't stand being in the same room with the guy, let alone seeing a teammate talking to him!"). How he would turn his contemptuous stare on any teammate who showed even the slightest sign of flippancy before or during a game ("He was as intimidating to our own guys as to the opposition," says Jean Beliveau).

"Where hockey was concerned," says Joan, "there was only one word to describe John—possessed. His only fear was losing, and wherever he could he passed that along to his teammates."

It hardly needs saying that Fergy was not a deft puck-handler or skater (he didn't don skates until the age of twelve), but he is quite justified in pointing out that his contribution as a player was by no means confined to adrenaline and ice boxing. Besides getting to the net when it counted and scoring his share of goals, he was an avid student of positional play and was a ferociously successful checker. In eight years of personally checking Gordie Howe, he didn't once permit Howe a goal. In fact, Fergy himself scored 145 goals in a five hundred–game career (the ratio extrapolated to a career the length of Howe's—2,186 games—would give him 634 goals). More remarkably, he averaged only 2.4 minutes per game in penalties (compared to, say, Tiger Williams, who averaged more than four minutes per game).

But no matter how the lily is gilded, or the record book interpreted, John will inevitably be remembered best as the man he wanted to be— the meanest, rottenest, most despicably miserable cuss ever to lace on skates. And as a five-star slugger. In a jingoistic exercise orchestrated by

> **"I was so cocky, I just never believed I'd lose to anybody."**

Canadian magazine during the late sixties, boxer George Chuvalo picked the top ten fighters in hockey and, not surprisingly, chose Ferguson as the heavyweight champion of the lot. A short time later, Fergy was more than willing to participate in a proposed exhibition bout with Chuvalo.

However, the Canadiens nixed the idea for fear that Ferguson would be hurt—or perhaps that Chuvalo would. It may even have occurred to them that if Fergy scored well against the famous boxer (he had, after all, taken boxing lessons as a teenager) he might, in the flush of victory, be tempted to abandon hockey for a more lucrative career in the ring. "I was so cocky, I just never believed I'd lose to anybody," Ferguson says with a shrug. "When Imlach was in Toronto, he'd often say he was bringing some guy up from the minors who was gonna do a number on me, and I'd skate by the Toronto bench, and I'd say, 'Who ya got this week, Punch? Send him out now!'"

"Fergy was the most formidable player of the decade, if not in the Canadiens' history," says Jean Beliveau. "He'd do what he had to to win, and he had to win—he wouldn't stand for anything less."

It was this indefatigable will to dispose of his opposition—as well as his success with Team Canada and with a professional lacrosse team he ran in Montreal during the early seventies—that, in 1975, brought Fergy to the attention of the floundering New York Rangers, who sent him a distress call and, within days, hired him as coach and general manager. Their hope was that he would imbue the team—a gang Ferguson characterizes as having massive salaries and massive hypochondria—with much-needed discipline and direction. Not surprisingly, one of Fergy's earliest moves in New York was to acquire Nick Fotiu, a 220-pound practitioner of hockey's darker arts. He also cleared the dressing room of its coterie of fawning doctors, hired a fitness expert, and began purging the roster of high-priced players who weren't pulling their (sometimes ample) weight.

But the book on Fergy's tenure on Broadway is by no means a slavish testament to discipline or old-style management. He was the first, for instance, to allow female reporters into the dressing room at Madison

Square Garden, declaring an unequivocal belief in what he calls "the practice of equal rights." He also responded to changes in the game, indeed influenced those changes, by advancing the boundaries of conventional scouting, chiefly in Europe, and by recognizing the talents of Scandinavian and American college players, who many in the game still viewed as fancy-skating, light-hitting irregulars. One of his last acts as Ranger general manager was to acquire Swedish stars Ulf Nilsson and Anders Hedberg from the Winnipeg Jets of the WHA.

Fergy's unexpected downfall in New York began four years after his arrival when he eased long-time Ranger hero Rod Gilbert, whom he considered overpaid and significantly overripe, out of the line-up and into a minor executive job with the club. Gilbert worked from behind the scenes to turn Sonny Werblin, a senior Garden executive, against Ferguson, and one morning in the spring of 1979 Fergy and the rest of the city awoke to a headline in the New York Daily News informing them that Fergy was no longer an employee of the Rangers.

The bitter turn of events was repeated in Winnipeg nine years later, after Ferguson's lengthy and successful term as general manager of the Jets. But this time the betrayal was perpetrated not by an obvious foe such as Gilbert but by Mike Smith, whom Ferguson had first hired in New York and had groomed as his assistant in Winnipeg. The duplicitous assistant convinced team owner Barry Shenkarow, a one-time business partner of Ferguson's, that Fergy was no longer right for the job, and Shenkarow fired the man who had led the Jets from the WHA into the NHL and had established them as a respectable and entertaining franchise.

"When John was fired in New York," says Joan, "I just told him, 'Don't worry about it—it's their loss.' I know it was painful for him, but it wasn't as if he'd been diagnosed with some fatal disease. Same in Winnipeg, really. It hurt him, and it's not at all like somebody getting laid off from a factory. It's headline news! You've given your heart and brains to this thing for so long, and it's over, and there's nothing you can do about it."

"And for that reason," says John, "we've never wasted any time thinking about the disappointments and disloyalties of the past. They come along, you deal with them, then it's on to the next challenge."

Asked if there are disappointments he has not dispelled so easily, Fergy thinks for a moment and gives a most unexpected answer on yet another topic that does not appear in his autobiography. "Quite a few years back," he reflects, "I was nominated for the Hockey Hall of Fame, and I heard from somebody close to the selection process that my nomination had gone through and I was in. Then when the new inductees were announced, my name wasn't among them. It's a very political process, and apparently there'd been a slight shift among the committee members at the last moment—enough to turn things against me. I wouldn't have felt so badly, except that I'd heard that I was in. It was very disappointing."

When it is suggested in jest that perhaps at some point in the past Fergy had beaten up someone he shouldn't have—a committee member? a committee member's friend or teammate? His face broadens into a smile. "If I did," he says quietly, "he probably deserved it."

*   *   *   *   *

Considering the proclivities of his early years, Fergy's face, at age fifty-six, is remarkably free of scars, and even of wrinkles. And despite the many injuries he suffered in the NHL trenches—inflictions of the sort that, for many NHL survivors, have led to debilitating arthritis—there is nothing about his gait or physical mannerisms that betrays even a hint of stiffness or incapacitation. He has an extraordinarily long nose with the contour of a skinning knife, thick brown hair, and the physique of a Kodiak bear. You cannot look at him without suspecting that at least part of his success as a pugilist must have come from his robust thighs and low center of gravity.

Fergy also possesses a less obvious pugilistic asset that, in the arcane realm of hockey warfare, may have cost him as much as it earned: "He was very slow to bleed," says Joan. "He could get clobbered on the head with, say, a stick, and he'd go to show the ref to prove it, and there wouldn't be a trace of blood, because his scalp, even the flesh on his forehead, is so extremely supple. You can pick it up between your fingers. He's like a shar-pei dog. A barber in Nanaimo once told him that, with a scalp like his, he'd never lose his hair."

Fergy has not punched anybody out in nearly twenty-four years, and he has no plans to do so. Yet when you ask him to show you the famous fists, the efficacious jack-hammers that rearranged so many noses and jaws during his years in the NHL, he doesn't hesitate to fold them and raise them. And even though it's only for show—and despite the smile on his face—you sense in the way he strikes the pose, elbows tucked, neck slightly scrunched, that way down deep, in the regions where the nerves think for themselves, he has not entirely forgotten the adrenaline thrill of vanquishing the many challengers who faced him.

> **"When they take the animosity out of the game, they can all go on strike, and nobody will miss them."**

Fergy once said the size of his hands was a significant factor in his stunning success as a fighter. And his hands are indeed large, the palms as thick as steak-house filets. But they are not so much big in breadth or length as they are stout hands, muscular hands, each a kind of mortar shell faced with knuckles an inch in diameter. As fists, they give the impression of being unarticulated extensions of his daunting arms and shoulders—and perhaps, more significantly, of the Draconian competitive temperament that, where sport is concerned, still lurks in the backwaters of his personality. On this particular afternoon, the old sensibility reveals itself in his low-key bridling over the buttery hockey being played by Wayne Gretzky and his band of All-Stars, on tour in Europe while NHL owners and players consume themselves and their season in wearisome labor negotiations. "That's not hockey they're playing over there!" Fergy scoffs. "There's absolutely no bloody intensity to it! When I played, we had pride! We did what we had to to win!"

For Fergy more than others, winning at any cost is an article of competitive faith. "As a hockey man," he says, "there's nothing worse than having to sit there and watch players float around and smile at one another and chit-chat during faceoffs. Our own NHL All-Star games are awful—imagine scores like 17–16!" He leans toward his visitor and taps his forefinger on the coffee table. "I'll tell ya something," he says, peering across the top of his reading glasses. "When they take the animosity out of the game, they can all go on strike, and nobody will miss them."

While her attitude toward hockey is somewhat less assertive than her husband's, Joan Ferguson, too, takes the view that pacifism is getting the upper hand in the game and is eventually going to give hockey a black eye. "What's the point if there's no drive to win?" she asks. "You might just as well draw straws and say, okay, your team wins tonight, ours'll win another night!"

Joan is a slim, insightful woman with an expressive face and an abundance of upbeat energy. Her outlook and attentiveness are a testimony to the range of domestic and psychological capabilities that must have been required to raise four children, often in John's absence, and to attend to John's hockey career as assiduously as she has. "He worked hard and I did, too," she says. "But I must say that I've genuinely enjoyed the hockey." During John's twenty-five years as a professional player, coach, and manager, she missed only a handful of the thousand-odd home games his teams played. Behind the scenes, she acted as dietitian, chauffeur, morale booster, archivist, and family ambassador to local charities and schools. "There were times when I even played doctor," she says. "I'd change dressings, make hospital visits, snip out sutures, whatever needed doing."

Today, she and Fergy occupy a stylish townhouse condominium in a newly developed section of Amherstburg, an historic town of ten thousand inhabitants, in the extreme southwest corner of Ontario, where the Detroit River flows into Lake Erie some thirty kilometers south of Windsor and Detroit. Within a kilometer of their front door, ocean-going vessels carrying grain and potash and wood pulp make their way up and down the St. Lawrence Seaway, while on the surrounding flatlands farmers and market gardeners grow tomatoes and vegetables for the canning factories in nearby Leamington and Chatham. The town's streets are gracious and verdant, its tax base solid, and, like the rest of Essex County, its topography is as flat as a sheet of gyprock. Amherstburg is, in large part, a retirement community—"a mini-Victoria" as resident Gerry Waldron describes it—and beyond its preponderance of medical clinics and retirement homes, there is little in the way of visible industry. The town's history and character are perhaps best represented by the partially restored (and eminently sedate) Fort Malden, a seventeenth-century British stronghold, which occupies a large waterfront park on the main street, attracting a quiet flow of tourists during the warm weather.

At the Ferguson home, large ground-floor windows look out past hardwoods and birdfeeders onto the expansive fairways of the Pointe West Golf Club. Inside, despite the comfy furniture and potted plants, the open-style ground floor is less a living room than a kind of indoor paddock for porcelain and bronze horses. There are dozens of them—trophies, mementos, antiques—some so small they could curl comfortably in a tea cup, others as big as border collies: thoroughbreds, standardbreds, Belgians, Lippezanners, Welsh ponies, jumpers, RCMP mounts, cart and sleigh horses. On a table in the corner shines a large Tiffany-style lamp, whose base is a bronze trotter and whose shade depicts another trotter in bright primary colors. Not ten feet away, by the piano, stands a knee-high likeness of a rearing stallion cast in icy green glass (and protected from galloping grandchildren by a strategically placed plant). On the walls and on available shelving are more horses, some in framed paintings, others fired onto ceramic commemorative plates.

"C'mon downstairs," says Fergy, and he turns up the lights on yet another level of the family equine museum: racing trophies, track citations, horses in paintings and in an extensive grouping of equine postage stamps arranged in a framed collage; horses on a tapestry and in photos, several of which show Fergy and Joan in the winner's circles of various racetracks, with some of the hundreds of winners they have raised and owned over the years. By comparison, there are few reminders of hockey: a couple of photos from the 1972 Soviet series, a Tex Coulter painting of John as a Canadien, and a brace of executive awards from the years in Winnipeg. Asked about his replica Stanley Cup trophies, John responds casually that they're "in a box in the garage somewhere."

The Fergusons would not be in Amherstburg were it not for horses. In 1988, after John was released as general manager of the Winnipeg Jets, he accepted a job as president and CEO of the Windsor Raceway, twenty-five kilometers north of Amherstburg on Highway 18. Joan, too, went to work at the track, running the gift shop and handling a variety of public-relations responsibilities.

For both of them, but particularly for John, it was a return to a cherished past. Fergy has had the smell of horses in his nostrils almost since he was born. Indeed, horse racing, perhaps more than hockey, has been the sustaining passion of his life.

John's dad, a Scottish immigrant, was an assistant trainer at Old Hastings Park, a Vancouver track, and John spent the summer of 1939, his first on the planet, in a bassinet at Willows Racetrack in Victoria, with his mom and dad. The Fergusons lived on Clark Drive in Hastings East, a rough (now derelict) section of downtown Vancouver, and long before he started school, John was making the daily streetcar ride with his dad either to Old Hastings Park or to Lansdowne Park, another racetrack. "Back then," he explains, "the tracks used to print what they called a 'green sheet' that carried all the past performances of the horses racing that day. I learned to read off that sheet. By the time I was five I knew practically every racehorse in Vancouver."

Although his dad died in 1949, John's affection for the horses never wavered. Even as an elementary-school student he would scoot promptly to the track after school, beg a program from someone who was leaving early, and be in the grandstand by post time for the third race. "Then I started working as an exercise boy," he says, "walking the horses in the morning, and hot-walking them after they'd run."

It was in the horse barns and on the turf of Old Hastings Park that Fergy gained his earliest appreciation of thoroughbred bloodlines and physical attributes and of the subtle equation that connects those factors to performance on the track—an appreciation that he has refined and expanded throughout his adult life. As a senior elementary-school student, he also picked up a hockey stick for the first time. "I could barely skate," he recalls, "but because I'd played a lot of soccer and lacrosse, I understood the patterns of the game, and, at thirteen, I made my first hockey team, the Lamoreux Concessions. I even scored a goal in my first game."

"One day in I guess the summer of 1952," says Joan, "I was on my way to figure-skating practice at the Vancouver Forum at eight o'clock in the morning. I was at the streetcar stop, and along came John—my friend Arlene McFarlane introduced us. I've always said John was on his way home from hot-walking horses. He says he was coming from rink-ratting at the Forum."

Throughout their early teens, the two saw one another regularly at social and sporting events. By 1953, they were attending rival high schools, John playing football, Joan performing on her school's cheerleading team. "We used to play Joan's school," smiles John. "It was the only time in my life that I ever fraternized with the enemy after a game."

By this time, Joan was training year-round as a figure skater, with hopes of becoming a professional. When the opportunity presented itself, in 1955, she tried out for the Ice Follies, made the grade, and at the age of sixteen was off to Los Angeles to learn her routines. Her mother, who had encouraged her skating, died in an accident without ever seeing her perform.

> **"I don't really think we believed we'd ever get out. All we were doing was going day to day."**

"Professional skating wasn't nearly as glamorous as you might think," says Joan. "It could be exciting, mind you, but there were endless hours of practice and touring, and as teenage girls it always seemed we were fighting off strange men."

After a year of it, she left the Follies and returned to Vancouver, where she and John were married in 1958.

The two spent their first year of marriage in a drafty apartment in Melville, Saskatchewan, where John was finishing his junior career, then spent a year in Fort Wayne, Indiana, John's first stop as a pro. In 1960, after a summer in Vancouver, they moved on to Cleveland, where, for three years, John refined his skills, and his increasingly frosty reputation, with the Cleveland Barons of the American Hockey League.

"When you're in the minors," says Joan, "you never completely lose the thought of making it to the NHL. But in those days, even very good players could spend their entire careers down there, and I don't really think we believed we'd ever get out. All we were doing was going day to day. We had the first of our children to raise, and John was doing what he wanted to do."

Joan describes their eventual move to Montreal as "sort of scary," in that the pressures and expectations, as well as the caliber of hockey, were suddenly "so much more intense."

But while the uniforms and caliber of hockey changed, John's obsession with horses remained constant. Whenever possible, wherever he happened to be, he would head almost instinctively to the track. "I'll never forget my first trip to Louisville with the Fort Wayne Komets," he says. "All my life I'd dreamed about going to Churchill Downs; I just couldn't wait to walk into the grandstand, go into the tunnel under the track and out onto the infield." Unfortunately, when John arrived at the renowned facility early in the morning, it was not yet open. "And I couldn't wait around," he says. "But just being there was a thrill."

On his next visit to Louisville, Fergy made another pilgrimage, this time to the famous Calumet Farms, where, during the late fifties, legendary horses such as Citation and Iron Liege were the farm's ranking studs. "I stood there for a long time watching the mares and foals," says John, "thinking about how much I'd eventually like to breed and race horses of my own."

In Montreal, Fergy soon became a regular at Blue Bonnet Raceway. But it was not until late in his years with the Canadiens that he and Joan found the capital to begin buying horses of their own—thoroughbreds and standardbreds at first, then gradually, exclusively standardbred trotters and pacers.

Since then, they have always owned horses, as few as seven or eight, as many as forty-four during the mid-seventies in Montreal. Sometimes they have had ownership partners, sometimes not. "We always seem to own a hundred percent of the ones that don't make any money," laughs Joan, "and only a share of those that do." At the moment, they have ten horses, some owned outright, some co-owned, all stabled in Toronto. "We have a trainer and a groom, and I stop by as often as I can to talk to them, see how things are going," says John. "I don't get to the races very often, but I try to watch them by satellite."

An esteemed judge of pacers and trotters, John is perpetually on the lookout for promising yearlings and, to that end, makes annual spring treks to farms and sales in Kentucky and Pennsylvania, as well as regular visits to Canadian farms such as Armstrong Brothers in Brampton, Ontario. He keeps a microscopic eye on the intersections of established bloodlines and, in the barns and paddocks, is an obsessive observer of the minutest details of growth and balance, knees and hocks, all in the interest of gaining a split-second advantage somewhere down the line.

"We've put a lot of money into horses over the years," confides Joan. "My guess is that we haven't taken as much out as we've put in, but we've sure supported a mini-economy of blacksmiths, vets, trainers, grooms, track employees, feed companies, sales people, government people. At one time I was paying bills in nineteen directions. The bad horses eat as much as the good ones. Of course, it's not that we didn't know it'd be that way. You have to be slightly mad to get into racing in the first place. And totally dedicated."

Fergy admits that, although the horses are supposed to be financially self-sustaining, even profitable, he and Joan have often been obliged to cover the high costs of the breeding and racing operation with money earned in hockey. "We've had terrible years, and we've had wonderful years," he says.

And they have had terrible and wonderful days. Fergy compares the reversals of the horse-racing world with those of hockey. "There's nothing like going into the Meadowlands with the best horse, the favorite, in a major stake race, being 1 to 9 on the board, with John Campbell on your horse, and the horse going offstride before it gets out of the gate and not getting into the race. That happened to us last August with our filly Hardie Hanover, and it was a horrible low! Thank goodness there was a consolation race the next week, which she won."

Largely because of Hardie Hanover (Canada's top two-year-old filly pacer in 1993), the racing year as a whole has been what John calls "a remarkable success." The prized filly won both the 1994 Fan Hanover Cup in Toronto and the Cadillac Breeders' Stakes at Garden State Raceway outside Philadelphia. "She earned $600,000 in total," says John, "and when we broke up the business relationship with her co-owners in November, we ended up selling her for half a million dollars."

By his own estimate, John "pays attention" to his horses about a hundred days a year. He would spend more time than he does with them except that, in 1991, when his friend Tom Joy, who had brought him to Windsor in the first place, was about to sell the Windsor Raceway, he weighed his prospects for the future and accepted a job as director of player personnel with the Ottawa Senators. As an indication of his priorities, it is worth considering that during his years at the track he turned down three offers to manage established NHL clubs.

He started with the Senators six months before their first draft of players and left the job abruptly in early 1996, over unspecified differences with the team's ownership and upper management. "On a lot of things, we just didn't see eye to eye," he says.

But Fergy is a valued member of the hockey fraternity, and he was barely resigned from the Senators when he was persuaded to join the San Jose Sharks as the team's senior professional scout.

Today, he spends as many as two hundred days a year on the road, scouting prospects, attending meetings, and supervising scouts in every corner of the hockey-playing world. A condition of his taking both the Ottawa and San Jose jobs was that he be allowed to work from Amherstburg, where he is comfortably established and has drivable access to hundreds of college, junior, and minor-pro games in southern Ontario and the north-central United States. "Besides," he says "We can see NHL hockey in Detroit."

His professional bible is a well-thumbed tome, published annually, which, as Fergy puts it, "lists every scheduled game in every upper-level league in every part of the world. I can go through it at the beginning of the year and coordinate my whole schedule: Here's a guy playing here that I wanta see, another guy the next night over here, another over there, and so on." Fergy watches up to half a dozen televised games a week, taping those he can't watch live, and professes to know at least something about every "upper-level amateur or pro" playing in North America or in Europe. He acknowledges with a grin that judging hockey players bears uncanny similarities to judging horses. "You're looking for strength, speed, balance, desire—one of the big differences is that, when I see a good horse I can often buy it. Good hockey players aren't for sale."

He makes as many as four trips to Europe a year, to scout tournaments and league play, and, by his own admission, derives as much pleasure from his side trips to the great tracks of Europe as from his hours in the arenas of Prague and Stockholm and Helsinki. "My ideal day," he enthuses, "is seeing the horses in the afternoon and a hockey game at night. And I guess you might throw in a good meal with a good bottle of wine. I love good wine; I go looking for it."

As befits a man of the track, Fergy also loves a good cigar, a hand-rolled Honduran cigar to be precise. He smoked his first cigar as a junior in Saskatchewan and now smokes three or four a day, imported for him by a Detroit tobacco shop. "Because of the grandchildren, I'm not allowed to smoke indoors anymore," he says solemnly (this explains the rain-swollen cigar butt by the curb in front of the condo).

"He can at least read about cigars indoors," says Joan, producing the latest issue of his subscription to *Cigar Connoisseur*, a perfect-bound glossy magazine with a slew of up-market advertisers and the panache of a journal of high fashion.

"He smokes continuously when he plays golf," says Joan. "I think that's why he likes playing so much."

> ## "I've always been one for challenges, and I guess if the right one came along I might still be tempted to consider it."

More than ever these days, Joan is an integral part of Fergy's professional life. Today, in fact, she is somewhat weary, having accompanied him to a game the previous night, in Toledo, Ohio—a trip on which she did most of the driving so as to allow John to concentrate on paperwork and scouting reports. "If I'm along, it gives him a chance to doze off," she smiles. "He gets up early, and he likes a twenty-minute snooze during the day, so he can keep functioning."

Tonight, she will be with him at a game in Sarnia and tomorrow night at the arena in Windsor. And the next night in Chatham or London or Saginaw. She has accompanied him to the past two winter Olympics in Norway and Japan. "He thinks if he doesn't take me I'll have nothing to do," she whispers, so as not to be overheard by Fergy, who is assessing scouting reports in the next room. "I have lots to do. But I don't like to see him go off on his own. Last week, he came through a terrible snowstorm on the way back from Barrie in the middle of the night."

While his name is occasionally proposed as a potential general manager for one NHL team or another, John has no immediate desire to be anything other than what he is. At least for now. "I've always been one for challenges," he says, "and I guess if the right one came along I might still be tempted to consider it." Even as he speaks, he is interrupted by a phone call from Sweden, from an official of the International Hockey League, who wonders if he'd be interested in investing in one of the league's proposed European entries, and perhaps playing a role in its development.

"It sounds intriguing," he says on hanging up the phone. "But who needs the stress? I had fifteen years of it in New York and Winnipeg. I'm not saying there's not some stress in what I do now, but it's nothing compared to being responsible for a whole franchise. Besides, Joan's the most important part of my decisions now. If I got back in the fast lane, it'd be hard on her, and I wouldn't get to see my children and grandchildren. They're very important to me."

The "children," all four of whom are married, range in age from early to mid-thirties. "The three girls all married guys named Paul," says Fergy. "Our oldest daughter, Chris, and her husband are in Vancouver; they have three children—Chris is into horses like Joan and me. Kathy and her husband and son are in Louisville (I have two reasons to go to Kentucky now). Our son, John, and his wife are in Boston. And Joanne, our youngest, works at Scotia-McLeod in Toronto and does choreography. She choreographed the Toronto production of *Oliver Twist*. It was just great."

Despite their current career stability and the high esteem in which John is held at both the horse track and the ice rink, Joan and John have seen enough of the vicissitudes of the hockey and horse racing businesses to know that nothing about the future can be taken for granted. "Sometimes I can't believe we've come through the past as well as we have," says Joan. "It took me years to realize that I'd married a riverboat gambler. We certainly didn't have much financial security for a long time. I guess, in some ways, we still don't. Mind you, there are always things and people to complain about if you want to look for them. I think our salvation has been that we've always understood how lucky we've been. It's hard to believe at times that the young people in hockey can be so callous about their good fortune. Of course, our attitude was influenced by growing up while the war was on; it made us grateful for what we had. Anybody who's enjoyed their interests as much as we have, and been able to make a living at them, has to be grateful!"

"It's been an adventure," says Fergy. "And we're still having fun at it. I know I'm not ready to retire. My current contract is good for a couple more years. Maybe after that I'll wind it down a bit.

"Then again," he shrugs, "maybe I won't."

* * * * *

Epilogue

Whatever else Fergy has done during the months since he voiced the aforementioned ambiguity, he has by no means "wound it down." He still spends a hundred days a year attending to his horses and as many as two hundred attending to hockey.

His job with the Sharks hasn't exactly been a hockey man's dream, inasmuch as the Sharks, an expansion team like the Senators, have undergone complex frustrations and growing pains on their route to respectability in the NHL.

John's contacts in the league were given a boost recently when his son, John Jr., who had recently graduated as a lawyer, was named assistant general manager of the St. Louis Blues, and then general manager of the AHL Worcester Ice Cats, outside Boston. "We talk a lot about what's going on in hockey," says Fergy, "about this or that player. But we're a close family—we talk a lot anyway."

John once made a TV commercial for a Canadian brand of bed sheets, but he has generally stayed away from commercial endorsements and has seldom appeared in old-timers games or made celebrity appearances at hockey events. So, it was something of a rarity when he participated in a recent Masters of Hockey game in San Jose (it is a seldom-mentioned fact that John played in two All-Star games, in 1965 and '67, and scored a goal in each). "A game like this," John said after his Masters appearance, "really reminds you of the great times you had during your playing days."

Whether or not John's presence in the game reminded his teammates of the great times they had playing against him went unrecorded.

As in his playing days, Fergy remains a strong "positional" man, rooted in Amherstburg, where he is still best located for scouting ventures into the United States and across Canada—and where he can be close to his beloved horses, which he acknowledges cost as much as ever to own, despite their occasional triumphs and payoffs.

Fergy's best and most constant companion is still his wife, Joan, who accompanies him on as many road trips as possible and (he admits) continues to regulate his cigar habit. "I keep thinking I'm going to stop and relax a little more, maybe get out of hockey," he says, echoing a sentiment he has voiced for nearly a decade.

"The problem," says Joan, " is that it's a lot harder to get out of horse racing than hockey."

"Horses are family!" John quips. "You've gotta care for them! And to do that, you've gotta keep going out and make a living."

CHAPTER
4

Gordie and Colleen Howe

The Flower and the Gardener

If Colleen Howe's dream comes to pass, there will one day exist a life-sized talking model of her husband, Gordie, clothed in the green and blue of the Hartford Whalers, or perhaps the red and white of the Detroit Red Wings. ("We haven't decided that yet.") The model's job will be to stand at the entrance to what Colleen envisions as "The World's Largest Exhibit of a Famous Athletic Family's Personal Memorabilia."

When people enter the exhibit," she explains, "this figure of Gordie will welcome them and tell them a bit about his career—how many goals he scored, how many games he played, that sort of thing. Then the people will go on into this incredible collection of our family's athletic effects: jackets, photos, trophies, skates, jerseys, pucks, sticks, art, everything. At each station, they'll be able to press a button and hear Gordie's voice, or the voice of another family member, telling them something about what they're looking at—these are the gloves I was wearing when I scored my one thousandth goal, and so on."

For nearly fifty years, Colleen has been collecting the immense volume of effects she intends to display. At the moment, she has them packaged, cataloged, photographed, and awaiting attention at a storage facility whose location she is reluctant to divulge.

> ## "I never saw myself as a housewife. I was a home engineer, a total camp director."

She says,"My plan is to get corporate sponsorship for this project. It's going to be expensive, and it's going to be a lot of hard work."

A glance at Colleen's resume would suggest that she is no stranger to a lot of hard work. Among other things, she has run for Congress; managed the first Junior A hockey club in the United States; written a book about her family; produced a series of hockey videotapes; owned a herd of Peruvian llamas (her CB handle at the time was Mama Llama); co-owned a restaurant; sold life insurance; comanaged a large team of Amway salespeople and Cambridge Diet Plan distributors; co-owned a hockey arena and a travel agency; owned a herd of pedigree cattle; and served as president of Howe Enterprises and Powerplay International, through which she currently manages all Howe family business endeavors.

Lest it be thought that she was dogging it in her spare time, she has also raised four children and done extensive work for a variety of charities. "I got the most wonderful letter when I ran for Congress," she enthuses. "A lady sent me a donation and said, 'I'm putting my money behind you, because you can raise kids, work at the same time, and do all the other things I know you're doing. And I feel you'd do a lot better job running the country than the current government. At least, you wouldn't let us get a trillion dollars in debt.'

"I never saw myself as a housewife," declares Colleen. "I was a home engineer, a total camp director."

In the interest of accuracy, it might be pointed out that Colleen's energy is not that of a camp director but of an entire camp . . . of marathon runners. Her appointment calendar is the sort of document whose appearance alone is enough to make the average nine-to-fiver feel the need of a nap. She rises most days at 5:00 A.M., works seven days a week, and has been known to work all night. "When she ran for the congressional ticket," says Gordie, "she wouldn't go to bed for two days at a time." (Recently, as Gordie watched a television documentary on the hammertop stork—a bird that, in the words of the documentary's narrator, "is constantly building, adding to the roof of its nest, plastering the walls"—he looked up and said softly, "If Colleen were a bird, that's what kind she'd be.")

Colleen owns hundreds of motivational tapes and has a bedside library that bristles with titles such as *Being the Best, The Other Guy Blinked, Don't Talk About It, Do It, How to Wake Up the Financial Genius Inside You,* and *How to Do Just About Anything.* Gordie's bedside literature consists of a couple of books on fishing and a book on seashells.

Asked about the roots of her drive and gumption, Colleen reminisces for a minute, stops suddenly, and tells this story:

"Just after I graduated from high school in 1950, I was interviewed for a file clerk's job at Bethlehem Steel. When I was asked why I thought I deserved the job over twenty other applicants, I said, 'Because filing requires a knowledge of the alphabet, and I'm the only one of all those girls who can say the alphabet backwards.' The guy who was interviewing me just roared. He said, 'Say it.' So I did. It was something my aunt had taught me when I was little—Z, Y, X, W, V, and so on. I got the job."

Colleen goes on to say that, during her term with Bethlehem Steel, she often spent evenings at the Lucky Strike bowling alley a few blocks from her home near the Detroit Olympia. One night as she bowled, she noticed a dark-haired young man with a high forehead and rather gentle smile. "He was wearing a western-style suede jacket with fringe on the arms, and I thought, boy, is that guy ever good-looking. When he came over and asked if I had a ride home, I nearly died. Here, I had a friend's car and couldn't accept. All the way home I just couldn't stop thinking about him. Fortunately, he got my phone number from the fella who ran the alley. I was so excited when he called the next night. Then he called every night that week! He'd talk for three hours at a stretch—about his home, his family, his childhood in Saskatoon, whatever. I felt as if I knew his whole family by the end of the week. It was really old-fashioned. The funny thing was that all through these conversations Gordie only mentioned hockey once, and I didn't pick up on it. I didn't have a clue that he was a professional hockey player—and here he'd been with the Red Wings five years! In fact, they'd just won the Stanley Cup."

Gordie says, "Finally I found the courage to ask her to a movie. Then in October she started coming to hockey games. I had a pair of tickets—one for my landlady, one for Colleen. I'd leave Colleen's at the ticket window, and she'd pick it up. I'd look for her from the ice."

On April 15, 1953, a week after the Red Wings had been eliminated from the Stanley Cup playoffs, Colleen and Gordie were married in Calvary Presbyterian Church in Detroit. "My only regret," says Gordie, "was that my roommate, Ted Lindsay, couldn't be my best man. He was Catholic, and they wouldn't allow it in a Protestant church."

Before the decade ended, Gordie had won five NHL scoring championships, had led the Red Wings to four Stanley Cups, and was widely recognized as the finest all-around player in hockey, some said the finest in the history of the game. The curious thing about Gordie was that, in spite of his vast talent, he didn't always appear to be doing that much on the ice. "My skating style was so smooth," he submits, "that a lot of people thought I was lazy." His stride was measured, his checking controlled, his shot a powerful but unexaggerated flick of the wrists. His strength and subtlety were such that he could often accomplish in one motion what other players took two or three moves to achieve. If, for instance, he was being checked from the right side (his shooting side), instead of shifting frantically, or whirling, or powering to a stop, he would often simply switch his stick to the other side of his body, change hands on it, and drill the puck ambidextrously from the left.

"You've also got to remember that I was crazy," says Gordie, in assessing his capabilities. "I was never afraid of getting hurt. And I was a good size, too. When I was a kid in Saskatoon, they called me the slope-shouldered giant. Everybody always seemed smaller than I was. Even if they were bigger they seemed smaller. And, oh, I was rough. It's one thing to be rough, but to be rough and crazy means the other guy is never going to get the last hit. Players knew that if they hit me, it was just a matter of time before I'd get them back. In the old league, we'd play a team fourteen times, so if a player did something dirty to me, I'd tell him I was going to get him. Sometimes I'd wait five, six, seven games. I'd play with him, tease him, but he knew that sooner or later he'd pay."

On occasion, Gordie's vengeance was less protracted, as Eddy Coleman of the Rangers found out during Gordie's early years as a pro. "He used to spike me in the back of the legs with his stick," recalls

Gordie. "And I'd be bleeding. So I told him one night that if he touched me again he'd be very sorry, and he laughed at me. We went down the ice, and I flipped the puck over to Lindsay, who was going to the net all alone. Everybody's eyes were on him.

> **"Everybody left me alone. Even the tough guys."**

Suddenly, I saw Coleman beside me and just turned around and nailed him with my gloved hand. Broke his cheekbone. A promise kept."

So as not to create any wrong impressions, Gordie makes it clear that under normal circumstances—that is, circumstances in which he was not in the process of a retributive strike—he found it impossible to cause anyone deliberate injury. He says, "Most of the time I played like an angel. I guess I could afford to after a while; almost everybody left me alone. Even the tough guys. There seemed to be a certain respect."

Given the tough defensive standards under which he played during his prime, Gordie's 1,071 career goals (NHL and WHA, including play-offs) are an almost unaccountable record for major league hockey; his 975 regular-season goals are the equivalent of nearly twenty fifty-goal seasons. His thirty-two-year pro career—a career almost twice as long as the Rocket's, nearly three times as long as Bobby Orr's—is an unprecedented record for any major league sport. By the time he retired at the age of fifty-two, Gordie had played NHL hockey in five decades. "People sometimes ask me how I lasted so long," he smiles. "And I always tell them the same thing: that I was totally in love with what I was doing. Even as a grown man, I could have played hockey all day. The sacrifices I made to keep my career going just never seemed that tough."

*   *   *   *   *

Today, nearly two decades after his retirement, Gordie looks as if he could still take a turn at right wing. He is about fifteen pounds over his playing weight of 205, but the added cushioning is by no means sufficient to disguise the extraordinary ropes of muscle that form his shoulders and arms and thighs. The only true signs of his aging are his snowy white hair, a few facial wrinkles, and a plum-sized hummock of arthritis on the back of his left wrist. His feet are a startling composite of sinew and calluses and boot hide (the toenails resemble thick purple and yellow sea shells), but their condition is less the result of aging than of sixty years of stuffing them into skates and having them battered by the rough and tumble of the game.

His hands, by comparison, are soft and supple. In fact, in a curious way, the hands are a totem of their owner's personality. They are so pliant that when you grip one of them in a handshake, you might easily imagine a quarter inch of sheepskin beneath the surface of the wide palm and fingers. At the same time, you cannot help but sense the vice-grip power that lies just beneath the sheepskin (these are most certainly hands that could crush your own fragile bones should they decide to do so). Likewise, you cannot help but be aware of the formidable tenacity beneath the gentle exterior of Gordie's disposition. "Oh, there are very definitely the two sides there," says Colleen. "And they can be traced almost directly to his parents. Gordie's father was a very tough, very resilient, stubborn man. The family didn't have a lot, and sometimes to get money he had to ride horses bareback, run down coyotes for the bounty, that sort of thing. He had a bit of a mean streak, too, and of course this came through in Gordie when he played hockey. Gordie won't hesitate to tell you that he and his brothers and sisters were scared of their dad. One time Gordie was playing on a pair of stilts that his dad had told him not to go on, and when his dad caught him, Gordie jumped off so suddenly that he impaled himself on a picket fence and was badly injured.

"Gordie's mother, on the other hand, was an extremely tolerant, understanding woman, and there was such a love between Gordie and his mother. Even when I first met him he'd talk about how wonderful she was. She was totally unselfish; she'd give and give, constantly concerned about her family. I remember how she'd rub Gordie's back, just loved doing things that made people feel good. It was this unselfishness and patience of hers—this incredible generosity of spirit—that I've always seen in Gordie in his life off the ice."

Indeed, it is this generosity of spirit that over the years has elevated Gordie above the precincts of mere sports idolatry and earned him an enduring portion of public appreciation and respect. He is a man not only of honesty but of the profoundly common touch. He is seldom happier, for instance, than when he is signing an autograph for a child.

Or a teenager. Or an adult. In fact, to watch Gordie sign autographs is to observe a perfect paradigm of his generosity in action. No matter how long the line-up of autograph seekers, he has a kind word, a joke, a reassuring smile for everyone.

During the 1960s, as an itinerant spokesman for Eaton's of Canada, Gordie would sometimes sign autographs from sunrise to midnight. "Literally!" he exclaims. "I'd be signing while I ate, while I watched TV, when I went to bed. I must have signed five million times." He recently signed the packaging on thirty-five thousand copies of a series of instructional videos that he made with goaltender Ed Giacomin and his sons Mark, Marty, and Murray. "It took me thirty-six hours," he calculates. "I can sign about a thousand times an hour."

As if by uncanny prescience, Gordie realized at the age of eight that he would one day be dispensing his signature in volume. "My older brother Vern's wife says she can remember me writing my name several different ways, then tugging at my mother's skirt, asking which one she liked best. The one she chose, the one I still use, I practiced like everything. When Mom said, 'What are you doing?' I said, 'That's for when I become famous.'"

Only once in more than forty years can Gordie remember being upset by an autograph request. "I was in the press box in Hartford the night my son Mark got pierced in the backside by the deflector plate on the net. When I saw him biting his hand I knew that he was badly injured. And I could see the blood, too. So I beat it out of there to get to the ice, and about halfway down the press table a guy held out a piece of paper to me and said, 'Sign this.' I looked at him and said, 'That's my son on that stretcher.' He said, 'It'll only take a minute.' At that point somebody else stepped in and told the guy to give it a rest.

"I guess there've been a few times when I've been too tired to keep signing, or have had to leave to catch a bus or a plane or something. When they can't get to me in person, I always hope they'll send a letter."

Many have. During the peak of his fame in Detroit, Gordie was receiving some five hundred fan letters a week. Colleen acted as his secretary, scanning and categorizing every piece of mail that came in: "Some people would want something for a charity auction (I'd take Gordie's old ties, and he'd sign them, and we'd send them out), some just wanted an autograph, some wanted a picture, some had sent something they wanted signed. Some people wrote pages, their life stories, and I'd have to skim these letters to see what the request was. There were some beautiful letters, too, of course. We answered all this mail at our own expense, postage and all. The Red Wings never offered a nickel." Colleen has saved every fan letter Gordie ever got, more than two hundred fifty thousand pieces of mail, some of which will eventually go into the big exhibit of the family's memorabilia.

And has Gordie ever gotten tired of the requests, the autograph signing, the adulation? "Never," he says solemnly. "I worked too hard for the privilege."

Today, Gordie has become not only one of the best-known and loved figures in the sporting world but also one of the more marketable. And Colleen is the ideal agent of that marketability. Where he is pliant, she is assertive; where he is quiet, she talks; where he waits, she scours the radar for action. She says, "Gordie's such a good guy, he can hardly ever bring himself to say no to people. So sometimes I have to be the bad guy, so to speak, if we're going to keep things in balance. Mind you, I don't deal rudely with people. I always try to find out what they want, and then give them what we can. I try to be as creative as possible."

With Colleen in charge of his appointments calendar, Gordie could hardly be busier. In addition to doing promotional work for a number of corporations, both large and small, he makes as many as a hundred banquet speeches a year and is in constant demand as a spokesman for charities and as a participant in media and athletic endeavors. To mark Gordie's sixty-fifth birthday, in 1993, he and Colleen embarked on a North American tour that took them to sixty-five minor and major league arenas for charity and personal appearances. A couple of years later, they hit the road again, in aid of their self-published autobiography, *And Howe!*, which, until recently, they promoted extensively across Canada and the United States.

"Colleen gets it all planned out," says Gordie. "All I have to do is show up."

"He's the flower, I'm the gardener," she grins.

*   *   *   *   *

Gordie is indeed one of the rarest flowers the game has ever produced. Unfortunately, the game has not always seen fit to cultivate him as such. Through most of his twenty-five years with the Red Wings, for instance, his salary was nowhere near commensurate with the effort he was making on behalf of the team. "Had I made more back then," he says, "I wouldn't have to work so hard today. But you don't see that at the time, because you want so much to be a part of it. It just never occurred to us that someone else was making a small fortune off our talents."

Even if it had occurred to the players of the fifties and sixties, they were generally not secure enough in their jobs to raise the issue with management. Gordie says, "Anybody'd think I wouldn't have had the same insecurities as most players, but they're dead wrong. I had serious injuries early in my career. I wasn't sure I'd last. And I wasn't trained for anything else—I'd devoted my life to hockey. On top of that you've got to remember that, until 1967, there were only six teams in the NHL and that they owned the rights to their players. You couldn't exactly pack up and move on if you didn't like the money you were making or the way you were being treated. If you balked—or weren't willing to play through injuries, say—there were always lots of players to take your job. And, of course, management used that to keep us in our place. My teammate Marty Pavelich once said, 'I never could understand Gordie Howe. Every training camp he'd show up worried about making the club.' I guess my true feelings showed. I'd go out there and work my butt off out of fear."

In 1945, Gordie was ecstatic to sign for $2,300 a year, plus a team jacket, with the Red Wings' Omaha farm club. That year, he bought a car, a couple of new suits, and returned home to Saskatoon with $1,700 in his pocket.

The following year in Detroit his salary doubled, and, over the next dozen years, it proceeded upward in marginal increments. But it was not until the late 1950s that he felt the first stirrings of his current disenchantment over what he was paid. "Here I was winning scoring championships, awards, Stanley Cups, and a friend of mine who sold insurance was making more than I was. He could afford to go away on weekends; I couldn't. He owned a boat; I only wished for one."

If there was financial hope for Gordie during the fifties it was that a pension plan had been introduced that would one day pay retired players $50 a month for every year of NHL service. "I remember thinking, That's pretty good," says Gordie. "If I last ten years, I could make around $500 a month at age forty-five—as much as I was making playing hockey."

Today, after the most distinguished career in the history of the sport, Gordie collects an NHL pension of some $1,300 a month, by far the largest pension for any player of his era. His benefits were given a boost recently with a lump payment of some $200,000, awarded by a Canadian court, because of longstanding owner misuse of pension funds. But the payouts to many players were not nearly so generous.

"What most people don't understand," says Colleen, "is that, because the basic monthly is still so puny, a lot of former players will have to work forever. . . . Someone once said to us, 'Maybe things would be better if you'd deferred money way back when.' But how could we defer money in an era when our salary barely covered our expenses? We had four children to support! We had to scrimp. I made our clothes. I cut the kids' hair. We used skate exchanges. It was strictly no-frills. I mean, I couldn't even afford to make long distance calls to Gordie when he was on the road. Then again, hockey wives—at least those in Detroit—were pretty well prohibited from contacting their husbands on the road, anyway. The wives were just nobodies in the grand scheme. I remember once when I wanted to reach Gordie during the playoffs, I had to explain to the general manager what I wanted. Just to talk to my husband. As far as they were concerned, my only purpose in life was to make sure that Gordie was well fed, well rested, and well taken care of. Total support of his career. There were times when I'd drive to the train station to pick him up at 2:00 A.M., with two kids in the car, in a snowstorm. Or I'd drive him to the hospital in the middle of the night. And yet when I'd show up at the rink the next day, I'd be treated like a schlock."

In September of 1969 Gordie learned his harshest lesson about the ethics and operations of his long-time employers in Detroit. Bob Baun had come to the Red Wings from Oakland during the off-season and had joined the team at its training camp in Port Huron, Ontario. "One day he took me out for lunch," recalls Gordie, "and the first thing he said to me when we sat down was, 'You're a stupid son of a gun, Gordie—I'm making almost twice as much money as you are.' This really stunned and hurt me, because I'd always had an agreement with the Red Wings that, because I was one of the best in the game, I'd always be the highest paid player on the team—in fact, the highest in the league. I was making $45,000 at the time; Baun was making $80,000. I owe a lot to Bob for setting me straight."

> **"You're a stupid son of a gun, Gordie— I'm making almost twice as much money as you are."**

Gordie subsequently discovered that another Red Wing, Carl Brewer, was also making far more than he was. His first inclination was to quit hockey and go into the insurance business, where he'd been guaranteed a job on retirement. Ironically, the company that had offered the job was owned by Red Wings owner Bruce Norris, who was primarily responsible for short-changing Gordie as a hockey player. "I phoned the manager of the agency," says Gordie, "and I said, 'How much will you pay me when I'm through?' And he said, 'Fifty thousand.' And I thought, For that kind of money, why should I beat my brains out here? I explained my situation to him, and he said, 'Before you do anything, let me phone Mr. Norris.' And he did. And, as a result, the Red Wings raised my salary to about $100,000. But they wouldn't have done it if I hadn't caught them out.

"What made it worse for me was that when Norris notified me of my raise, he said, 'I hope that makes Colleen happy.' I said, 'Colleen has never scored a goal or backchecked or taken a penalty in this league, Bruce, and it has nothing to do with her or her happiness. In fact, because you people have been lying to me indirectly, it doesn't even make me happy.'"

Beyond the large duplicities, Gordie was regularly affronted by a host of smaller deceits and antagonisms on the part of the Red Wings' ownership and management. "There were just so many things," he says. "For instance, a little while before I retired, my dental work was getting pretty bent up, and I wanted to get it fixed. But the Red Wings said to me, 'Don't get it done now. Wait till you retire and we'll fix it all up so it'll last forever. When the season was over, Colleen and I went away for a while, and when we came back, I asked them about the teeth, and they said, 'Oh, it's too late now. You're not with the club anymore.' They wouldn't put a new plate in for me. So the team dentist, Dr. Muske, said to me, 'Gordie, I heard them make that promise, and I'm embarrassed—I'll put the plate in for you at my own expense.' They just seemed to think so little of us."

It might have helped reshape Gordie's opinion of the club that, upon retirement, he was invited into the front office as a vice president. But before long, that, too, turned sour. He says, "I'd always been told that when I was through playing, I'd be involved in running the team. And I guess I was naive enough to think that that was what they had in store for me. It turned out that in two years on the job all they ever asked me to do was run around and show my face at banquets and promotional functions—'Go represent the club,' they'd tell me. Half the time, they didn't even have the courtesy to tell me in advance where I'd be going. Some days I did nothing at all. It was pathetic. I was floundering."

"It didn't help matters," says Colleen, "that they gave him the tackiest little office in creation. It was a joke. When he had an interview or had to get his picture taken, they'd move him into someone else's office. They didn't even give him a secretary."

"One day," says Gordie, "they sent me out to an awards event being held by the Food Caterers of Michigan—the Red Wings had purchased a table. They told me, 'You won't have any responsibilities; just go sit at our table. Enjoy yourself.' So I showed up, and sure enough they'd bought a table for ten, but there was nobody sitting at it but me. So I just walked away from it. It turned out that I was the recipient of an award, and the Red Wings hadn't even told me. They knew—they just never bothered letting me know. They were so bush-league about it all. And if I complained, they'd say, 'What are you belly-aching about now?'"

Gordie came to refer to the club's attitude toward him as "The mushroom treatment—which is where they keep you in the dark and come in once in a while and throw manure on you."

Colleen says, "When Gordie resigned from this travesty of a job, and we were about to leave Detroit, we went down to say good-bye to some of our special friends at the Olympia. While we were there, Gordie picked up his final paycheck, and he opened it and started to laugh. He said, 'You're not going to believe this.' As a favor to Bruce Norris we always booked our travel through his travel agency, and the agency would bill us at the end of the month. And here they'd gone and deducted our last travel bill from Gordie's check. His pay had been reduced almost to nothing. That's what twenty-five years of commitment to that organization got us. Someone gave that order—'make sure they're paid up before they leave this building.'"

The league's treatment of its former stars has improved dramatically in recent years, but even into the mid-1990s Colleen and Gordie frequently ran afoul of those who operate the game. Just prior to the departure of the Quebec Nordiques for Colorado, for example, the Howes were invited to appear at Rendez-Vous, a two-game series between Soviet and NHL All-Stars in Quebec City. "The league offered to pay our expenses," says Colleen, "and a $100 fee—that's right, one hundred big ones for three days' work. I told them to forget the hundred dollars, but that we'd come because we wanted to see our son Mark play in the games. As it turned out, Mark was injured and couldn't play, but we went anyway, and we found out that the Rocket had blatantly refused to go and had finally been paid thousands of dollars to make an appearance. So had Guy Lafleur and Vladislav Tretiak. There were even athletes from other sports who had been paid to be there—Gary Carter, Wilt Chamberlain, Nancy Greene, Pele the soccer player, and a number of others. One of these athletes told Gordie that he'd been paid $5,000 to attend. In fact, so much emphasis was put on these other athletes that attention was deflected away from the real stars of the show."

Colleen explains that Bernie Geoffrion was invited to attend Rendez-Vous for the same $100 fee that had been offered the Howes. "He told them, 'Look, I don't make a living from hockey anymore. Do you think I just sit here in Atlanta waiting for you to call?' He wouldn't do it for $100, but to accommodate them he contacted his sponsor, Miller Brewery, and they organized some paid events for him in Quebec and sent him. Bernie didn't score all those goals for Miller, but they take care of him, even when the hockey moguls won't. And he's grateful for it. But when he got to Quebec City he was so busy with his obligations to Miller, plus what the league wanted him to do—they were holding autograph sessions at the city armories, where they had a display of Hall of Fame artifacts set up—that he collapsed with the stress."

Gordie says, "He was just finishing his autograph-signing shift when he felt faint, and his chest started hurting. He said, 'Excuse me, I've got

> **"The sad truth is that the league is far more concerned that its corporate sponsors be taken care of than it is about the players who have made the league what it is."**

to go to the washroom and have a drink.' And suddenly he was on the floor. As it turned out, he was all right, but the episode might have been avoided if he'd just been treated in the same way that the organizers treated the big stars from other sports—if they hadn't been so insensitive. What made it all even harder to accept was that Rendez-Vous ended up making a big profit, and you can be sure some of it came from the admission charges to this Hall of Fame display."

Colleen says, "Gordie has done a great deal of work for change. And so have I. For one thing, we've done our best to convince the league administration that when they put on a big production—whether it be an All-Star gathering, a televised awards night, the Hall of Fame induction ceremony, whatever—and they pay so many technical and promotional and staff people to work on these things, they should also compensate the former players who show up and participate. So often the players who give these events their character are older fellas who don't always have a stable income. Then there are those who never show up at all, aren't even invited—great Hall of Famers, and they haven't been seen at a league function for years! The step that Gordie has taken is to tell the people in the league office that he is no longer available for league appearances unless he and any other players who appear are properly compensated."

Gordie says, "Once when I was with the Whalers, I attended an NHL marketing meeting and discovered they'd scheduled twenty-one appearances for me without a word of consultation. I had to refuse them. I simply said, 'I work for the Hartford Whalers, not for the NHL.'"

Colleen says, "I've said to these people in the league office, 'Don't you see that a backlash will develop if you don't start paying a little more respect to some of these guys?' The sad truth is that the league is far more concerned that its corporate sponsors be taken care of than it is about the players who have made the league what it is. We ourselves never hear from them unless they want Gordie's services. We do get a Christmas card, but it wasn't until very recently that we ever got an invitation to the All-Star game or the Hall of Fame dinner. One year, we were taken to the Hall of Fame dinner by Avie Bennett, the publisher. He seemed shocked that we hadn't been invited by the league.

"At the last All-Star game that Gordie played in, in 1980, I wasn't even given a seat. I had to roam the halls of the arena until one of the people from the league office saw me and rescued me. But I'll tell you, there wouldn't have been a corporate sponsor who didn't have a seat. After the game, a friend of ours from Chrysler said to us, 'Come on, we'll walk with you to the reception.' We said, 'What reception?' It was a thing the league was putting on for their corporate friends—the All-Stars weren't invited. We've just never been able to figure this sort of thing out—do we cramp their style? Are they afraid the players are going to say something that will embarrass them? The corporate people would far rather meet players than NHL functionaries. As it turned out, nobody from the league asked us to leave, but they obviously hadn't planned on us being there. We felt about as welcome as a dead mouse in a punch bowl."

What Gordie and Colleen didn't realize at the time was that the league had not even wanted Gordie to play in the 1980 All-Star game. Colleen says, "Gordie found that out later from Scotty Bowman, the coach, who'd had to fight to have him on the team. The league said there were more deserving players, with better records. I mean, the game was to be held in Detroit! It was almost certain to be Gordie's last All-Star game. Bowman simply told them that it was important to hockey and to the people of Detroit that Gordie be there."

"It was the only game I ever played," says Gordie, "in which the opposing team was cheering for me to score. They were saying, 'C'mon, take a shot—put the sucker in.' Oh, I had a great time. And the fans loved it."

Colleen says, "Later that night as we lay in bed at the hotel, Gordie said, 'Isn't it funny how the people we've done the most for are often the people who show the least regard for us? I don't even want to be around these people anymore. We can't operate like that.'" Colleen reflects for a moment and says, "Maybe we should have been a little tougher years ago. We've given way and given way to these people. Yet if I speak up, I'm labeled a troublemaker. When they say I'm difficult to get along with they mean I don't fall over dead like I'm supposed to when they do something they shouldn't have done."

Of all the things NHL officials shouldn't have done, few have piqued Colleen as much as the actions of those officials in mid-February 1982. "They made arrangements for several players, including Gordie, to have lunch with Ronald Reagan at the White House before the All-Star game," she explains. "But they made it crystal clear that no wives or female companions would be attending this function, that women simply weren't welcome. And this really bothered me; it stung me. It was the first time Gordie had been invited to the White House without us going as a couple. I've always said that players' families share in the bad times and should be welcome for the good times, too." In this case, Colleen's grievance was not just with the NHL but with Gordie. "He didn't agree with what was going on," she says, "but because he felt an obligation to attend and didn't take a stand on my behalf, it put a heavy strain on our relationship at the time. If I'd been invited to the White House for some reason, I never would have gone without him. I'd rather have offended the president than my partner in life. As it turned out, when Gordie got to the White House, he discovered that there were women there. We both felt badly deceived."

Gordie says, "Someone once told me he'd heard a league rep say, 'You don't want to deal with Gordie Howe because you'll have to deal with Colleen.'"

"And yet," says Colleen, "our business associates from outside the league deal with me all the time. And we've had a wonderful relationship with them. They don't see me as some sort of interfering Jezebel. They treat me with respect and openness. What we want—what anybody wants, I guess—is to be with people who make us feel welcome and good about ourselves, the way the fans do. The fans have always been our salvation, and we love them for it."

It is hardly surprising that Gordie and Colleen's fondest memories of hockey are not from their NHL days but from the six years Gordie spent in the World Hockey Association upon coming out of retirement after his two-year stint in the Red Wings' front office. In the WHA he was free of the restraints and narrow-mindedness with which the old league had bound him for decades. The move also gave him the opportunity to fulfill a long-held dream of playing with his sons Mark and Marty, both of whom were too young to sign with NHL teams at the time. What's more, it afforded him the generous remuneration that had for so long eluded him in Detroit. The contract that Colleen and a business adviser negotiated with the Houston Aeros during the summer of 1973 brought the family nearly $2.5 million in exchange for four years of service from Gordie and the two boys.

"The WHA was so much more relaxed than the NHL," says Gordie. "There just wasn't the pressure. Hockey was fun again. And I know the hockey was every bit as entertaining as what we played in the old league. I told the management in Houston that if I'd known it was going to be this much fun they wouldn't have had to pay me. And yet I never worked harder in my life. A lot of my enjoyment, of course, came from playing with the kids. It made the work seem easy." Gordie considers it one of the saddest facets of his career that after four years with the Aeros, the franchise was sold, resulting in what he calls "financial problems and personality conflicts" that left the Howes no choice but to move on. He says, "When they asked us to take a big cut in pay, I knew it was over. It hurt more than ever because the kids were involved."

As they waved good-bye to Texas, there was some possibility that the Howes would return to Detroit. "It was either there or Boston," says Colleen. "The Red Wings asked us what we'd expect if we came back, and I gave them a proposal as to what Gordie would consider an ideal role in the organization. The general manager's job wasn't out of the question. The boys would play, of course, although their rights would have to be obtained from the NHL teams that owned them. The thing was, we wanted to go back there—our hearts were still in Detroit. But just as our negotiations were climaxing after months of talks, Bruce Norris went out and hired Ted Lindsay as general manager without telling us he was even thinking of it. So we knew they had an agenda of their own, and we had no way of knowing what other surprises might be on it. As it turned out, Ted refused to negotiate with me and refused to trade a draft pick to acquire Mark's rights, which were held by Montreal. That was that. We weren't going back. And I took the fall-out. The Detroit headlines said something like, Colleen Howe makes decision to keep family out of Detroit."

When negotiations with the Boston Bruins also fell through, the Howes of Houston became the Howes of Hartford, and Gordie and his sons enjoyed another three years in matching uniforms with the Hartford Whalers of the WHA. At the end of year two, however, the Whalers were absorbed into the NHL, and suddenly the Howes were back in the old neighborhood.

Until recently, Gordie and Colleen maintained a four-thousand–square-foot home and office on a wooded acreage just east of Hartford in Glastonbury, Connecticut. But for most of the past dozen years, their true home has been on a twenty-mile-long spike of land that points north into Lake Michigan's Grand Traverse Bay, a few miles north of Traverse City in northwest Michigan. That home is a resplendent place, a state-of-the-art kind of place, with an exterior of treated cedar and architecture somewhere between Frank Lloyd Wright and Rubik's cube. The interior is a multilevel showpiece that features a sunken living room, a twenty-foot-high ceiling, and ubiquitous tracts of oak trim. Several generous expanses of plate glass look out onto the West Arm of Grand Traverse Bay—icy and sullen in winter, piercing blue in summer.

"We liked the place in Connecticut," says Colleen, "But Michigan is my roots, of course; it's the kids' roots. Strictly speaking it's not Gordie's roots, but it might as well be after all those years in Detroit."

Even before the couple made their permanent move from Connecticut, Colleen would often travel to Traverse City on her own and was sometimes known to drive hundreds of miles for a weekend's respite. She says, "I've always loved the tranquility—being able to get out on the water or go for walks. Or just sit and read."

When Gordie and Colleen are alone in the place during summer, one of their preferred activities is to take the power boat out to rugged Marion Island on the bay for an evening picnic. "Or we just drift and enjoy the water," Colleen says. "We also like sailing. And Gordie fishes further up the bay."

As often as possible, the younger generations of Howes—three married sons, a married daughter, and seven grandchildren—make their way to Traverse City to spend time with Gordie and Colleen. But even when the scions and sprouts aren't in residence, they inhabit the place through dozens of framed family photos: on shelves, on tables, on walls and bedroom bureaus.

While family business is conducted these days from a converted bungalow across the road, Colleen cannot always resist the temptation to do a little business in the main sanctuary. In fact, on a mild mid-winter Saturday she has exposed the place to more than a little figuring and phoning. Throughout the afternoon she burns up the phone line, and as the day wears on, her pertinent papers and correspondence spread themselves

> **"So many people have told me they were at that All-Star game, I figure there must have been half a million people there."**

gradually across the kitchen table and bedroom table and onto the bedroom floor. As she works, Gordie and a guest take a walk along the waterfront, picking their way through beached floes of ice, keeping their eyes peeled for "Petoskey stones," smoothed chunks of colony coral exclusive to the pebble beaches of northern Lake Michigan.

When Gordie and the guest return at sundown, Gordie plays solitaire for a while, eventually suggesting to Colleen that they make plans for dinner (they have not eaten since breakfast).

Within twenty minutes, the threesome is in the Howe's eight-seater van, and ten minutes later is casing the streets of Traverse City, trying to decide on a restaurant. Traverse City was built by the lumber barons of the nineteenth and early twentieth centuries, but it is now supported largely by tourism and by the Michigan oil industry. It has twenty thousand inhabitants and ninety-three restaurants.

At Shelde's on Munson Avenue, the diners remove their coats and are escorted to a comfortably upholstered booth. Even before the waitress arrives to take their order, a heavyset man from a neighboring table approaches and addresses Gordie jovially as "Number Nine," explaining that he was present at Gordie's retirement festivities in 1972 at the Detroit Olympia. The man produces a paper placemat and asks if Gordie would mind signing it: "Make it out to Sam."

A minute later, a younger man approaches: "I was at the All-Star game in 1980. Could I get you to sign this?"

When the man is just out of earshot, Gordie whispers, "So many people have told me they were at that All-Star game, I figure there must have been half a million people there."

The next man to the table claims to have seen the first game Gordie played with his sons.

"They all have a story," says Gordie. "They saw me score my five hundredth goal; my eight hundredth; saw me in the '62 playoffs; went to school with one of the kids. A ton of them went to school with me," he smiles. "We must have had an awful big classroom.

"The other day a guy said he saw me play with Eddie Shore. I told him, 'If I'd played with Shore, I'd be a hundred years old!' The guy said, 'No, I saw ya.' All right then, he saw me."

During dinner, three more autograph seekers materialize beside the table, and when the first-course dishes have been cleared away, the manager appears with a complimentary dessert—a tasty (and enormously caloric) mound of apple pudding. The waitress moves in and, as if a major breach of protocol had been committed, explains, "I'm sorry—I didn't know who you were. "What she would have done had she known is not clear, although a minute later she returns with five sheets of paper: "Would you mind signing these for the guys in the kitchen?" She pauses just long enough and says, "To Carl, to Mike, to Terry, to Marty, and to Tony."

When it seems that everyone in the restaurant who cares must surely have an autograph, and Gordie is set to pay the bill, a woman tiptoes up to him with news that her husband would like an autograph and would like to shake Gordie's hand but is too shy to ask."Where is he?" chirps Gordie, and she points across the room at a balding Danny DeVito look-alike, wearing a sheepish smile. Gordie walks over to him, extends his hand, and says, "Nice to meet you." It is all the man can do to stammer, "I saw you in the All-Star game in 1980."

On the way home, the talk turns to the future, to finances, to retirement—"final retirement," as Colleen calls it, to distinguish it from Gordie's two previous retirements from active hockey and his retirement from the front office of the Hartford Whalers during the early 1990s.

Colleen reveals that she and Gordie are somewhat concerned that, at the moment, a major chunk of their income is derived from Gordie's personal appearances and services. An average week's work might well take him to as many as three or four cities, at the request of one or another corporation or charity. "A time will come," says Colleen, "when he just isn't going to want to spend all this time traveling, or perhaps when he isn't able to." Colleen submits that she, too, will eventually want to cut back on her seven-day work weeks and extensive travel. "Right now I'm doing almost as much traveling as Gordie. By the end of the year we're both exhausted."

According to Colleen, the pair's "five-year plan" is to develop business interests that will gradually take the emphasis off Gordie's personal appearances and her own consuming labors and put it where it belongs—on golfing and snorkeling in Florida, where the two enjoy annual winter vacations; and on time at home. "And, of course, on family," adds Colleen. To accomplish this, she and Gordie hope to develop increased amounts of "passive income"—earnings that can be nurtured without significant outlays of time or effort.

Gordie sums up his hopes for retirement in two words: total security. "I want financial comfort for myself and Colleen, I want to be debt-free, and I want to be able to assist the family if necessary, particularly some of the older members. I don't want a one hundred-fifty-foot yacht; I just want a home, a boat, and some time to enjoy them. Above all, we don't want to have to rely on anybody but ourselves."

But while Gordie is thinking relaxation, Colleen is girding for further productivity. Among other things, she has plans to collaborate on a pair of videos, one about Gordie's boyhood on the Prairies, the other a feature-length account of the life and times of the Howe family.

"In the meantime," she says, "I'm working on some new corporate affiliations, and of course I want to get the display of Howe memorabilia going. I guess I've got the next few years pretty well cut out for me. And I intend to enjoy them.

"God willing, our most exciting years are still ahead."

*   *   *   *   *

Epilogue

Whether or not the past year has in fact been one of "the most exciting" for the Howes, as Colleen might have hoped, is open to debate. Certainly the time has been a hectic continuation of the life the pair established from pretty much the point at which they met in Detroit half a century ago.

For one thing, the year has brought drama in the form of illness and surgery. But despite having had double knee replacement surgery in early 1999, Gordie still crisscrosses the continent, making public appearances that range in setting from corporate conferences to charity golf tournaments, to small-town mall or storefront visits. In December 1999, for instance, Gordie and Colleen visited a Hallmark card shop in Holland, Michigan, where Gordie spent two hours signing miniature glass Christmas tree ornaments of his likeness in a Detroit Red Wings uniform. And, as they have done for a decade or more, he and Colleen continue to make appearances for Zellers' department stores in Canada.

"Making a living helps," Gordie once quipped. But, as always, he is as willing as ever to lend his name and reputation to any cause he might happen to believe in. He was a featured participant at a recent WHA reunion dinner, the proceeds of which went to aid former WHA players in need. And he was one of sixteen members of the Hockey Hall of Fame who, last year, threatened withdrawal from the Hall if the institution did not expel one-time Players Association boss Alan Eagleson, who had been found guilty of stealing from the players' pension fund.

Despite ongoing rehab for his knees, Gordie was a featured guest at NHL All-Star celebrations in Toronto, in February 2000, and participated in a televised pond hockey game with, among others, Wayne Gretzky, Eric Lindros, and Mario Lemieux.

While Colleen's health has suffered periodically of late, it was Gordie who made headlines when he was diagnosed with skin cancer in late November 1999. He had discovered the cancerous lesion on his left shin three months earlier but assumed it was the result of a cut he had received from a piece of coral while swimming in Florida. Colleen eventually persuaded him to consult their son Murray, a radiologist in Toledo, Ohio. Murray, in turn, referred Gordie to a cancer specialist who

Yvan Cournoyer

Yvan Cournoyer joined the Canadiens for the 1963–64 season. He is seen here in his official team photo from that year.

Yvan on a mission against Eddie Giacomin, Harry Howell, and Arnie Brown of the Rangers.

Yvan Cournoyer

During fourteen years with the Canadiens, Yvan played on ten Stanley Cup winners.

Yvan and Evelyn.

Yvan and Kurt on Lac Labelle, in front of the family chalet, 1994.

Phil, Gordie, and Bobby prior to a "Masters" game, 1983.

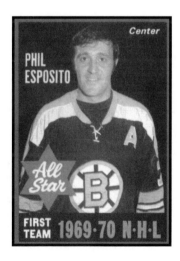

Phil Esposito.

John Ferguson

John Ferguson (right) and linemate Ralph Backstrom with the Price of Wales Trophy, awarded to the Canadiens for their first-place finish in John's rookie season, 1963–64.

Fergy with coach Toe Blake and teammates Ralph Backstrom, Jean Beliveau, and J. C. Tremblay, after defeating the New York Rangers in the first game of the 1967 semifinals.

Fergy with Claude Provost, Jean-Guy Talbot, and Gump Worsley. Fergy is holding the good luck charm that helped the Canadiens win the Stanley Cup in 1969.

John with Hardie Hanover, the North American champion three-year-old pacing filly for 1994. (Michael Burns)

John and Joan showing off the silver medal won by Team Canada at the World Hockey Championship in Stockholm, Sweden, 1989.

Gordie Howe

Gordie Howe Right Wing

DETROIT RED WINGS

The Howes on their wedding day, 1953.

Three generations—Gordie, Travis, and Mark—at the '86 All-Star game in Hartford, Connecticut.

The Howe team.

Bobby Hull

The Golden Jet.

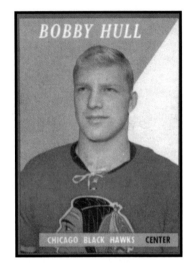

Bobby Hull, the first NHL player to score more than fifty goals in a season, with his sons Bobby Jr. (left) and Blake.

Reggie Leach

Reggie Leach with the Flyers during their 1974–75 Cup-winning season.

Reg and his son, Jamie, in 1982. Jamie has played for four NHL teams and is currently with the Buffalo Sabres. He was a member of the Stanley Cup champion Pittsburgh Penguins in 1991.

Reggie Leach

Brandon (Debbie's son) and Brandie (Reg's daughter). Brandie played for the Canadian Women's national lacrosse team in 1992. She is a student at Rowan Community College in Glassboro, New Jersey. Brandon attends elementary school near Sewell, New Jersey.

Reg and Jamie at Arnes, Manitoba, near Reg's hometown of Riverton.

Reg with Flyers Alumni team, on tour in Switzerland in 1993. At left is former Flyer Rick MacLeish, at right Al Secord.

Reg and his fiancée, Debbie Cooper, in Switzerland in 1993.

Stan Mikita

(Clockwise from left) Jane, Stan, Jill, Chris, Meg, Scott, and the family pet, Mandy, Christmas 1988.

Jill and Stan Mikita.

Eric Nesterenko

Eric Nesterenko in his prime, with the Chicago Blackhawks.

Eric flies down the slope at Vail, Colorado, 1995.

Maurice Richard

A pair of nines—the legendary Gordie Howe and Maurice Richard.

Maurice Richard

The Rocket and Lucille arriving at Rideau Hall.

The Rocket (or "Rock," as he was known to his teammates) in his office at S. Albert Fuels.

MAURICE RICHARD

Maurice Richard

The Canadiens' all-time dream team at the Forum, 1984 (clockwise): the late Jacques Plante, Larry Robinson, Toe Blake, Jean Beliveau, Dickie Moore, the late Aurele Joliat, Doug Harvey, the late Maurice Richard, and Bob Gainey.

diagnosed the disease and performed successful surgery on November 29, 1999.

The couple's other major diversion of 1999 came five months earlier when they unexpectedly severed ties with their beloved Traverse City and moved permanently back to Detroit, where they are now living, near their son Mark and his family.

"I just loved Traverse City," says Gordie, "but the weather can be a problem up north, and the travel back and forth was getting to be too much." The trigger point for the decision to move came during the early months of 1999 when Gordie was unable to fly out of Traverse City because of a two-day blizzard and had to drive for nearly sixty hours to get to an ESPN television taping of a show on the top one hundred athletes of the century.

"We had a dozen good years in Traverse City," says Colleen, "and the area is always going to be a part of us."

In the meantime, Colleen's dream of founding a family museum is coming closer to reality. The plan now calls for a privately owned Howe arena that will also serve as a showplace for the treasures Colleen continues to collect. Seven years ago, Traverse City named an arena in Gordie's honor, but it was not a business venture in which the Howes shared.

"We're still looking for a site," says Colleen. "But I believe it'll be in Michigan, and I believe it'll be soon." For now, Colleen admits she and Gordie are counting their blessings and living at a pace that is somewhat relaxed relative to what they kept in the past.

"If Colleen gets any more relaxed," Gordie once observed, "she'll be operating at the level of the average sixteen-year-old."

Which is a point well taken from a man who played twenty minutes a game in the NHL at age fifty-one, and, at seventy-two, is fit enough to play pond hockey with the likes of Wayne Gretzky and Eric Lindros.

CHAPTER

5

Bobby Hull

A Kind of Dream

THE POWER: "Do you know what I used to think when I was playing? I used to think that I must be going to die soon, and that these people were just allowing me to do these things before I died. It was a kind of dream. So many people would have loved to live my life. As to what it all meant, I don't know, I can't say. In many ways it was magical—does magic have meaning? I do know that when I'd pick up the puck behind my own goal and start up the ice with my jersey fluttering and go the whole length of the rink and slap one in the net—when I did that, if the fans had sat there twiddling their thumbs, I'd have felt it was all for naught. But to hear those people, to almost feel them charging down the ice with me was the greatest feeling in the world. I can't tell you how it felt to have power over twenty thousand people in that way."

THE PRAGMATIST: "The problem with leaving the game was not being able to find any replacement for it—anything that was even a distant second to it in terms of excitement. I searched around for a while, but eventually I had to accept that I wasn't going to find anything that I could go at with the same energy that I'd always gone at hockey. It just wasn't there. So I've been biding my time from then to now—almost ten years. I mean, there's always been the cattle, but beyond that I've never wanted to get involved with anything, jump in with both feet and then find out I didn't like it. So I said, I'll just do this and that, stay busy, make a buck here, a buck there, wait until that one thing comes along again. With a little patience maybe it will. Maybe it never will. Maybe I'll just continue for another five years or so, if I live that long, doing a bit of this, a bit of that. There's always something that comes along to pad the bank book."

THE WIFE: "There's nothing I'd love more than to see Bob back in hockey, because he adores it, just like he adores his cattle. He's so obsessive and so creative about it, I just know that he could do something wonderful if he was given the chance. But for that to happen, hockey people would have to start treating him like a human being. I've been around Mr. Wirtz and his buddies a number of times, and I think they really respect Bob's athletic abilities and achievements. In fact, they see him as this athletic god. But they just don't take his views or opinions seriously. They don't have any regard for his intelligence—it runs entirely counter to theirs. It's sad, because Bob could do so much for hockey. He's available, they could use him, but they don't."

*   *   *   *   *

To get to Bob and Deborah Hull's, you drive south from Belleville, Ontario, across the bridge that spans the Bay of Quinte, and out onto the sprawling rural island that forms Prince Edward County. From the village of Rossmore you follow an ever-narrowing series of roads across sparsely populated, low-lying pasture and woodland. There is something primitive, even haunting about the landscape. It is not so much farm land as an amalgam of moor and range, close-cropped and dotted with cedars that emerge from the ground like random pegs in a game board. Chunks of limestone dot the sparse soil. If you follow your directions closely they will eventually lead to a tastefully modest beige bungalow that sits within twenty meters of the Bay of Quinte on the island's north side.

Two sturdy brick pillars greet the visitor at the end of the driveway, and close to the house sits a white Chrysler New Yorker. The place is shaded by tall blue spruces and, while carefully groomed, has a summery insouciance about it, a cottagelike quality, accentuated by the vast body of water that laps up to the shoreline in front. In the distance, across that water, is a low ridge of mainland; and out of sight, somewhere to the northwest, are the remains of Point Anne, once a lively company town where Bob's father worked in the cement plant and where the young phenom grew up with his ten brothers and sisters. There is an air of wistful relinquishment in Bob's voice as he explains that, with the cement plant gone, Point Anne is "practically a ghost town."

Bob bought the lakeside house in 1959 and, since then, has occupied it sporadically, mostly during summers. At one time he farmed neighboring land, and it was here nearly three decades ago that an enterprising photographer shot the famous beefcake photo of the brawny young Black Hawk pitching hay.

Today, Bob shares the house with his wife Deborah and his teenage daughter from a previous relationship. In the several years since her arrival, Deborah has worked hard to put her signature on the place, refurbishing it room by room. "My father was a contractor," she smiles, "and I used to love going to the new houses and driving nails and so on. My idea of a good time around here is tearing up a room and putting it back together the way I want it."

Deborah is a pretty woman in a pleasingly unconventional way. She has a high forehead and fine sandy-blonde hair, cut off with geometric precision at the nape of her neck. Her face is a study in focus (she has a way of looking at you that gives the impression she is either intensely interested in or intensely skeptical of what you are saying). She wears no makeup and her somewhat studious mien is accented by a pair of stylish red-framed glasses.

Her tastes in decor are a discreet hybrid of rural charm and old-world refinement. Regency hardwoods are crossed with Quimper china and back-country antiques. It is only in the newly finished rec room and bar—an artfully converted garage—that she has acceded to a more vernacular style, well-suited to the room's use as a showplace for Bob's trophies and mementos. Here, hockey photos share wall space with photos of champion bulls. And along one wall are perhaps fifty bronzed pucks, representing a variety of Bob's goal-scoring achievements. By no means, however, are all of the mementos of his spectacular career given wall space, or even preferential lodging. Some twenty-five landmark sticks—commemorating a fiftieth goal, a five hundredth goal, a first WHA goal—are stuffed helter-skelter into the furnace room. Some are marked with ballpoint or pencil scratchings indicating what

> **"I always defended with my left arm as I cut toward the goal on my backhand, and, oh, it got an awful pounding."**

achievement they represent; some are unmarked. ("I haven't got a clue what they all are," smiles Bob.) The more intimate pieces of his gear—the shin pads and shoulder pads and elbow pads, all of which he wore from day one in Chicago to the day of his retirement twenty-three years later—are in a canvas bag in a portable garden shed in the backyard. In the name of literature, Bob retreats to the shed and produces the fossilized equipment, declaring as he pulls a few pieces from the bag that it is "held together with dust"—not very cohesive dust, as it turns out. The shoulder pads, threadbare relics that would surely provide no more protection than the shoulder pads in an average Armani sports coat, fall into two pieces as he attempts to untangle their laces and straps. The cracked shin pads are wadded up with cotton batting and look like something a pick-up player might dig out of his basement for a game at the community rink. "Actually, my legs never took that bad a beating," Bob muses as he throws the shin guards back in the bag. "But my arms! I always defended with my left arm as I cut toward the goal on my backhand, and, oh, it got an awful pounding."

As he nears the end of his sixth decade, Bob himself is considerably better preserved than his equipment. Although he has not played hockey in some two decades, he has not forfeited the physique that, throughout his career, made him one of hockey's strongest competitors. His chest is a boulder of muscle, his forearms as big around as fenceposts. Nor has he forfeited the Duracell smile that once signalled his role as hockey's most gregarious ambassador.

But there is also a pensiveness to Bob these days—a more shadowy sense of himself than has perhaps been present in the past. During a day of conversation, he several times makes reference to his mortality, as if it has been on his mind. Asked about the references, he passes them off, purporting not to have noticed that he has made them. They may be a function of his age; but it is difficult not to speculate that they are equally, subliminally, connected to the recent death of his and Deborah's infant son Ryan.

All of which is not to suggest that Bob has been anything less than a complex human being in the past. He has always had a broad emotional contour—part of which is a capacity for impetuosity—and a broad, poetic range of expression. His conversation is laced with graphic verbs and vivid turns of phrase. Nowhere is his lyricism more evident or appealing than in his evocation of working on his relatives' farm near Marysville, Ontario, as a boy: "It was just across the water here," he says, giving his head a cursory toss in the direction of the bay. "From the age of ten on, I spent my entire summer holiday there, haying, then thrashing—oh, I loved that thrashing; they used to stook thrash. I loved pitching on the sheaves. Then the older fellas used to have me carrying grain the length of those big Ontario barns and dumping it in the bins. They used to fill those bran sacks to the top with wheat, so that I could hardly get a handhold on them. The older guys used to laugh watching me stagger around trying to get those big sacks on my shoulder. They must have weighed one hundred fifty pounds each—and me just a pup. It's a wonder my guts didn't bust. But I loved it anyway. And the meals! Oh, they were just heaven! See, the farmers along the road from about Shannonville to Marysville used to exchange help at thrashing time. I'd take the team and wagon and go wherever the thrashing machine was. And the gals on these farms would always try to outdo one another at mealtime—they'd have anything from beef to pork to chicken to duck to lamb, and about sixteen different pies and cakes; it was just fantastic the way those farm girls could cook. And I loved to eat—I needed it, I was working so hard. I was very ambitious as a kid—on the dogtrot all the time, never walked anywhere. I remember once during thrashing I was out in the field pitching sheaves with two older farmers, and they jawed all morning and smoked their pipes, never took their pitch forks off their shoulders. I'd run from one shock to the next, and before they'd get there, the sheaves were all on the wagon. At noon hour these older fellas came in for dinner at my mom's cousin's—her name was Hemmy Topping—and I'll never forget them saying, 'Hemmy, you better get that kid out of that field or he's gonna kill himself!' And here they'd done absolutely nothing to help me all morning!

"I loved those summers. That's where my love of agriculture and cattle comes from. And also from just driving through the country in the old 1930 Model A Ford, with my mom and dad and sisters and brothers. I'd see those old red-and-white Herefords out there on that green meadow, and they looked kinda nice to me, and I thought that if I was ever able to afford some, I'd buy 'em. And as soon as I could, I did."

Since 1959, Bob has farmed, either on his own or with partners, in half a dozen locations in Ontario, Saskatchewan, and Manitoba. He is currently part-owner of a good-sized Hereford breeding operation, through which he shares cattle with the owners of three central Ontario farms. Although he has no formal schooling in agriculture, he has learned his lessons well enough that, not long ago, he was invited to lecture on Hereford breeding at the Agricultural College of the University of Guelph. He is an unofficial spokesman for the Polled Hereford industry and an internationally respected judge of quality cattle. "It's an art," he says, "and I've worked hard at it for thirty years."

And never harder than now, although no longer at the end of a hay rake or manure shovel as in years gone by. Nowadays, Bob logs endless miles of travel selling the unlikely commodity, bull semen. "That and my breeding program, B and C Polled Herefords," he says. He produces his engagement calendar—"my little book"—a roughed-up, conspicuously unofficial-looking promotional handout from a greeting card company, and flips through it, calculating that he spends at least a hundred days a year on the road in aid of semen sales. "We sell all over the United States, Europe, South America, Japan—I'm doing more traveling now than I did when I was playing hockey. I go to sales, shows, to visit herds, sometimes just to keep abreast of what's going on, seeing which of our bulls are doing the job. It all takes lots of time, lots of effort, lots of money. A lot of money comes in, a lot goes out." Which might suggest a rather narrow margin of profitability. But Bob considers the breeding business less risky than most farming (which is perhaps not saying much in an industry that regularly bankrupts even its thriftiest practitioners). "This isn't the beef business, where you never know what you're going to get per pound. All our animals are pedigree. The only ones that go down to the golden arches are those that we don't feel are good enough to be breeding stock."

As effusive as Bob is about his business, it is not until he takes out his stacks of cattle photos and begins to rhapsodize over bulls with names such as Rhett Butler, Excalibur, The Stick, High Noon, and Moonraker that you sense the true extent of his affection for his animals. "Here's High Noon's mommy—isn't she beautiful!" enthuses the doting squire, displaying a color photo of an animal that the average punter might mistake for any healthy Hereford cow. "And here's The Stick. Isn't he something!"

The Stick is something—or at least was until he broke his leg several summers ago and was reluctantly dispatched to bull heaven. "I knew he was special the moment I laid eyes on him," says Bob, who spotted him as a calf in a Connecticut field nearly a decade ago and bought him for $2,500. "He brought in more than $100,000 a year in semen sales for more than five years running. He was the daddy not only of our current operation but of a whole new breed of Polled Herefords. In fact, The Stick will probably go down in history as the most influential sire in the Polled Hereford industry. He had that kind of impact."

Never one to withhold praise (or its opposite, if he feels justified in dispensing it), Bob ascribes at least a corner of his niche in the Hockey Hall of Fame to agriculture and his long-time love of it. "I spent my summers throwing bales around and wrestling cattle, and it kept me in terrific shape. You've got to understand that the success of my game depended entirely on physical strength. I was powerful, I could skate, I could shoot."

For hockey fans during the 1960s and 1970s, Bob's magnificent skating and shooting were the very definition of the game of hockey at its best. Fitness king Lloyd Percival once measured Bob's shot at nearly two hundred kilometers per hour. And his skating speed has seldom if ever been matched. Bob entered the NHL as an eighteen-year-old in 1957, and during twenty-three professional seasons was named to seventeen All-Star teams, won four scoring championships, and was the first player to score more than fifty goals in an NHL season. In 1974–75, with the Winnipeg Jets, he scored a remarkable seventy-seven times. His signature move, the one for which his fans best remember him, was accelerating across the blueline on the left wing (either with the puck or to receive a pass), raising his stick to an exaggerated height, and then pounding his slap shot at the net. "When his shot hit you," says Hall of Fame goaltender Johnny Bower, "it was like being walloped with a sledgehammer." In the words of goaltender Les Binkley, "When the puck left his stick, it looked like a pea. Then as it picked up speed it looked smaller and smaller. Then you didn't see it anymore."

By no means, however, was Bob's impact on the game confined to his skills as a player. As much as anything, it was his radical defection from the Chicago Blackhawks to the Winnipeg Jets of the then-fragile World Hockey Association in 1972 that marked him as the most influential player of his generation. By signing with the Jets he gave instant credibility not only to his new team but to the entire WHA. In fact, had he not lent his formidable presence to the new league, whose solvency quotient at the time was approximately that of distilled water on marble, there would quite likely have been no WHA after a season or two; and the Edmonton Oilers, Phoenix Coyotes (once the Winnipeg Jets), Colorado Rockies (once the Quebec Nordiques), and Carolina Hurricanes (the former Hartford Whalers) would almost certainly not be part of the NHL today.

Of more significance to his peers, Bob's daring migration dramatically altered the game's salary structure. In the competitive open market between the two leagues, many players increased their income four- and five-fold. Even journeyman players, who might have been earning $20,000 in the NHL, were given $100,000 contracts by WHA teams. Other NHL players were given large contracts not to defect. "We all owe him a lot," says Stan Mikita, who was courted by the new league but chose to remain with the NHL Chicago Blackhawks. "For a while there, every morning when I got out of bed, I tried to figure out where Bob would be, bowed down in that direction, and said, 'Thank you, Bob. Thank you for doing what you did.'"

Bill Wirtz, the owner of the Chicago Blackhawks and a senior NHL governor, once told Bob's brother Dennis that the All-Star winger's defection cost the Blackhawks and the NHL a billion dollars over a ten-year period. "I didn't believe it," Bob scoffs. "But one day I mentioned it to Harvey Wineberg, my accountant in Chicago, and he said, 'Well, let's see—the Hawks went from crowds of twenty-two thousand down to an average of eight thousand . . .' Harvey just makes that old adding machine smoke. And by the time he went through salaries, loss of attendance, everything else, he tallied up a billion dollars. So you can understand that the NHL wasn't too happy with me.

By way of punishing the departed star—and a nasty spanking it turned out to be—the Blackhawks immediately obtained a court injunction preventing him from joining his new team. "I couldn't even practice with them," says Bob. "I missed eighteen games and, for weeks, didn't know whether I'd ever play again. Wirtz had the judge in his back pocket. The Hawks thought that because of a certain clause in the standard NHL contract their hold on me was perpetual—that they owned me. But when it came to a final ruling, a judge in Philadelphia, a guy named Higginbottom, said, 'Nobody owns anybody!' And I was free to play."

> **"If I hadn't been so busy trying to get settled in Winnipeg, I'd have sued them blind."**

In the meantime, the NHL had approached the Ford Motor Company, CCM, and a number of other corporations that advertised on *Hockey Night in Canada* and that also held endorsement contracts with Bob, and told them that if they did not jettison Hull, the league would jettison them as sponsors. "If I hadn't been so busy trying to get settled in Winnipeg, I'd have sued them blind," says Bob. "But I had too much else going on at that point.

"Then there was the '72 series with the Russians—it was called a Canada–U.S.S.R. series, not an NHL series, but the organizers wouldn't let me play because I was no longer in the NHL. Bill Wirtz, Alan Eagleson (president of the NHL Players' Association), and Clarence Campbell (then NHL president) were behind that. Eagleson's such a fart, and Campbell was the crookedest old snake that ever was. He was the guy putting pressure on Ford and CCM to throw me out. He was acting for the league owners, of course. He was just a puppet."

Bob makes it clear that, even up to within days of his signing with the new league, he had no intention of leaving Chicago. "As far as I was concerned it was the greatest city in the world, with the greatest fans. But the Hawks were giving me contract hassles. They always had. Back in '67 when I'd signed my last contract, they'd promised to leverage my income and invest this and do that, and they'd never done anything about these promises. The foot-dragging went on for several years, and finally at training camp one year, I said, 'If you don't clear all this up, I'm not going to be here at the start of the season.' And I wasn't. I sat out nearly twenty games."

During the one-man strike, Bob deeply antagonized his employers by calling Wirtz "a bumstead" and Hawks' general manager Tommy Ivan "a puppet"—names that found their way into the Chicago newspapers. "I had quite a go with the Wirtzes over it all," he chuckles. "I was talking to old Arthur and young Bill at one point, and I said something, and the old man objected, and Bill said to his father, 'But Bobby's right, Dad!' And the old man hollered, 'Shuddup, Bill!' And I said to him, 'Bill, you're forty-five years old—are you going to let that fat old putz tell you to shut up when you know you're right?' And he said in this whimpery voice, 'Well, you know, Bobby, he is my father.' And I said, 'What's the matter? You're right, and he told you to shut up! I wouldn't take that from my father!' It was just a bad scene all around."

When it came to offering a new contract at the end of the 1972 season, the Blackhawks were as sluggish as ever. But this time Bob had a career option that had never before existed for NHL players. In fact, the WHA had made its initial pitch to him several months earlier: "I'd flown to Vancouver for a game in the middle of the season, and as we checked into our hotel, Bob Turner, an old teammate of mine, came up to me in the lobby. He said, 'Bobby, would you mind meeting a friend of mine from Winnipeg?' I said, 'Not at all. Who is he?' He said, 'Ben Hatskin— he's my boss; I'm in the pinball and vending machine business with him. He's across the street in the hotel.' I'd never heard of Ben Hatskin, but after I'd cleaned up I went across the street with Bob, walked in, and there was big Ben. We talked for a couple of minutes, and suddenly he said, 'I want you to come and play for the Winnipeg Jets.' Just like that. Apparently they'd put the names of all the NHL players in a hat, and Winnipeg had drawn my name. Ben said, 'I'll give you $250,000 a year for as long as you want to play, and $100,000 a year after that, if you want to stay and coach.' I was making about $100,000 a year in Chicago. I said, 'That's an awful nice offer, Ben, and I appreciate it, but there are two problems—I've got half a season still to play with the Blackhawks before I even want to talk and, furthermore, I think I can get $250,000 a year in Chicago.'"

No sooner did Hull get back to Chicago than numerous phone calls began coming in from Hatskin's office—as many as two or three a day. Hatskin also began hectoring Bob's accountant, Harvey Wineberg. "When the playoffs ended it just got crazy," says Bob. "At that point, I was meeting with Arthur Morris, a lawyer who the Blackhawks had sicked on me to try to sign me up. He'd say, 'What do you want, Bob?' And I'd say, 'Look, Arthur, I've busted my tail for this organization for fifteen years. You guys have to try to sign me. You make me an offer, and I'll respond to it.'

"By this time the media was beginning to get excited about the WHA and how they were romancing me, the whole deal. The phone calls were coming in so thick and fast by now that finally I said to Harvey, 'Look, they've gotten their million dollars' worth of publicity out of this. Tell them to get lost! I'm sick of their badgering! I mean it! I'm not going!' An hour later, Harvey called back and said, 'They want to know what it would take to bring you to Winnipeg.' I said, 'There's no way I'm going to cart an extravagant wife and five kids across the continent to a city I've never even been to.' Harvey said, 'They still want to know what it'll take for you to go.' So I said, 'Harvey, I can get $250,000 a year in Chicago for the next five years.' I'd made up my mind that that was going to be my salary. I said, 'What if I go to Winnipeg for the same money, and the league folds. They're not going to want me back in Chicago or anywhere else—I'm out a million bucks.' So I said, 'Go tell them I want a million dollars up front.' This was just to scare them, to get rid of them. A while later Harvey called me back and said, 'They don't want us to do anything until we hear from them.' I said, 'You mean they're considering raising a million bucks?' He said, 'Yep!' I said, 'I should have asked for ten—I don't want to go to Winnipeg!'

"All I ever wanted was a contract from the Hawks! And they didn't offer one until well into June. They hand-delivered it—$250,000 a year for five years. And I said to the guy who brought it, 'You can take this back to Mr. Wirtz—it's too late.' A few days earlier, the WHA had been in touch to say they'd raised half a million. The next day they phoned to say they were at $750,000. At that point I said, 'I'm gone, Harvey. If they've got that much, Ben Hatskin himself will ante up the other $250,000. I've given my word that I'll go for a million.'"

*   *   *   *   *

The World Hockey Association was certainly no Jerusalem for the million-dollar man. The league expected a return on its money, and, within months, the pressure of promotional obligations—a steady schedule of interviews, speeches, and rubber chicken—had afflicted Bob with a painful ulcer. Playing conditions, too, took their toll: eight- and nine-day road trips on which as many as eight games were scheduled, second-rate facilities, and, in some cases, second-rate opponents. "It got pretty rough," says Bob, arching an eyebrow. "I mean, in Chicago, I was just a member of a team in a well-established league with a good reputation.

In Winnipeg, I was with a league that had to take second and third dates in arenas that were sometimes just horrible. In New Jersey it was hilarious—we'd put on our equipment in the Holiday Inn, then bus over to the arena in our street shoes and go into a little dressing room in shifts to put our skates on. The room was so tiny we couldn't all go in at once. And the rink was tilted! By the end of a period, with the snow built up on the ice, you really had to be able to shoot the puck just to ice it.

"And of course they let in a lot of incompetent coaches and players. We used to call the Birmingham Bulls "the Birmingham Circus." Most of them were just goons, kookaloos, brought in to harass the better players, and they had a kookaloo coach, Glen Sonmor. And here I was supposed to be promoting all this to the world!"

The ultimate hardship for jumping leagues—and, in a larger sense, for being such an inveterate individualist—would not be known to Bob for a number of years. In fact, it was not until sometime after the two leagues had amalgamated in 1979 and he had retired that it became clear there was no place for him, and probably never would be, in what was now the only game in town, the NHL. Asked if "black-balled" is too strong a word to describe his current status relative to the NHL, he quips, "It's probably not strong enough. Certainly there are powerful people in the league who don't want me around. Eagleson was certainly against me before he went to jail. And Bill Wirtz once said in print that there's no place for me in the Chicago organization. Then again, Bill may not even be in control in Chicago. I wouldn't mind working with the Blackhawks, because I wouldn't mind living in Chicago. But I doubt it could ever happen."

Bob also believes that his long-standing commitment to fair and creative play, to the eradication of violence and intimidation, is too radical, too impractical for most NHL organizations. "There are a lot of people in pro hockey who'll tell you that the fans enjoy blood. But, let me tell you, they only want blood if you give them bad hockey. They will not stand for mediocrity; blood is more exciting. But if you replace mediocrity with good hockey, they'll buy it. Soon that's all they'll want, and if anyone impedes that good hockey, it takes away from their entertainment, and they won't stand for that. If you're going to give people bad hockey then you'd better stick about fourteen fights in with it, because that's the only way they'll watch it."

Bob admits that he would "love to put together a bunch of guys" who know how the game should be played. "I don't need to be a coach or a manager, or even have a title—just let me loose."

During the late 1980s and early '90s, Bob toyed with the idea of

> # "I still have this wound-up spring inside of me, tight as a bowstring."

helping create another new league. "We did it once, we could have done it again," he reflects. "But we'd have needed somebody like a Mario Lemieux to make it work. When Mario was having contract troubles in Pittsburgh a number of years ago, I thought, boy, if only we had something in place right now. We had the cities and the facilities. Look at Hamilton—great rink, lots of people. I'm sure we could have gotten people to take on a team in Hamilton, and I was pretty sure about Milwaukee, Indianapolis, Chicago, San Francisco, maybe the East Coast. I know we could have done something every bit as interesting, or more interesting than the NHL. And I damn well hope somebody will before long."

Over the years, Bob has also imagined a quieter, more genial life for himself as he approaches his sixtieth birthday. He says, "Sometimes I think I should just start enjoying what time I have left. I don't want to be patted in the face with a spade before I do a lot of the things I want to do. I'd certainly like to get to a point where I'm a little better organized than I am now—not so much helter-skelter, here and there, cattle sales, appearances, endorsements. I get tired of it all, tired of the travel. Whether I'll ever be able to shut down entirely and be happy, I'm not sure. I know I can't stay here in the country for all that long before I get an itch to get to the city. I guess that's my problem—I still have this wound-up spring inside of me, tight as a bowstring. Nervous energy. It compels me to keep going. Probably the only way I could have released that energy after hockey would have been to channel it into one all-consuming pursuit. And I don't mean cattle. As much as I love the cattle business, it's never really demanded or gotten my full energy or attention. It's not quite enough. The problem always lay in finding that all-absorbing pursuit. No matter which way I ever looked at it, the closest thing I could imagine to it was hockey."

*   *   *   *   *

One afternoon during the winter of 1983, as he worked around the house, Bob received a telephone call from a young woman in Bensenville, Illinois, a western suburb of Chicago. The young woman explained that she worked in advertising for a drug store wholesale company and that her boss was the sponsor of an annual hockey tournament for the hearing impaired. She wanted to know whether Bob could be persuaded to attend this year's tournament?

"I hadn't even wanted to make the call," says Deborah. "In fact, when my boss, who was a real promoter, told me to call Bobby Hull, I blurted, 'I'm not calling Bobby Hull! There's no way I'm getting on the phone and calling Bobby Hull.' I mean, Bob is this legendary character in Chicago, right? My boss said, 'No, call him. I want to get him down here!' I kept saying I wouldn't do it, but you can only say no to your boss so many times.

"As it turned out, Bob initially agreed to attend. But then he phoned and cancelled. Well, my boss just went through the roof. He said, 'That is not acceptable. I will not hear of it. I have to have him. Get him on the phone again, Debbie. Ask him how much he wants.' I was pretty embarrassed by this time, but I got Bob on the phone, and my boss spoke to him, and they settled on a fee for the appearance. As soon as he hung up, my boss said, 'Get the air ticket, get the check cut, and get it to him Federal Express, so he can't say no.'

"Before the tournament, I had a last phone conversation with Bob, and he said, 'I'll have to meet you when I get to town.'"

For a year following their meeting, Bob and Deborah saw one another every few months, during his visits to Chicago. "But we never saw one another or spoke between times," she says. "Who knows where he was? Just gone! But when he'd get to Chicago, he'd call, and we'd go out, eat, whatever."

At Easter, 1984, Bob surprised Deborah by asking her to return with him to Ontario. "By this time," she says, "I'd quit work in Bensenville, and I thought, What a great deal! I've never been to Canada. I have nothing to lose, everything to gain. I mean, I really did sincerely like the fella.

"So I came up here to the island—I remember driving in from Belleville, weaving and turning, and thinking, Where on earth am I going? It seemed so desolate.

"I ended up staying three months, then returned to Chicago, and Bob left for a trip to Alaska. When he got back he had a bunch of little gold nuggets from which he planned to make a ring for me. I thought, oh, no, this guy's getting serious."

*   *   *   *   *

Over the years, marriage has not been an easy road for Bob. An ill-advised teenage marriage while he was playing Junior hockey in St. Catharines ended quickly in divorce, but not before producing a son. His subsequent marriage to Joanne in 1960 lasted nearly two decades and engendered four sons and a daughter before ending in a protracted and hostile divorce. A relationship during the early 1980s produced another daughter and another difficult separation.

On August 17, 1984, Bob and Deborah drove to Picton, Ontario, some fifteen miles from home, and took their vows. "Bob never remembers the date," winks Deborah, "and last summer I decided not to remind him. And sure enough it went past without him remembering. Then on August 19th, 20th, and 21st, we were in Toronto for the Arlington Million horse race, and we were sitting having dinner one night, and there was a guy from Chicago with us. This guy tells us how wonderful his wife is to let him come up here and not be home in Chicago on their anniversary. And Bob's going, 'Well, that is something! That's really nice!' And I say to him, 'Bob, I can't believe you're saying this! Our anniversary was three days ago, and you didn't even acknowledge it!' He would never have known if I hadn't told him. Mind you, he's very observant in other ways. He can be a real sweetheart."

Asked for an elaboration on Bob's personality, Deborah volunteers that there is a "very sensitive guy" behind Hull's sometimes rather prickly exterior. "I've seen him cry—he cries just like the rest. Of course, there's a tough guy in there, too—a very opinionated guy who believes it's his way or no way. Because his way is the right way. I don't know how many times I've heard him say that. His kids make fun of him over it. But he believes it! There's no way you can argue with him when he believes he's right. Although I do," she laughs. "I can be pretty strong-willed, too. I'm certainly not afraid to stand up for myself, although I can also be very accommodating and forgiving. I'm like Bob in that I'm usually pretty up-front in my attitudes."

Deborah is certainly up-front in describing the challenges of being married to a man who for millions of Americans and Canadians is an athletic icon. "It's not always easy to preserve my identity in this relationship," she says. "So often, for instance, people refer to me as 'Bobby Hull's wife.' I mean, it may seem insignificant, but it's the sort of thing that robs me of my sense of self. Not long ago, one of Bob's friends was talking on the phone, and I heard him say, 'Well, Bobby Hull's wife is here.' And I screamed at him, 'Jay! I have a name! It's Debbie! I'd appreciate your using it!' Not that I want to be front and center—I don't. But you can't allow yourself to become lost in another person. It just doesn't work."

Deborah also rues the lack of what she calls "private time" with Bob. "Almost everywhere we go, whatever we do, there are always other people involved. And of course there are always the autograph seekers. After all these years with Bob, it's still amazing to me how much adulation he gets. As soon as he leaves the driveway he's public domain—people swarm over him."

To escape the swarm, Deborah hopes that one day she and Bob will own a home in Florida, where people are not so much aware of hockey and of Bob's glittering past. "Down there, it's possible for us to be out on the golf course and actually enjoy ourselves. . . . I'm not saying we don't do lots of enjoyable things now. We get out to dinner and, occasionally, to live theater when we're in Chicago or New York. And I love going to events where there are other former players and their wives. We were in Calgary recently for a get-together, and we'll be in Phoenix next week for a charity golf event. I really like getting together with Jill Mikita, Colleen Howe, Evelyn Cournoyer, all the girls. They've been very good to me, accepting me, the new kid on the block."

*　　*　　*　　*　　*

You could talk to Deborah Hull for hours, about everything under the sun, and the subject of her son Ryan's death would never come up. She has made it clear in the past that she does not want to talk about it—that it is too personal, too private. "It's like, Here's my heart; it's broken; take it," she once said. "It's just not something I care to discuss."

That is why when the subject was broached on a warm afternoon last April, Deborah's intense, freeflowing candor came as such a surprise. It was as if after four years of harboring the pain in her heart, sharing it only with her closest friends, she was ready to let some of it go. "Talking about it is certainly less painful than it used to be," she said that day. "But there's still only one word to describe the effect it's had on me, and that's 'devastating.' All the more so because Ryan was in perfect health. He was eight weeks old. I put him to bed one night at 11:30, and the next morning he was dead. Sudden infant death syndrome. The autopsy showed nothing."

As Deborah felt her way through a maze of wrenching memories and emotions, Bob stood across the room, leafing through business papers, occasionally glancing up at her, somber-faced. But he showed no inclination to interrupt or add to what she was saying. As much as he shares her pain, he seemed to allow that the story was hers to tell.

"It's changed my whole emotional makeup," she said. "I just haven't handled it well at all. I guess if I'd taken the time and gone through support groups and spent more time with people who understood, it might have helped. But I didn't. I did talk to people on the phone—on these hot line numbers that you can call for various difficulties—but that didn't mean anything to me. There was no comfort in it."

Deborah volunteered that a day hadn't passed in years when she had not re-experienced the agony of Ryan's death. "Every single day," she emphasized. "Some days are worse than others. In fact, the whole thing haunts me so much that most of the time it bothers me just to see other little babies. I know I can't pick them up and hold them. Even the thought of it is just too much for me. I don't even want another one of my own. I look at it in very black-and-white terms—where we are in our lives, what our lifestyle is like—and I can't see it. I know how it was when I had Ryan. Bob was away a lot, and he still is. He was gone the day Ryan died. That's Bob's life—I'd never ask him to change it or stop traveling. But I don't want to be left while he goes—not anymore. And with an infant, I don't have any choice; I'm left.

"Maybe if we were living in Chicago it'd be different. I mean, in Chicago I had friends, I had family. I could pick up the phone and call

> **"He was growing like crazy. He would have been a big boy."**

someone. Or I could go somewhere and not be lonely. Bob's being away wouldn't bother me. But up here it's very isolated. I simply don't have anyone here when Bob's gone. I heard it took two hours for an ambulance to get here from Belleville once. Knowing what I know, how could I possibly have another baby here? Believe me, there are days when I really wish I had my own. Oh, yes, there are. But it's a dream, and I have to tell myself to snap out of it. It just wouldn't be good family planning right now."

Deborah falls silent for a few seconds, then says quietly, "I deal with it all day by day. I go over it and over it, and there's nothing that can be done—nothing that could have been done. We've gone through every move that we made with Ryan the week before, trying to figure it out—detail, detail, detail—but there's nothing. It's not there."

"It's been pretty rough for us," says Bob, looking up from his work. "But I guess I'd have to say that I'm in a slightly different position than Deborah, in that I have kids of my own—I've had the feeling. Deborah's only had one."

"And he was such a pretty one," says Deborah, "styled right after Bob. Big chest, nice big hands. And he was growing like crazy. He would have been a big boy."

Asked what effect Ryan's death has had on her sense of her own mortality, Deborah reflects for a moment and says, "You'd think it might have made me more accepting of it. But in fact it's made me terrified of dying. Because I've seen death; I know what it looks like. I think about it often, and it makes me shiver. The one constructive thing I can say about the whole experience is that it's made me realize how precious life is. Every single moment of it."

Asked how the experience has altered his view of mortality, Bob tells a story: "Deborah and I were in Hawaii four years ago. Almost no one knew we were there. One night the telephone rang in our hotel room. A guy said, 'My name is detective so-and-so, FBI. I hate to be the bearer of bad news.' Right away it went through my head, which one of the kids is it? I never thought about anybody else—just, which one of the kids? The guy said, 'Your mother has passed away.' Well, I just fell back on the bed in relief. She was eighty years old. I loved my mom very much, but she'd lived a good life. Ryan was different. Never had a chance.

"I'll tell you one thing, I don't take life for granted anymore. I used to live as if time was never going to run out. Now I've seen it run out, and I know how valuable it is. You've got to do what you can to make it count."

*   *   *   *   *

Epilogue

In the months following the writing of this profile, Bob and Deborah separated and began divorce proceedings. She returned to Chicago to live, and he stayed on the island, where he still makes his home.

Bob's life, in the aftermath, is a continuing round of promotional appearances, product endorsements, and occasional old-timers outings, sometimes on skates. He is occasionally seen on television doing late-night advertisements for a muscle-toning and weight loss machine and is still passionately (if not always profitably) involved with the cattle business.

As ever, Bob is no stranger to controversy. During a recent trip to Moscow, he was reported to have made racial remarks to a reporter from the English-language *Moscow Times*, suggesting, it was claimed, that Adolf Hitler had "some essentially good ideas," but that he went a little too far in putting them into practice. The former star is also said to have disparaged African Americans.

Bob aggressively denied making the remarks and, with guidance from his lawyer Timothy Danson, launched a suit against both the Moscow newspaper and the *Toronto Sun*, which brandished the story on its front page. Bob also embarked on a campaign of elaborate damage control, which included a well-publicized conciliatory meeting with Jewish and black leaders, under the auspices of the Canadian Jewish Congress. He also voiced support for a museum to commemorate the Holocaust. (I might add in Bob's defense that, during several days with him, in preparation for the preceding profile—including several very personal conversations—he did not once make a remark even remotely detrimental to Jews or blacks.)

The nineties have seen the rise of Brett Hull, Bob's son, to NHL superstardom. However, despite Bob's attempts to portray his relationship to Brett as intimate and fatherly, Brett's own feelings are perhaps more ambiguous. When Brett's Dallas Stars won the Stanley Cup in June 1999, Brett, who scored the overtime Cup-winning goal, was asked following the victory whether there was anyone in his life who was particularly in his thoughts at that point—who had influenced him especially, or to whom he particularly wanted to pay tribute? The expectation seemed all too obvious that Brett might mention his father, calling forth the past heroics and nostalgia so beloved of the medium. But, without missing a beat, Brett responded, "Not really. I owe an awful lot to my teammates and to the management here in Dallas."

On the other hand, Brett has called for a recognition of his father's WHA goals and assists in the calculation of Bob's career statistics. For his part, Bob gave public encouragement to his son when the latter suffered a recent goal-scoring slump.

Between his athletic heroics and private antipathies—including divorces, court dates, and financial reverses—it is no stretch to say that Bob has lived a complex life. And his sense of humor tends to reflect that complexity, inclining often to sarcasm or to put-downs of himself as well as of others. Hull was never a man to turn down a beer or glass of wine—or to refuse to acknowledge the darker side of his behavior. So it should hardly have come as a surprise that, when asked recently if he had regrets about his past, he responded, perhaps facetiously: "If I had it to do over, I'd probably do more drinking."

"Sure he's done some questionable things in his day," a long-time friend in Chicago said recently, "but he's done some damn well unquestionable things, too—a lot of very good things. You couldn't count the number of kids out there who've had their self-esteem raised by some encouragement from Bobby Hull. Or the charities he's supported. Or the entertainment he's given fans. So when I hear somebody knocking Bobby, I always want to say, Go ahead—he never claimed to be a saint, and he never wanted to be treated like one. But he doesn't deserve to be treated like crap, either—by the press, or by the hockey authorities. But that's too often the way he is treated! Frankly, I don't blame him for saying that if he had it to do over he'd do more drinking."

"What I meant," Hull joked later, "is that I'd do more thinking! Write that! Then again," he quipped, "thinking can get you into just as much trouble as anything else."

CHAPTER
6

Reggie Leach

In the Wilds of New Jersey

By the time Reg Leach headed west to play for the Montana Magic, a Central Hockey League franchise in Billings, Montana, in the autumn of 1983, his playing career had lapsed into a stifling and irreversible aimlessness. He was thirty-two years old, not exactly a fossil, but of an age when any pro hockey player who has suffered heavy injuries or has not taken particularly good care of himself is likely to be in decline.

Reg's hockey career had been almost miraculously free of injuries; he had last been laid up at the age of sixteen, with a separated shoulder. But to say that he had not taken care of himself is a truth of such gasping proportions that it can barely be addressed without a significant stretch of the imagination. He had been binge drinking since the age of twelve, for example, and acknowledges having been hungover for at least half of his nine hundred big-league games. "On average, I probably played at about 75 percent of my capacity," he says. "Sometimes less, sometimes more."

One is left to guess what a player of Reg's talent might have accomplished had he not consumed up to a dozen bottles of beer the night before virtually every game he played as a pro.

Even amidst his alcoholic blackouts and sweats, he scored more than four hundred NHL goals and had his name inscribed on the Stanley Cup in 1975. The following year, he led the league in goal scoring, was an All-Star right winger, and played for his country in the Canada Cup tournament. He won the Conn Smythe Trophy as the outstanding performer of the 1976 playoffs. The postseason achievements for which he was honored that year included a remarkable nineteen goals (in sixteen games) and a record five-goal game on May 6 against the Boston Bruins. The *Philadelphia Inquirer* used the words "stunning," "pulsating," and "electrifying" to describe the five-goal performance. *The Hockey News* wrote, "Philadelphia hockey fans were treated to the greatest single-game scoring exhibition put on by a National Hockey Leaguer in the last thirty-three years as Reg Leach single-handedly blasted the Boston Bruins out of the Stanley Cup playdowns."

Readers of the aforementioned rave could hardly have been aware of the unintended irony of the writer's choice of verbs. For the Boston Bruins were by no means the only "blasted" party at the Philadelphia Spectrum that day. The star of the show, Reggie himself, had consumed so much alcohol the previous night that, at ten o'clock the morning of the game, as the team gathered to prepare for its 1:00 P.M. faceoff, (the Sunday game was to be shown on national television), he was lying in the basement of his suburban home in a state of alcoholic unconsciousness.

When his whereabouts were discovered a couple of Flyer teammates were dispatched to the Leach residence where they coaxed their felled comrade through a cold shower and poured a quart or more of galvanizing coffee down his throat. Within half an hour, he was alert enough to realize that his best chance of making it through the afternoon was, as he puts it, "to have a drink or two."

With a couple of fresh Budweisers awash in his system, he and his teammates headed for the Spectrum. There, however, Fred Shero, the team's coach—himself a drinker of considerable reputation—pronounced his leading scorer unfit to play. "I was still stone drunk!" exclaims Reg. "Except by this time I was starting to feel really loose, actually pretty good, and I said to Clarky [team captain Bobby Clarke], 'I think I can go,' and he went to Freddie, and Freddie said, 'Suit him up, then.' So I got my stuff on, and the last thing I remember telling Clarky before the game was, 'Just get me the puck. I'll put it in.'"

And that is what Clarke did. And what Reg did. And by the end of the afternoon the Bruins were gone from the playoffs, and the Riverton Rifle was coholder of a historic record that has yet to be broken.

The lessons of that afternoon are ambiguous at best. As Reg himself notes, "Some of the guys probably weren't all that happy about my showing up plastered for a playoff game. But there wasn't much they could say when I went out and scored five goals." In fact, a number of them helped Reg celebrate by accompanying him to a favorite team oasis and continuing the party they had begun the night before.

In all, Reg's party lasted twenty-two years—from the time he was twelve to the time he was thirty-four. It swallowed up some twenty thousand bottles of beer and took in towns as small as Riverton and Flin Flon, Manitoba, and just about every notable city in North America. "In the end, there weren't many places where I didn't know the bars," says Reg.

But by the time he got to Billings, Montana, the lessons of his profligacy were far more apparent than they had been on that heroic afternoon in Philadelphia. His agent, Frank Millen, had been busy all summer trying to get him a last-ditch gig in the NHL. Reg had spent the previous year as a member of the Detroit Red Wings, with whom he had signed a one-season contract worth $145,000. Under the severe eye of coach Nick Polano, he had tried to curtail his drinking. But he had argued with Polano over other matters, had fallen out of favor, and now no other NHL team was willing to take a chance on him. "I knew the booze would eventually catch up with me," he says. "What surprises me, looking back, is that I lasted as long as I did."

Whatever the condition of Reg's baggage, the owners and coaches of the Montana Magic were more than happy to have him on their team. For one thing, they were a new franchise in need of a marquee player. For another, the team was half-owned by an oil-rich Aboriginal band from Hobema, Alberta—the same band fictionalized and made famous by Canadian writer W. P. Kinsella. "They were determined to have some Native blood in their line-up," says Reg, whose mother is Ojibwa and whose late father was Metis.

While, to date, he had shown little interest or pride in his Native roots, he was happy now to accept the cultural accountability of his new role (he was happy just to have a job). But he was no more inclined to devote the best of his energies to hockey than he had ever been. He continued to party with Dionysian abandon, drinking nightly, deeply, and, by this time, at significant risk to his health. Whereas the previous year he had taken his family with him to Detroit, he was now missing the moderating presence of his wife, his thirteen-year-old son, and his eight-year-old daughter, whom he had left at home in the Philadelphia suburb of Cherry Hill, New Jersey. "It was the beginning of the end of my marriage," he allows. But almost before he can complete the thought, he is laughing. "What are the first two things to go on a hockey player?" he grins, pausing for effect before answering, "His legs and his wife! Which is pretty much the way it happened with me."

On the ice, the man who seven years earlier had scored sixty-one goals during a single NHL season had to content himself with a season total of twenty-one, against players who, five years earlier, would not have been deemed worthy to appear on the same ice as the one-time scoring champ.

"To make matters worse," says Reg, "the band council in Hobema stiffed me on my contract." When he had arrived in Billings in the autumn, a group he calls "the big shots of the tribe" had traveled to Montana and had worked out an agreement with him whereby his salary of approximately $90,000 would be split in two, half to be paid by team management in installments throughout the year, half to be paid directly by the tribe at the end of the season. The band council, he was told, would draw up a contract to cover its part of the bargain. "But they never did!" says Reg. And in the spring of 1984, when he attempted to collect his money, the council informed him that because there was no signed contract he should not expect to be paid. "I gave them a few phone calls at the time," he says, "and they promised to have another look at the matter, but they never called back, and I never went after them legally. I couldn't really prove anything. I trusted them and they screwed me. They still owe me $45,000."

What made the shafting doubly painful for Reg was that, over the years, he had made a number of visits to Hobema, at the band's request, to speak to students, attend banquets, and endorse a variety of Native causes. "I haven't been back since," he says, "and of course they don't call, although, once in a while, I still see the boss, Larry Mine, at Native functions. When we end up in the same room he just hides, I guess out of guilt."

In the end, the lessons of Billings and Hobema were no less ambiguous than those of the five-goal binge in 1976. Even today, eleven years later, the Billings fiasco poses an unsolvable moral conundrum for Reg, who would still be happy to see his money, or even a portion of it, but prefers to tip-toe around the issue so as not to be seen to raise his hand against the Native community, or to cast even the slightest shadow over it. "These days, I do a fair bit of promotion for Native causes and sports," he says. "The last thing I want is to create a situation that reflects badly on Natives, which is exactly what would happen if I took the matter to court. Everybody'd say, 'Oh, look, these Indians are robbing their own people.' I have no argument with the band out there; it's just a few guys who for some reason decided not to keep their word."

> **"On the hard stuff, I could get hammered in half an hour instead of an hour and a half."**

Within days of the end of the hockey season that year, Reg returned to Cherry Hill, where his drinking continued unabated. "I guess in a sense it got worse, because I started drinking liquor," he says. "I'd always been strictly a beer drinker. On the hard stuff, I could get hammered in half an hour instead of an hour and a half." He had saved little or no money from his hockey days and in the monthly grope to make a living, he turned to selling cars. "That lasted two months," he says. "I couldn't stand being inside all the time, and I just hated all the lying you were expected to do to the customers." He took courses to become an insurance salesman like his fellow Flyers, Orest Kindrachuk and Rick MacLeish. But he was no happier selling term and investment policies than he'd been selling automotive fantasies. And no better at it either. "The only thing that made insurance preferable to cars," he says solemnly, "was that it was easier to drink on the job. After a few months I was doing more partying than selling. I'd go for days without even making an appointment."

By this time, Reg had begun to experience alcoholic blackouts, the result of blown synapses and brain cells that, in their journey to the bottom of the bottle, carried with them all recollection of hours of bar-hopping and socializing.

By mid-1985, he had taken a bachelor apartment in Cherry Hill, and he and his wife of sixteen years had initiated divorce proceedings. "I gave up everything I had," he says with no apparent bitterness. "The house in Cherry Hill, our cottage up in Canada, whatever was worth anything." The liquidation included the sale of a summer ice cream parlor that the Leaches had opened in Arnes, Manitoba, near the family summer cottage just a few miles from Reg's hometown of Riverton. "The only thing I kept," Reg says, "was my NHL pension. . . . At the time all I wanted was to get out of the marriage and get on with my life."

What Reg did next would not jibe with most people's ideas about getting on with life. "I decided to take a year off and do nothing," he says. "As long as I was drinking, there didn't seem to be much I could do anyway."

At this point, his self-destructive slide might have seemed headed toward flat-out disaster, if not tragedy. His story, however, is not one of ruin but of redemption. And of remarkable self-renewal. As he has demonstrated throughout his forty-five years on the planet, he has extraordinary physical and psychological powers when he commits himself to using them (the five-goal game in Philadelphia is, in itself, a microcosmic paradigm of will over wobble). Nevertheless, in 1985 few would have bet on his chances for long-term salvation. "I'd always just thought of myself as a guy who did a lot of partying," he says, "but I can see now that I had a serious problem. I wasn't well at all."

*   *   *   *   *

By the time I met Reg in the late 1990s, he was in robust health, and the signs of it were as obvious as the signs of his sickness had been a dozen years earlier. During the years since his recovery from alcoholism he had built a successful business that now grosses nearly half a million U.S. dollars a year; had gained a measure of domestic contentment that he had not known in years; and had become a respected spokesman against drugs and alcohol in the Native community. "Most guys play sober and drink after they retire," he told me at the time. "I played drunk and sobered up afterwards."

That redemptive sobering began not with the sort of moral or mystical revelation one might expect would trigger such a dramatic turnaround but with a fierce bout of vomiting on a long weekend in August during the summer of 1985. "I'd been drinking pretty heavily the night before," he explains, "and for the first time in my life, I woke up sick—really sick.

So I went to see a doctor friend of mine. He sat me down, gave me a shot, and said, 'Reg, you're going to have to quit drinking. If you don't you're going to be in very deep trouble. Your liver's still okay, but it won't be for long; you're right on the edge.' This was a Sunday. On Tuesday, I checked into the rehab center in Marysville, New Jersey."

During the next thirty-two days, Reg was obliged to confront aspects of his inner and outer life that, by his own admission, he had never before considered. "I got a whole new view of my past, from childhood right through to the present," he says. "And a lot of what I saw I didn't like."

More importantly, he got a new view of his (alcohol-free) future. He says, "I still wasn't sure what I wanted to do with my life, but I've always known that if I put my mind to something, give it all my energy and focus, I'm going to be able to do it. The trick was to find something I'd like."

To understand what Reggie did, and why, it helps to know that during his teenage summers in Riverton, and during summers early in his NHL career, he had been an all-but-constant presence at the Northernaire Golf Club near the tiny settlement of Arnes, Manitoba, a few miles south of Riverton (his daughter, Brandie, who attends college in New Jersey, now works summers in the Northernaire clubhouse). The place is owned by the Luprypa family, a Riverton clan that had befriended Reg as a youngster and given him part-time work in their general store. By his mid-teens, Reg had become a skilled golfer, as well as something of an expert at seeding and cutting grass, laying sod, tending shrubs and trees—in effect, doing whatever landscaping was required on the breezy, rural links.

During the mid-seventies, he applied the skills he had developed at Arnes to beautifying the large suburban lot that surrounded his home in Cherry Hill. "One day, after I'd come out of rehab," he recalls, "I was talking to a former neighbor, who said, 'Why don't you go into landscaping, Reg? You're good at it. Look what you did at the house!'"

Reg glimpsed a future in the advice, and by the following spring had founded a bare-bones company named Reggie Leach's Sports Lawn Service. Head office was Reg's bachelor apartment in Cherry Hill, and by the time he had canvassed his ex-neighbors and sporting associates, he had corraled fifteen clients, all of whom he knew personally.

As the weather warmed up he started making house calls. Fifteen dollars bought a client a weekly mow and snip. A few dollars more bought anything from gardening to patio work to tree pruning. At the time, the company assets totaled two Lawnboys, a Weed Whacker, and a tiny Mitsubishi truck that Reg had obtained in a trade for his car. Asked recently whether it was humbling to cut grass for people who had once cheered his exploits as a sports hero, Reg responded without hesitation that it "wasn't nearly as humbling as being an out-of-work alcoholic."

By the following spring he had ninety customers, the price of a visit had risen somewhat, and his weekly gross often totaled more than two thousand dollars. "The problem with having so many clients," he says, "was that I was racing around all the time and finding it harder and harder to collect my money. I didn't have a clue who a lot of the people were—they were friends of friends, and when I'd go to the door and tell them they owed, say, eighty bucks, they wouldn't wanta pay."

On a fateful day in 1988, Reg was introduced to a pair of natty strangers at a Philadelphia golf tournament. As it turned out, they were senior executives with Interstate Realty Management, a multimillion-dollar corporation that controls hundreds of low-cost housing projects all over the eastern United States. "Because these properties are full of people on welfare," says Reg, "the government pays Interstate hundreds of thousands of dollars a year to keep the grounds around them landscaped and tidy." Interstate, in turn, spends the money to hire independent landscapers who do the grass-cutting and tend to the shrubbery and fences. "So these fellas asked me if I'd like to do some work for them," says Reg, whose response was so unequivocal that the pair immediately assigned him landscaping duties on the grounds around their main office and at the enormous Salisbury housing project in the nearby city of Camden, New Jersey.

"By the next year, I had five Interstate properties," says Reg. "Then nine, then eighteen, now twenty-six." Many of the properties are multi-unit tenements that cover a city block or more and include dozens of acres of lawn. They range in location from southwest New Jersey and Philadelphia to as far north as the outskirts of New York City. To take care of them, Reg employs a foreman and ten crew members. He owns six trucks with trailers, five or six sit-down mowers, earth-moving equipment, and truckloads of smaller implements. "If I were to put all my mowers side by side," he says, "I could cut a swath forty feet wide across a field."

But that day on the golf course, he could not have known the dimensions of the job he was about to take on—that it would eventually place him, for instance, in some of the most

> ## "Your life isn't worth much at the best of times and isn't worth anything after dark."

dangerous and degenerate ghettos in North America, places where, by his own estimation, "your life isn't worth much at the best of times and isn't worth anything after dark." (One day in the slums of central Philly, he had to leap for cover to avoid being picked off in the cross-fire of a gun fight.)

On the second day of my visit with the former Flyers star, he took me to visit the Salisbury housing project on the south side of Camden. It was an experience for which nothing I had seen to that point in my life could possibly have prepared me . . . except perhaps the previous evening's conversation, a dinner-hour primer on the staggering abuses and injustices of the ghetto, and on the poverty, defiance, and dissipation (and the seemingly irrepressible good humor) of Reg's own remarkable boyhood and youth.

*   *   *   *   *

Today, Reg lives with his wife, Debbie Copper, and her teen-aged son, Brandon, in an antique shiplap house on a rural sideroad in the township of Sewell, New Jersey, some twenty miles southwest of Philadelphia. For anyone who does not know the area, it is not an easy place to find. When my wife, Betty, and I traveled to Sewell to visit Debbie and Reg last year, I was so hopelessly confused in my attempts to locate their home I was forced to call from a house less than a mile away and have them come and fetch us. It was explained to me later that even people who have spent their lives in central New Jersey suffer flop-sweats at having to find their way through the insufferable tangle of poorly marked highways, sideroads, and freeways that dissect the countryside into a zillion inaccessible fragments—and on which the traffic seems always to be moving about thirty miles an hour above the (rarely) posted speed limit. The area's countless towns and villages, once a day's ride by stagecoach from Philadelphia and Camden, are now bedroom communities for the affluent bondservants of the Philadelphia skyscrapers. By and large, these are places that once had boundaries and identities, but they have spread during the past half-century to form an amorphous, semirural subcity, a vast municipal protozoan, that gloms onto the east bank of the Delaware River, providing both an escape dream and an alter ego for the city of Philadelphia. "Most of the people who live in these places can find their way comfortably onto the nearest freeway and into Philly, or out to Atlantic City," I was told by a gregarious Amoco attendant near Glassboro, "but ask them to get from Jefferson to Glassboro or Sewell to Runnymede, and they'll look at you like, don't be ridiculous, I'm not an explorer." A map of the area, photocopied for me by Reg, reminded me of the winter windows of my boyhood, covered in an infinite network of delicate frost tracings. Except that frost tracings generally show signs of a pattern. The roads in New Jersey show none.

But if the cartography is uncertain, the hospitality at Debbie and Reg's is not. Debbie, who has known Reg for ten years but has been married to him for just four, is chatty, outgoing, and has a happy capability for making her guests feel instantly comfortable and relaxed. She has a motherly smile, an easy laugh, and a striking pile of long blond hair. Part of her considerable facial charm resides in the slight leftward deviation that the bridge of her nose takes as it descends in an otherwise flawless line from her brow to her upper lip.

Reg is equally friendly but, in the tradition of Ojibwa society, is somewhat less forthright in extending himself conversationally. He speaks when he has something to say. And yet there is nothing awkward about the silences that occasionally occur in his presence, sitting, say, in a restaurant or car, or even in his own living room. He is such a gentle and unassuming man, so intuitive and good humored in his communication with the world, that when the silences occur they seem less like holes that need filling than like breathing spaces, natural punctuation, in a dialogue that is unfolding at some rhythmically predetermined pace and will recommence when the time is right.

Reg is part of the last generation of helmetless hockey players, but, considering that he has suffered countless nicks and cuts between the chin and hairline, his face is remarkably free of visible scars. He has hair the color of ravens' feathers and warm dark eyes, the lids and corners of which crinkle softly when he smiles. At first glance, he does not seem to be a particularly big man. Compared to most hockey players, he is decidedly narrow through the hips and thighs; and his hands are lean and graceful. But he has the strength of a blacksmith in his forearms, shoulders, and rather sturdy torso. His weight these days is about ten pounds above his playing weight of 205.

Mention Reggie around anyone who knows him and they'll tell you pretty much the same thing: that he's one of the most decent, genuine, and generous men on the planet. "He'd give you his last dollar if you needed it," says Debbie. "He's always giving away money and buying things for everybody. Beautiful gifts. A few Christmases back, he bought me a Ford Explorer, but he bought it a little early, so that when Christmas came, he figured I'd better have some Christmas presents, so he went out and bought more. I said, 'Reg, please!' He'll just give, give, give. I think some of it goes back to his boyhood, when they had so little. There were certainly times when there wasn't much food in the house."

The difficulty with Reg's generosity, as Debbie sees it, is that people are inclined to take advantage of him. "He's such a soft touch," she says. "Guys he hasn't seen for twenty years will phone up out of the blue and ask if he can lend them five thousand dollars. They think that because he was a pro hockey player he's some kind of financial institution. He always tries to help out, and when he does, of course, so many of the people are right back asking for more." Debbie pauses, smiles self-consciously, and says, "I've kinda tried to protect him from some of that. I mean, Reg is famous for giving it all away, and now he's at an age where he has to think about his own future. You can't just keep making unrepayable loans."

Debbie acknowledges that it's a little more difficult to stand in the way of those who come asking for favors rather than money. "They say, 'Oh, Reg, you're in the landscaping business, can you design some little thing for my backyard?' And of course they expect it for nothing. Reg'll get a shipment of shrubs or chrysanthemums, any number of things for the job sites, and people will come over and say, 'Do you mind if I just take this little bush or these flowers for my mom? It's her birthday.' And Reg'll say, 'Sure, go ahead, take what you need.' It doesn't seem to occur to them that he's paid a lot of money for these things and needs them himself. I mean, he likes to help people out, and that's great. It's just when people want so much that it's hard."

Reg and Debbie first crossed paths in 1990, in Wilmington, Delaware, at a Flyers' alumni charity game. Debbie had gone to the game with a girlfriend because her girlfriend's boss, the one-time NHL goaltender Roger Crozier, was playing that night for the Flyers' alumni. "They had a buffet after the game," says Reg. "Funny thing is, I usually don't go to the meals after these games because of the socializing. I try to avoid places where people are drinking. But I was so hungry that night, I decided to swing by the hotel for a bite."

Debbie had not intended to be at the postgame party, either. "But then we got invited," she says, "and I happened to get seated at a table beside Reg. The room was pretty loud, and Reg was so sweet and quiet, I thought, this guy must really be from Canada. It was funny, because I'd always had the impression that hockey players were guys with no teeth and no brains, and here was this guy being so sensitive and nice. We didn't really say all that much, but during the months after that I kept running into a fella who works for Reg, and I'd say, 'Tell Reg that Debbie from Delaware says hi.' Then my girlfriend and I got invited to attend another alumni game in Philly. Reg played, and we saw one another afterwards, and one thing led to another, and we started going out." The two married in late 1995.

Debbie, a former legal secretary, now handles the Sports Lawn accounting and helps Reg in whatever ways she can with the clerical aspects of the business. They have decorated their home in Sewell in a way that pretty much represents their respective tastes in furnishings and bric-a-brac. The ground floor combines Debbie's preferences for bucolic antiques and contemporary rustic charm with Reg's giant television and a varied display of remembrances from his hockey career. A tiny antique highchair used by Debbie's grandmother stands in the dining room among other piney throwbacks to the beginnings of the century. A trophy case at the far end of the living room is chock-a-block with family photos, hockey medals, and commemorative silverware, while the walls are crowded with Reg's extensive collection of "limited edition" framed prints of Emmett Kelly, the original sad-faced clown.

The windowless cellar below is by no means a typical office (it is by no means a typical cellar), but it is Reg's domain, the low-level wheelhouse from which he pilots the ever-expanding affairs of Sports Lawn Service. Its walls are mortar and stone, and its appurtenances include a photocopier, a fax machine, and an elaborate computer. At the leisure end of the office, a comfortably battered chesterfield faces an equally world-weary television. It is from this rather eccentric substation that Reg coordinates the ordering of shrubs, flowers, fencing, mulch, and sod; figures costs, labor, square footage, invoicing, and equipment needs; sets staff schedules and deployment routes—everything required to contain the human and botanical forces that threaten constantly to make chaos of his twenty-six job sites. "What surprises people," he says, "is that I never write anything down; I keep it all in my head—thirty, forty, fifty things that I have to remember to do on a given day."

> **"I never write anything down; I keep it all in my head—thirty, forty, fifty things that I have to remember to do on a given day."**

The house is surrounded by old trees, newish gardens, and, out back, perhaps an acre of rolled gravel that makes a parking lot both for employees and for company trucks and machinery.

On our first evening in Sewell we drove with Debbie and Reg through monsoon rains to a first-rate rural roadhouse called The Library. Rows of old books lined the walls of its various nooks and ramifications, and its menu included beef filets that could be ordered custom-cut off the loin to any size the customer might want. In the habit of the pro hockey player whose years in the game were fueled by outlandish infusions of protein, Reg began his meal with an appetizer of mussels and followed with a strenuous filet mignon that in mass equalled five stacked hockey pucks and, in leaner times, might well have been called upon to feed the entire table. As he ate, he told us first about the ghetto to which he planned to take me the following day . . . and then about his boyhood.

There is about Reg's early years a kind of woolly implausibility, a truth stranger than fiction, that suggests the wild plotting and texture of a

John Irving novel: sometimes funny, sometimes outrageous, sometimes tragic, sometimes triumphal. As he recounts the details of those years, it quickly becomes clear that he remembers every setting and circumstance, apparently every soul, that made him what he is today.

*   *   *   *   *

Reg was born in 1950 in Riverton, Manitoba, a town of some six hundred people on the low-lying borderland between the prairies to the south and the boreal forests of northern Manitoba. If you stood atop the town's lone grain elevator and looked east across a couple of kilometers of marshland and willow, you'd see Lake Winnipeg, a shallow body of water roughly the size of Lake Ontario. To the west you'd see the thin-soiled hardscrabble of the Manitoba Interlake. ("You don't so much farm the Interlake as play it as it lays," Winnipeg writer Ted Allan once wrote.) The town is a low-built flat-lying place where the wind—off the lake or off the prairie—almost never stops blowing. Its gravel streets are dotted with smallish frame houses surrounded by large gardens in summer and even larger snowbanks in winter. A ways south of town, on Highway 9, stands a conspicuous plywood sign bearing a freshly painted likeness of a black-haired young man in the sweater of the Philadelphia Flyers. Accompanying the image are the words "Riverton. Where the Rifle scored his first 500. Reggie Leach."

By the time Reg was born, his father, a hard-drinking itinerant, had left Riverton for work in the northern mines. His mother, barely more than a child herself, departed for Edmonton shortly after his birth, leaving Reg with his paternal grandparents, who adopted and raised him with twelve children of their own in a wood-heated house on William Avenue. Reg's grandfather was physically disabled and was incapable of holding a job, although Reg no longer recalls the nature of his disability. Throughout Reg's childhood, the family limped along on welfare payments and whatever bits of income his grandmother could generate. He says, "I remember her bringing in the town's minor hockey sweaters and repairing them by hand and washing them up."

Reg maintains gamely that he was largely unaware of the poverty and that it did not particularly affect him. "I guess I just thought it was normal for a whole bunch of people to be crowded into one house, drinking in the afternoon," he says. Being the youngest, he was, for the first fifteen years of his life, the last stop in an endless cascade of hand-me-down clothes. At times, his second- or third-hand shoes pinched his feet so badly that, even today, he occasionally suffers intense cramping in his toes.

"Things weren't all bad," says Reg. "We had good times, too. It's just that there was so much to deal with and overcome. . . . One of my stronger memories of childhood was when my older brother wrapped a car around a tree—killed himself." A second brother, an alcoholic, froze to death, drunk, in a Riverton snowbank, and a sister died of asphyxiation in the front seat of a car. "Another sister," says Reg, "died in a mental hospital in Portage la Prairie."

By his own assessment, Reg was "no good at all" in school. "By the time I got to grade eight," he says, "it was either high school or hockey, and I chose hockey." It was a choice that must have been applauded by the staff of the local high school. For Reg's years at elementary school had been distinguished by mischief making of a sort that outflanked even the thorniest peccadillos of Bart Simpson or the Little Rascals. "In grade four or five," he says, "my two best buddies and I had a contest to see who could get the strap the most times, and I won; I got it fifty-six times. I used to pull my hand out just as the strap was coming down, and the principal would hit himself.

"I remember one time," says Reg, "a buddy and I got shut in the cloakroom for acting up. By the time they let us out at the noon hour, we'd eaten every lunch in there—fifteen or twenty of them."

For two weeks every summer, Reg attended catechism school, in preparation for service as an altar boy at the local Catholic Church. However, he admits to having spent most of his time kneeling outside the church door "as a punishment for goofing around."

It seems extraordinary in retrospect that, until Reg was nearly eleven years old, no one thought to harness his energy, or at least diffuse it, by putting a pair of skates on him and introducing him to the sport of hockey, which was played by virtually every male kid in Riverton. But it was not until the autumn of 1960 that he was given a pair of battered blades and his first hockey stick. Immediately, the game became not just a focus for the rampant energy that was threatening to consume him but a welcome respite from the poverty at home and from his continuing failures at school. He took to it with such passion that by the spring of 1961 he was the most accomplished young player in Riverton, if not in central Manitoba. "Every chance I got," he says, "I'd sneak into the arena and skate—with whoever happened to be on the ice. When I couldn't get in, I'd skate outdoors, for hours a day: on ponds, on the river, anywhere I could find ice. I even built a rink behind the house. It wasn't big enough to skate on, but I could use it to shoot pucks against the little shack my mom kept out there. Shoot, shoot, shoot, every spare minute, morning, noon, and night. After a few months, I'd knocked all the siding apart."

To maximize his ice time at the arena, Reg joined Riverton's predominantly female figure-skating club, which monopolized the ice on Wednesday evenings and Saturday mornings. He stayed with the club for four years. "I had the little picks and all," he says—and credits the experience with giving him the balance and speed that would eventually distinguish his skating in the NHL.

In warmer weather, the boys of Riverton played street hockey. "We'd divide the town into four segments," says Reg. "Each had its team. We'd have a schedule, playoffs, fights, everything."

Shortly after his introduction to hockey, Reg was introduced to what quickly became the other great influence on his young life—alcohol. "I guess I kinda blame my adoptive parents," he says. "I wouldn't say they gave me my first drink—they weren't really drinkers—but they were aware of my drinking, and, by the time I was twelve or thirteen, they'd always allow me to have a beer or two, homemade wine, whatever my older brothers and sisters were drinking. I mean, it was my fault, too, but I was a kid; I didn't know any better. I thought it was normal for kids to drink at home. I see now that if my parents had given me a little advice instead of just watching me drink, things would probably have been a lot different for me. When I go to speak to Native groups I always stress the role of the parents in helping the kids along." Reg recalls occasions on which he and his best friends pooled their winnings from skating races at the local winter carnival and gave the cash to "a local drunk" who would in turn buy the youngsters twelve-packs of beer.

Booze or not, Reg was sufficiently skilled at hockey by the age of thirteen that he was able to play regularly for the Riverton senior men's team, in a league that was about as close as sport can get to legalized criminality. "Oh, it was rough," laughs Reg, who was perhaps spared the worst of that roughness because of his great maneuverability and speed. "I weighed 185 pounds at that point," he says. "But I didn't have the strength of the men, so I had to be

> **"They'd call me something, and I'd just go down and score a goal. Take that, white man!"**

sharp—mind you, I had to be tough, too, or I couldn't have played at that level."

Along with his introduction to high-level hockey came a grisly introduction to the realities of racial discrimination. "I'd been exposed to it in low-key ways pretty much since I was a kid," he says, "but when I'd get on a hockey rink, where there was something at stake, it seemed to get a lot worse." In senior hockey, and then Junior A, Reg grew accustomed, and eventually inured, to taunts such as "dirty Indian," "smelly Indian," and "drunken Indian."

"As much as possible I tried not to let it get me," he says. "At the time, I was one of the best players in western Canada, and I'd say to these guys who'd give me lip, 'Look, fella, I've got the puck; you've gotta chase me.' They'd call me something, and I'd just go down and score a goal. Take that, white man!"

In the winter of 1963, during a senior game in Winnipeg, Reg was spotted by a Detroit Red Wings talent scout, who the following autumn enticed him to attend the training camp of the club's junior affiliate in Weyburn, Saskatchewan. "I was the last guy cut from the team," says Reg, "so they sent me to their farm team in Lashburn, Saskatchewan." The fourteen-year-old prodigy endured two months of intense homesickness in the dreary farm community before pulling up stakes, boarding the bus, and returning to Riverton. "At that point," he says, "I wasn't sure I'd get another chance, or whether I even deserved one."

The most stabilizing influence on Reg during his years in Riverton's minor-hockey program had been his coach, the late Siggi Johnson, a descendent of one of thousands of Icelandic immigrants who settled the Manitoba Interlake during the nineteenth century. "My dad spent a lot of time with Reg at the arena," says Siggi's daughter, Sigrid Palsson, who is now Riverton's librarian. "He really thought the world of Reg. He was very proud of him, and concerned, too, that perhaps he wasn't getting the direction he needed."

As a way of encouraging Reg during the weeks after his return from Lashburn, Siggi bought him his first pair of CCM Tack skates. "Till then," says Reg, "I'd never even had skates that fit me right. . . . Siggi told me that the town bought them for me, but I've always figured he bought them himself. I know he couldn't afford them, either."

At the same time, Siggi gave Reg the most important motivational lecture he has ever received. "Basically," says Reg, "he asked me whether I wanted to be a bum for the rest of my life, or whether I was prepared to get out of Riverton and do something with my talent—make a name for myself."

The following August, an opportunity arose to join another Detroit affiliate, the Flin Flon Bombers. With fifteen dollars in his pocket and Siggi Johnson's words smoldering in his skull, Reg boarded a bus that took him first to Winnipeg, then north to Flin Flon, Manitoba, where, after fifteen hours on the highways, he disembarked at the local bus depot at 6:00 A.M. "There was no one there to meet me," he says, "so I just sat in the bus-station restaurant and waited for the coach, who was supposed to be there." Eventually, the restaurant owners, Mary and Jack Reid, asked Reg if he needed assistance. "I told them who I was," he explains, "and even though they had nothing to do with hockey, they told me I could stay at their place for a few days, until I got settled."

By Reg's estimation, meeting the Reids was "one of the best things" that ever happened to him, and he ended up staying three years in their home. During the weeks that preceded training camp, he also struck up a friendship with the hometown hockey hero, a sixteen-year-old diabetic named Bobby Clarke, who would dramatically influence the rest of Reg's career. "We were close right away," says Reg. "We even bought our first car together, a '55 Chevy that cost us eighty-five dollars. We drove it all over the countryside." The pair particularly enjoyed trips across the provincial border to Creighton, Saskatchewan, where the drinking age was eighteen, instead of twenty-one, as it was in Manitoba.

Clarke was a classic alpha centerman, a team leader and an extraordinary playmaker, who set up nearly every one of Reg's several hundred goals as a Bomber and would eventually set up hundreds more as a Philadelphia Flyer.

Away from the rink, Reg worked mornings as a steward for the Hudson Bay Mining and Smelting Company, which operated the Bombers as a winter diversion for the town's residents, most of whom lived in Flin Flon because of the mine. "The tougher the hockey, the better they liked it," said Reg. "In fact, our guys were so rough, some teams wouldn't even make the trip up to Flin Flon to play us." Fist fights and brawls were commonplace in games involving the Bombers, and coach Pat Ginnell was practically sadistic when it came to keeping his team in pitbull trim. "One time we were on a three-week, twelve-game road trip," recalls Reg. "It was just go, go, go, on the bus, all over western Canada. We'd won eleven in a row and were ahead, 6–2, during the second period of the twelfth game in Saskatoon. But we were so exhausted from all the travel, we ended up losing 7–6. After the game, we bused straight through to Flin Flon, seven hours, got in at about 6:00 A.M. But before we got off the bus, Ginnell ordered us into the arena, made us put our wet equipment back on, then worked us like dogs for an hour. I'll tell ya, we never blew another lead like that."

Despite his continued drinking, Reg quickly became one of the league's best players and a top NHL prospect. In his second to last year with the Bombers, at the age of eighteen, he scored eighty-seven goals, and in each of his last two seasons he won the Western Canada League scoring title.

But his transition into the National Hockey League was by no means a flawless progression. The Boston Bruins, who drafted him in 1970, had won the Stanley Cup the previous year and had an all but impenetrable line-up that included the likes of Phil Esposito, Bobby Orr, Ken Hodge, Derek Sanderson, and Johnny Bucyk. As a result, Reg played more than half of his initial pro season with a minor-league team in Oklahoma City, just blocks from the now-tragic site of the Alfred P. Murrah Federal Building. After polishing the bench for most of his second season in Boston, Reg was traded to the Oakland Seals, a club whose collective ambition was so desultory that he was unable to persuade himself even to get properly fit to play.

Meanwhile, in Philadelphia, Bobby Clarke, the captain of the Flyers, had been quietly agitating to have team management bring his one-time linemate to Philly.

> **"When I'd shoot, it was as if my eyes were out on the blade of my stick."**

When the deed was accomplished in a three-for-one trade on May 4, 1974, Clarke announced to the press that, "even in a bad year," Reggie Leach could be expected to score forty-five goals for the Flyers.

But by Christmas of his first season with the team, he had scored just five, and skeptics questioned the wisdom of the previous spring's trade. In the new year, however, Reg reeled off forty-one goals in some forty-five games and ended the season as the team's leading goal scorer. He added ten goals in the playoffs, helping the Flyers win their second straight Stanley Cup.

The following year, he led all NHL scorers, logging sixty-one goals during the regular season, nineteen more in the playoffs. The team's general manager, Keith Allen, dubbed his star winger "the Riverton Rifle," a fitting moniker for a man whose shot seemed indeed to possess the speed and accuracy of a bullet. "One of my advantages," explains Reg, "was that I could get the puck away extremely quickly. I didn't take a full wind-up, just about three-quarters of the way back. I'd get the puck from Clarky, take a couple of strides, and let 'er go. Always the slapper. I could shoot about 115 miles an hour—the same speed as Bobby Hull. In those days I could stand at the top of the slot and put nine out of ten pucks into an imaginary six-inch square in either of the top corners of the net." Every day after practice, Reg took two hundred slap shots and, at times, would intentionally ding as many as ten shots in a row off the goal post or crossbar, from thirty feet away. "When I'd shoot, it was as if my eyes were out on the blade of my stick," he says. "I'd make allowance for the difference in perspective between the stick and my actual vision. In other words, if my eyes could see a two-inch opening, my stick could probably see four inches, and that was enough to put the puck through. I used to tell the guys to imagine their eyes out there on the blades of their sticks; a lot of them had never considered it."

Reg is neither long-legged nor notably strong-legged, but he was nonetheless a deceptively fast skater, a smooth skater who, like a figure in an Alex Colville painting, seemed at times almost to float an inch or two above the ice. "I imagine there were a few guys in the league who might have been a little faster than I was," he says. "But probably nobody at that time who was faster and had quite my feel for the puck."

While the combined skill and brawn of the Flyers of the mid-seventies made them largely unbeatable on the ice (they won Stanley Cups in 1974 and '75), the team's collective proclivity for after-hours dissipation may well have stubbed their chances of becoming a longer-standing force at the top of the NHL. "Pretty much the whole team was into partying and drinking," confides Reg. "It just seemed to be part of what we did. There was beer on the bus, on the airplanes, in the dressing room. It was always available to us. On the road, we often seemed to have nothing to do but drink. Freddie Shero's rule was that if the players came into a bar where he was drinking, we could say hello and stay for one drink, then we had to go—that was his bar for the night. And if he wandered into a bar where the guys were drinking, same thing, one drink; that was our bar for the night. We did have a curfew of eleven o'clock, but the guys never really bothered with it. Once in a while, management would do a room check, but they'd always warn us in advance, and we'd all be in our rooms like choirboys at eleven. But we'd leave again around midnight, and we'd drink till three or so.

"If I'd had a particularly bad time the night before a game, I might say to [defenseman] Ed Van Impe, 'Could you watch my side a little closer tonight? I'm not feeling too good.' And, similarly, he'd say to me, 'Reg, I was out a little too late last night—could you make sure to come back?' We worked together that way."

At the time, Reg thought of his drinking—rationalized it—as a means of coping with the intense pressures of life in the game. "It wasn't till later," he says, "that I realized I was using the pressure as an excuse for doing what I was probably going to do anyway—or was addicted to doing. But there was never anyone around to give us any advice about that sort of thing. From time to time, some of the guys would encourage me to cut back, but they didn't have a clue about the nature of addiction, and it was pretty hard to convince me to rein it in when I could score sixty-one goals on the sauce."

Reg played nine seasons with the Flyers, making at most $145,000 a year. He feels, in retrospect, that he was considerably underpaid, given what he accomplished. "Guys who weren't doing any more than I was were making as much as $250,000 a year with other teams," he says.

"What you've gotta understand is that, with the Flyers, no one could make more than Clarky. And that was right—he was our best player." But Clarke, according to Reg, was on an extremely long-term contract that amortized his salary at an artificially low annual rate. "When his numbers were used as a yearly ceiling for other players," says Reg, "it kept their pay lower than it should have. Don't get me wrong; I have no argument with Clarky—it wasn't his fault."

Reg's disgruntlement toward the Flyers' management by no means extended to his coach, the late Fred Shero, whom he remembers not only as a talented hockey coach but as "an intelligent, honest man," a man unafraid to give his players the news, in whatever form it took. "He'd sometimes give Clarky and Bill Barber the day off," says Reg, "and I'd be out there working, and he'd come up to me and look me right in the eye and tell me that all players weren't created equal; some needed more work than others. He'd leave little sayings and quotations on my locker, always trying to teach me something, get me thinking about things. One day during the year I scored all those goals in the playoffs, he wrote on the board, 'No man is an island.' He was referring to me— suggesting, I guess, that if we were going to keep on winning I'd need some support from the rest of the team."

But the Flyers did not keep on winning. They lost the finals that year to Montreal, in a four-game sweep, and over the next half- decade would mount just one more serious challenge for the Stanley Cup. By 1981, they were little more than a ghost of their once-fearsome selves.

Reg's years with the team ended in 1982, in a way that was neither as happy nor as dignified as he might have wished. In March of that year, general manager Bob McCammon had fired coach Pat Quinn and his assistant and had taken over at the bench. "I had a chat with him," says Reg. "I told him that, in spite of the changes that were going on in the organization, I'd like to finish the year with the team, and he said that was fine."

Two nights later, without consultation, Reg was scratched from the line-up before a game in Hartford, and was scratched again the follow- ing night in Philadelphia. "The next thing I knew," Reg says, "they told me they were releasing me. They were going to pay me until the end of the year, but they didn't want me around the rink."

Reg has always believed the key to his dismissal was that he had scored twenty-nine goals so far that year and that a contract he had negotiated the previous autumn called not only for a substantial bonus if he reached thirty goals, but for a year's extension on his contract if he achieved a total of fifty goals and assists. "I sat home for the rest of the season, collecting my paychecks," he says, "and when the team got knocked out of the first round of the playoffs, I was the happiest guy in Philly. At that point I had absolutely no use for them. The owner Ed Snider was a good man in many ways, but hockey players are no more than cattle to the owners. There's no loyalty. You can give everything to an organization for years, and they'll still dump on you and toss you out the door without giving it a thought. I mean, I realize now that I wasn't exactly the greatest guy in the world to have on the team. You're not much good to them when you're drunk half the time. Anyway, I had nothing to do with the Flyers for years after I left."

And the Flyers had nothing to do with Reg . . . until one afternoon in the late autumn of 1991. At that point, a representative of the team's front office phoned to congratulate the disposable star on his election to the Flyers' Hall of Fame and to notify him that he would be inducted with flying colors into the Broad Street shrine on the night of Thursday, February 13, 1992.

*   *   *   *   *

Camden, New Jersey, sits on the east bank of the Delaware River and, these days, is less a city unto itself than a kind of back door to the city of Philadelphia, which towers above it on the west bank of the Delaware. Settled in 1681, it is, among other things, the home of Rutgers University, Campbell Soups (founded in 1869), and Del Monte canned goods. It is a port and shipping center for the farms and orchards of central New Jersey and was the last home of the great American poet Walt Whitman, who lived in the city from 1884 until his death in 1892. It was in Camden that Whitman produced the final version of his life-long opus, *Leaves of Grass*.

The Salisbury housing project on Camden's south side lies in the shadow of the gargantuan Walt Whitman Bridge, the main link between the state of New Jersey and the city of Philadelphia. The project was

Reg's first assignment in reclamation landscaping and tends to typify the sort of places in which he works.

And so we toured Salisbury and the surrounding ghetto, street by street, in a company pick-up, on a sweltering August afternoon. The area is infested, quite literally, with rats, cockroaches, and termites—and, more visibly, with block after block of alarmingly degenerate tenements, three- or four-room flats, their windows smashed, their doors busted, their porches rotted or burned. The assumption evoked by such places is that nobody could possibly live in them (who could survive the winter without heat, windows, or doors?). But people do live in them—not just the walking dead of the drug and alcohol wars, but, in some cases, whole families, generations of families, who simply have no place else to go. At one time, the buildings made solid fronts along the streets, but these days they are interspersed with empty lots, sometimes two or three in succession, where the buildings have seemingly been vaporized out of existence and where the remaining patches of hard-packed dirt support a potentially lethal debris of hypodermic needles and broken glass, as well as the more benign trash—the chunks of concrete and scrap steel, the tires and cans and endless piles of plastic and paper—that accumulate anywhere there is a space that can be turned into a makeshift dump.

"This is a main street, so you're not likely to get hurt here during the day," says Reg, as we motor along Eighth Street, past brick walls dense with hateful graffiti, past men collapsed in doorways with their bottles, past junkies, crackheads, and grim-faced prostitutes on the beat in their platform shoes at three in the afternoon. "But you get off onto some of these side streets and, even in broad daylight, you can get yourself into big trouble." Seconds later, we turn down precisely such a street—an alleyway posing as a street—and almost immediately are among conclaves of contemptuous young men in outrageous haircuts and clothing, and among the filth-ridden carcasses of twenty-year-old roadboats that sit along the curbs, some so thoroughly ravaged it is impossible to tell that they ever had paint, windows, or tires. There is no grass, no trees, no greenery, either on the boulevards or in the yards; and garbage of every description lies strewn across the dusty clay. Bored faces stare balefully from the buildings, while the emaciated forms of other unfortunates lie in doors or on steps, even on outdoor couches, apparently in drug-induced or alcoholic stupefaction.

Such ghettos are frequently depicted as war zones or battle zones. But the depiction is inaccurate, in that it suggests a kind of closure on the attendant horror and desperation, a sense that this is where the war goes on, confined, self-limiting, destructive to itself but little more than a sound bite or news item to those of us who live safely on the outside. But to get up close to such places, even for an hour or two, creates an impression by no means of limits or definition but of a boundlessly degenerate no-man's land, a (barely) demilitarized zone, between affluent North America and some enormous social lesion that is unlikely to stop festering just because it has expanded to the boundaries of south Camden, or central Philly, or Newark.

> **"Every second guy down here has a gun. Even the kids have guns."**

Reg has been working in these areas for a dozen years and submits that their economies are based almost entirely on drugs, alcohol, and any variety of minor or major crime, from petty theft and prostitution to extortion, armed robbery, and murder. And of course on welfare payments, which are inclined to dovetail with everything else. "Every second guy down here has a gun," he says. "Even the kids have guns."

In the context of south Camden, the Salisbury project, which houses approximately a thousand people, is a relatively stable habitat. Its two-story row-houses, block after block of them, have functional windows and doors, working appliances, and facades free of graffiti. Because of Reg and his crews, the project has landscaping—not just lawns, fences, and shrubbery but *cut* lawns and *trimmed* shrubbery.

"But don't get it wrong just because it looks good," says Reg. "A lot of the people who live here are either users or dealers, and most of them have guns. When you cut grass in here, you're constantly cutting around beer bottles, crack piles, needles, whatever." He points out a late-model white Cadillac and beige Mercedes-Benz parked among a half-dozen rusted-out beaters. "Dealers," he says. "I tell the guys when they come in here, 'Always be polite, always agree with everything anybody says.' If you argue, some of these guys'll just shoot ya."

Every second week, Reg sends a crew of eight men into Salisbury. "Four of them cut," he says, "the rest do trimming and weed whacking.

They're in at seven in the morning, out by one. I often go with them; I get the easy job, riding around on a big mower."

On the rare occasion that the crews are called upon to plant gardens at Salisbury or other sites, the flowers are frequently torn up within hours, by teenagers or older addicts who sell them to buy crack. "Even stuff that can't be sold," says Reg, "gets ripped up just for the sake of it. When I order shrubs for these places I always get barberries, or something with heavy thorns, so they'll at least stand a chance. Even chain-link fence gets ripped right out! I have to use wrought iron."

Reg admits to discouragement at seeing the repeated wreckage of what he and his crews have painstakingly created. His frustration, however, is tempered by empathy for the people who would seem to be frustrating him most. "I know what they're going through," he says. "What bugs me is that so many of them don't care; they don't wanna do anything to help themselves out. Some of them, mind you, are great people. I even know drug dealers who are good people; they're just trapped."

Perhaps because of his own disadvantaged boyhood, Reg shows a particular affinity for the children of the ghetto. "I certainly can't say I blame a lot of them for dealing drugs," he says. "They understand that's where the money is. They're ten or twelve, they're making $500 a week! What hope do they have otherwise? Who's gonna convince them to go to high school, so that they can make six or seven bucks an hour when they graduate? That's no way out. The worst thing is, most of them don't live to see eighteen."

Many of the inhabitants of the ghettos in which Reg works know him as a professional athlete, which he believes gives him "a bit of an advantage" in his dealings with them. "I know it helps me get the kids on my side," he says. "I can sit down and talk to them. I let them help us with the work if they want; buy 'em a Coke or a candy bar, or something. Once in a while, I'll offer a bit of advice, but you can't really do too much counselling; it's too crazy down here. You make a false move, put somebody off, and they'll whip the gun out."

If Reg has an additional advantage in the ghetto, it is, of course, that he, too, has known poverty, addiction, and discrimination. "These people are a lot like Canadian Indians," he observes, "except these guys are trapped in ghettos, while the Indians are trapped on reserves—or some-times in ghettos of their own. There's a lot of similarity in the disadvan-tages and hopelessness." Reg feels that what he can best show them from experience is that their situation "is not necessarily permanent," and that there are ways in which they can help themselves. "They can't all be pro athletes, obviously—maybe none of them can," he says. "But they can quit drugs and drinking, and if they do that, you never know what else they might be able to do for themselves."

Ghetto relations notwithstanding, Reg attributes his business success to hard work (he frequently rises at 5:00 A.M. and does not finish his day until suppertime), to efficiency (he manages his time and maintains his equipment almost religiously), and to his easygoing personality. "I don't let too much bother me anymore," he says. "I guess it's partly an A.A. philosophy: get through the day; there'll be another one tomorrow."

He is somewhat more sanguine about his ambitions for Sports Lawn Services. "My goal," he says, "is to get the business to a point where I can leave it alone, let it run itself. I wanta get to where I'm grossing a million or so a year—that's the plan. I'm getting there fast. You've gotta remember, this is an expensive business. Hundreds of thousands of dol-lars go into wages and equipment and materials. I'm always taking on new properties. My aim is to be able to travel more with Debbie and Brandon, go south in winter, north in summer."

Reg also wants to spend more time working for the betterment of Canadian Natives—"especially the kids," he says. "I know what it was like for me, and I hate seeing the same mistakes repeated." He admits to feeling guilt that he has not been more involved with Native causes or been a better model for children and young adults. "When I was play-ing," he says, "I'd often get held up as an example of a Native guy who was making it out there in the world. But of course I wasn't a good example. When I'd visit a reserve, I'd know the kids were drinking, but I wouldn't say anything about it—what could I say? I've got some ground to make up. I only wish the various bands would use me more than they do."

As it is, Reg makes anywhere from five to ten trips a year to speak to Canadian Native groups, largely in Saskatchewan, Manitoba, and Ontario. "The exposure to the culture has been good for me," he says. "When I was playing I really didn't have much interest in it. Native pride

> ## "I'll never be able to lift my arm over my head again. No more slap shots."

wasn't big back then. In fact, if you were an Indian you did your best to cover it up. So, I'm learning."

Reg's message is not complicated: "I tell them what happened to me, then I tell them what I did about it, and then I tell them what I think about it. I often get told about this Indian or that Indian who had all this talent and could've been this or that. 'That's great,' I say, 'but there are all sorts of couldabeens. And why didn't they make it? Because they drank too much.'"

During recent summers, Reg has conducted a week-long Native hockey school in Gimli, Manitoba, just a few kilometers from his hometown. "Sixty or seventy kids," he says. "We teach hockey, we talk about drugs and alcohol, we keep 'em busy." Reg's son Jamie, who has played for four NHL teams, most recently the Buffalo Sabres during the mid-1990s, assists with the school. "One thing I'd like to do somewhere down the line," says Reg, "is get a big Native men's tournament going in central Manitoba. Mid-winter. Promote Native hockey. For the number of good Native players out there, there are very few in the NHL. Somewhere along the way, we're losing them."

At the moment, Reg is committed to an assortment of public-service ventures in the Philadelphia area. The Flyers' alumni organization, of which he is a member, supports some forty charities through benefit sporting events, and Reg personally hosts a charity golf tournament that raises some twenty thousand dollars a year for the Easter Seals campaign.

He seldom plays hockey these days, largely because of a serious shoulder injury he incurred during the spring of 1995. "I'd gone to Brandon's skating class to demonstrate a few things," he explains, "and I got horsing around, skating backwards, and I fell over a kid. Three hours of surgery. I'll never be able to lift my arm over my head again. No more slap shots. I still like to get the skates on when I can, though."

One thing Reg does not do is watch the game, either on television or live. "We didn't go to a single big-league game this year," says Debbie. "Last year we went once. And, ya know, even after all these years, as soon as we got in there, you could hear the people whispering, 'There's

Reg Leach, there's Reg Leach.' We can go to the most remote restaurant in Maryland, and people will go by and say, 'Hi, Reg!' At first, I thought, boy, this guy has a lot of friends. I used to wonder why he never introduced me to people he'd be talking to, and I got kinda upset at him one day. I said, 'Why don't you introduce me to your friends?' And he said, 'Because I don't know who they are.' They often tell him they met him somewhere, and he tells them he remembers. But he doesn't. He just doesn't want to seem rude."

On our second evening in Sewell, Debbie served a heaping meal of fried chicken, after which Betty and I and our year-old daughter, Georgia, got into the car and headed north on the New Jersey Turnpike. As we said our good-byes, Reg allowed that, at some point in the future, he'd be quite happy to return to Canada full-time to get involved in Native causes, athletic and otherwise. "I'd sell the business here," he says.

"Back to Manitoba?" I asked.

"Probably around Riverton somewhere. If you're going home," he mused, "you might as well go home."

The exchange reminded me of something he had said earlier in the day as we drove through the back streets of Camden. "I look back," he'd told me, "and it seems as if I've been saving up lessons in life for forty years, or so—mostly on how not to live it. . . . Now that I'm doing a little better at it, I guess I've reached a point where I figure I've got something to tell people."

Something they are not very likely to hear from anyone anywhere else.

*   *   *   *   *

Epilogue

Reg and Debbie's life has not changed substantially during the months since the preceding profile was written. Their business continues to grow in and around Philadelphia, and Reg is increasingly involved in Native hockey in his home country. "One thing we're doing is traveling more these days," Debbie said recently. "Reg takes a little more time off just for him and me."

Reg's desire to return eventually to Manitoba is unabated. "Right now," he says, "I'm as tied up in the business as I was with hockey twenty years ago. But it's not always going to be that way."

Meanwhile, he continues to take on the toughest of landscaping assignments in the Camden and Philadelphia ghettos . . . and, as he learned in rehab nearly twenty years ago, to be grateful for what he has and is, and to take life a day at a time.

CHAPTER

7

Stan and Jill Mikita

Stops along the Way

"If you can't take stress," says Jill Mikita, *"don't marry a professional hockey player."*

Knowledgeably spoken.

Consider the evening of December 16, 1967. Jill was at home in Elmhurst, Illinois, paying casual attention to a televised hockey game between the Pittsburgh Penguins and the Chicago Blackhawks. She vacated her chair by the television and returned a minute later to the sight of her husband Stan's face filling a good portion of the twenty-one-inch screen. Actually only part of his face was showing. Nearly half of it was swathed in a blood-spattered towel. The shoulder and chest of his jersey were stained bright red, and the ice suggested the aftermath of a hatchet murder.

"I always worried about his eyes," says Jill, recalling the incident. "He'd had a lot of cuts around the eyes, and my first thought was that he'd injured or lost his eye. Stan always knew that I'd be watching his road games on television, so when he'd get an injury he'd call me as soon as he could. That night it was twenty minutes before he called. I was two months pregnant at the time. Between the injury and the call, I went into shock and lost the baby."

As it turned out it was not Stan's eye that had been injured but his ear. In his own words, the ear had been "sliced off" and took thirty-five stitches to restore.

"I always allowed that injuries were a part of the game," says Jill. "And yet I was never quite ready for them when they happened. Then again, I wasn't one of these wives who went around worrying about them before they happened either. It may seem odd, but what bothered me more in a general way, caused me more day-to-day stress, was when the team got on a losing streak. Not that Stan ever brought his problems home. I myself wanted him to win, couldn't stand it when he didn't."

Jill allows that a lot of things can "get to you" if you're married to a professional athlete. "You're alone a lot, your family life isn't always normal, you have added responsibility for your children. . . ." On the verge of plunging deeper, she stops, as if her frankness had suddenly been kicked in the shin by some deeper urge for tact. "But you can't go around complaining," she smiles. "You knew what was involved when you got into it."

The same cannot be said for a hockey player's children. Yet they, too, face hockey-related stresses and challenges. For the most part, even the least of these are not apparent to them until the age of seven or eight, when it is suddenly evident that their father spends an inordinate amount of time away from home. Play time. Story time. Holiday time. Indeed, it was only in recent years that the NHL ended it's Draconian practice of scheduling games on Christmas Eve and Christmas night, which forced players to be away from their families—sometimes two thousand miles away—at that time of year. But New Year's, Easter, birthdays, graduations, and any number of special family occasions are still up for grabs. "You might say I had a father, but I didn't always have a dad," reflects twenty-year-old Jane Mikita. "Every year, for instance, my elementary school had a father-daughter banquet, and in all my years at school, my dad was only able to attend once. And when he did go people lined up for an hour to get his autograph. These were my friends. It was so weird."

Jane finds it equally weird that nearly two decades after her dad's retirement, his career still impinges regularly on her life—not always positively. "At one place I used to work downtown, 90 percent of the people were men, and they were always, 'Like, wow, is your dad Stan Mikita?' I don't know how many times a day. . . . One day a guy said to me, 'You get special treatment around here because of who your father is.' And I looked at this guy and said, 'You're wrong. And don't say that again.'"

Jane is an outgoing young woman of dark complexion and striking height. She is a graduate of the Chicago Academy of Design and Fashion Merchandising and works in the Chicago fashion industry. She has inherited a healthy dollop of her mother Jill's assertiveness and is a model agent of Jill's view that Stan's fame as a hockey player must be kept in perspective. "I mean, I'm proud of my dad for what he did," she says. "But, you know, it's not a big deal. People come up to me and say, 'What's your dad like at home? Does he cut the grass?' I've seen people drive slowly past the house, looking for my dad. I can't accept this, and yet in one way or another I've always got to deal with it."

Jane also has to deal with an occasional challenge to her identity. She says, "It really annoys me when somebody introduces me as 'Stan Mikita's daughter.' I always say, 'No, I'm Jill Mikita's daughter.' It may seem snotty, but it makes the point. In high school, I was on the golf team, and I did pretty well, and when articles were written about me, they always referred to me as 'Jane Mikita, daughter of famous ex-Blackhawk Stan Mikita.' Around some people, your identity can just disappear."

Even more irksome to Jane are people who buddy up to her with the hope of meeting her father. "I once went on a date with a guy who said, 'When I take you home will I get to meet your dad?' I said, 'Look, pal, you're not taking me home. When you ask me out, you go out with me. If you want to go out with my father, you ask him.

"My older sister Meg had a hard time always being identified with Dad. And my older brother Scott gets it in his theater reviews—he's a professional actor here in Chicago: 'Son of Stan Mikita.' Meg lives in Boston now, so she doesn't get it anymore.

"I want people to get to know me and get to know my mom and dad through me, not the other way around."

*   *   *   *   *

It hardly needs saying that the most persistent hazards of the hockey life are reserved for the players themselves. The physical pain alone can be an outrage. And yet it is routinely minimized by coaches, managers, and media, who measure it not on a scale of suffering but in lost games or minutes of games. Players regularly perform with broken jaws, broken noses, plate-sized bruises, multi-stitch cuts—injuries that, should they befall the average human being, might well prevent him or her from getting out of bed, let alone participating in a game that Canadian poet Al Purdy called a "combination of ballet and murder."

Stan Mikita is unequivocal in declaring pain the most oppressive aspect of professional hockey. "I once had a broken heel," he says, "and I remember waking up in the middle of the night literally crying in agony. I had so many injuries I can't name them—lacerations, broken bones, muscle tears; everybody gets them."

Jill Mikita reveals that Stan once played with a broken shoulder that had gone undiagnosed by team doctors. "They X-rayed it and told him it was fine," she says. "It was only later that an independent X-ray showed it was broken. Another time, he was having trouble with his arm. He had no strength in it. He was told by a team doctor that he had tennis elbow. But Stan didn't buy it. He went to other doctors, orthopedic people, and they told him his triceps muscle was torn off the bone. Stan told the Blackhawk management that this is what he'd found out, and that no matter what they thought, he was going to have surgery on it."

Even a player's retirement from the game seldom puts an end to the cumulative physical discomforts of his career. Stan suffers chronic back pain, the legacy of being sledgehammered into the boards nearly twenty-five years ago while jumping to avoid a bodycheck.

In a broader sense, retirement can create more discomforts than it relieves. Some players find it an emotional dead zone, a restless vacuum, bereft of the camaraderie and attention of the big-league game.

For others the problems are practical. "You've got to understand that the system never gave us any useful education," says Stan. "I'm not talking about typical schooling; most of us learned more playing hockey than we would have in a classroom. But we're ridiculously uneducated when it comes to making a living after our legs give out. See, in hockey, everything is done for you—airline reservations, hotel reservations; these days, even your business is often done for you by your agent. I've heard stories of guys who, after years in the game, don't even know how to book a flight. Our Blackhawk alumni group has tried to counteract some of this by bringing in speakers every month to address us on different topics. We're making this available to active players, too. I took a university course for six weeks in 1980—Business 101. I was thirty-nine; I felt like a grandfather. I only wish I'd started at nineteen. My belief is that education should be mandatory for the young guys. We older guys have made our mistakes. I accept that I could have gone to college and didn't. I take responsibility for it. I regret it. It would have changed things for me after I quit."

As implied, Stan's retirement was by no means a stroll into the Peaceable Kingdom. He was nearly a decade out of NHL hockey before even beginning to find his feet. Had he not been a man of strong will and intelligence—a man accustomed to surmounting obstacles—he would not have come as far as he has since playing his last NHL game in April of 1980.

*   *   *   *   *

Born Stanislav Gvoth, Stan faced his first major challenges as an eight-year-old boy in the village of Sokolce, Czechoslovakia. "My dad was a menial laborer in a textile factory," he recalls. "My mother worked in the fields during the summer." Stan's earliest memories are of going with his parents in late August to load hay and sometimes to pull potatoes outside the village.

During World War II, Sokolce was occupied by the Germans, and young Stanislav's family was obliged to billet two of Hitler's soldiers. "We had a little two-room house," he says. "One room was a kitchen with a bath and an outhouse off of it; the other was for eating, sitting, sleeping. The whole place was about the size of our current living room. Anyway, one of these soldiers had lice, so we had to burn our bedding. We talked to the captain, and he gave us new billets, higher in rank, very clean. I remember going to the mess hall to bring back their lunch; I'd walk very gingerly so I wouldn't spill too much. I'd go out to target practice with them; they'd rest their guns on a fence post and let me pull the trigger."

Unknown to Stanislav, as the war consumed Europe, an uncle and aunt he had never met were quietly mapping his future in a faraway country. Joe and Anna Mikita had emigrated to St. Catharines, Ontario, during the 1920s. "When my older brother was born in 1937," says Stan, "my uncle wrote my mother a congratulatory note, joshing her that the next baby she had was his, that he'd come and take the child to Canada. He and my aunt couldn't have children of their own."

In 1940, Stanislav was born, and eight years later the Gvoths received a letter from Uncle Joe, informing them of his impending visit to Sokolce. "He showed up with gum and candy and toys, and we thought he was God," laughs Stan. "Everybody has dreams, and we always dreamed of going to Canada or the United States. We thought the people over here lived in paradise, that they didn't have to work, that if they needed money they just plucked it off trees.

"My uncle was still keen on taking me with him back to Canada—in fact, I guess that was the main reason he'd come—but my mother kept putting him off as if he were joking. But he was very persistent, explaining what life was like in Canada and the opportunities that were available.

"One night, he and my mom and dad were sitting around talking about him adopting me. I was in bed in the other room, and I was hungry, so I asked for a piece of bread and jam. My mother wouldn't give it to me, and I started to cry. They thought I was crying because I'd overheard her saying that she wouldn't let me go to Canada. So she told my uncle, 'Okay, Joe, he can go.' That was that. As far as I knew I was just going for a visit."

It was not until Stanislav reached the French port of Le Havre, about to embark by ship for Montreal, that it occurred to him that he might never see his parents again. But his uncle reassured him that was not the case.

Not quite. "By the time I saw them again, I was playing for the Chicago Blackhawks," says Stan. "I'd just finished my first season, and I went back for a visit with my aunt and a cousin. By this time my sister Viera had been born—she was ten years old—and I'll never forget the first words my mom and dad said to us when we reached their place in the middle of the night. They took me aside and said, 'Watch what you say; we don't know whether your brother and sister are in the Communist Party.' Then they asked if I was angry at them for giving me up. I let them know right there that I couldn't thank them enough for having allowed me to go."

His gratitude notwithstanding, there were times when young Stan would have been quite happy to put the boots to life in St. Catharines and return to Sokolce. After initial placement in grade three, he was quickly demoted to kindergarten, unable to speak more than a few words of English. "About all I knew was that my name in Slovak had been Stanislav and that now it was Stanley. Fortunately, an older Slovak girl in St. Catharines took me under her wing and became my tutor. Within a few weeks I'd learned enough English to go back to grade three. But even so, there was always somebody making fun of me for the way I spoke, or calling me a DP."

> **"I'm sure my life wouldn't have amounted to much over there."**

Stan has poignant memories of watching the neighborhood boys play street hockey during his first winter in Canada. "For a few days I watched from the window, then from the porch, then from the sidewalk. Then one day they were short of people, and they asked me to play. . . . Once I got involved in sports and in school, and made some friends, I pretty well forgot about home. And of course I loved my new mother and father. I'm not saying I didn't have homesick moments. In fact, for about two years after I got here I had an occasional fantasy that one day I'd join the Canadian Air Force and steal a plane and fly home. I figured it was the only way I was going to get there."

Although he had come to terms with his adoption many years earlier, it was not until 1964 that Stan caught a glimpse of the parental emotion—the extraordinary bittersweet commitment—that made the adoption possible. "I walked into my daughter Meg's bedroom one night when she was tiny, looked at her in her crib, and I just wondered how anybody could give up a child. Then it hit me that it must have taken an awful lot of love for my parents to give me up. They knew that after the war, with communism taking over, with all the poverty and destruction, there was very little for me in Czechoslovakia. And they were right—I'm sure my life wouldn't have amounted to much over there."

Over here, Stan's life has amounted to far more than he ever could have imagined. The physical evidence alone is impressive. The Mikitas live in an expansive five-bedroom home in the affluent Chicago suburb of Oak Brook. The beige brick facade of the place is fronted by tall white pillars, creating an architectural effect that is part colonial, part baronial, part southern antebellum. A circular driveway arcs past the front door, and a swimming pool occupies the backyard. The interior of the house is a comfy aggregation of marble, broadloom, and wood paneling that Stan admits would at one time have seemed like a palace to him.

If anything, the plush surroundings belie Stan and Jill's essentially unassuming view of the world. The two are straight-thinking, hard-working people whose sense of order encompasses a deep belief in family togetherness and family responsibility. There is a manifest sense of warmth and caring among Jill and Stan and their now-grown children. At the same time, there have never been any free rides for the kids. At Jill and Stan's insistence—and in spite of the family's affluence—all of the Mikita children held part-time jobs while attending high school. "When they got to college or university, we paid their tuition, nothing more," says Jill. "I don't like that sense of self-importance that some athletes' kids get, so I've always tried to make ours realize that they're just normal people, that they have to make it on their own. Naturally, you want them to do well, but not on the back of their father's reputation."

The struggle to impose normality upon the scions has had its low points and its laughs. Jill says, "When Meg, our oldest, was five years old she had her father sign some of the little postcards that the Hawks make up for each player. The next day I caught her outside selling the autographed cards for a nickel. So I brought her in and did my best to let her know why you didn't do these things. I thought I got the point across. But then a few days later I caught her out there signing her name and selling it. The funny thing was that, without realizing it, she was signing 'Gem,' her name spelled backwards."

*　　*　　*　　*　　*

Jill's rigorously unassuming attitudes are rooted in the hardworking ethnic neighborhoods of Berwyn and Cicero on Chicago's west side, where she grew up. Her father was a welder, her mother what she describes as "a life-long housewife." Jill studied physical education at the University of Illinois and by the age of twenty was doing full-time organizational work for Congressman Harold Collier of the Tenth District. "It was the sort of job I'm good at," she says. "I'm a very orderly person. Always have been—in everything I do." The self-assessment is beyond dispute. The Mikita home is impeccably scrubbed and vacuumed. The books are shelved, the flowers arranged with a florist's fastidious touch. Jill herself is neatly, fashionably turned out, morning, noon, and evening. In summer, she rises at 4:30 A.M. (no alarm clock necessary) to do her housework and to prepare the evening's dinner. By 7:30 A.M. she is at her favorite spot on earth, the first tee of the Medinah Country Club, fifteen miles from home. She golfs six days a week and would make it seven but for one reason—the club is closed on Mondays.

In winter, she replaces golf with bridge, another game that, by her own admission, she could happily play seven days a week. In the corner of the den a sturdy, official-looking bridge table is encircled by chairs, ready and poised for occupants. There is a suggestion that a game could break out at any moment. Another bridge table sits in Stan's office.

Stan shares his wife's fascination with golf and bridge, and to a degree her sense of neatness. His slacks are well creased, his shoes polished, his shirts and sweaters invariably neat and new. His hair is carefully combed. Facially, he bears more than a passing resemblance to the actor Charles Bronson—or at least to what Bronson looked like fifteen years ago. High cheekbones, dark narrow eyes, angular jaw. For a man who has been nicked and cut and stitched so many times, Stan's face is remarkably free of scar tissue. His only noticeable scars are two fine horizontal white lines that abut one another in the middle of his upper lip to form a rakish-looking (and nearly invisible) moustache. He wears granny-style reading glasses and has the vocabulary and language skills of an English teacher. "The vocabulary came from doing crossword puzzles," he volunteers. But you get the feeling while listening to him—to the grammar, the syntax, the orderly progression of thoughts and sentences—that the concern for language runs deeper than mere vocabulary.

"Oh, yes," says Jill, "he always wants to say the right things in just the right way. That's why he's such an excellent speaker. He plans his speeches very carefully, writes them out, and for two weeks before a speaking engagement he's an absolute nervous wreck. But when he gets up there he's incredible."

*   *   *   *   *

Stan's sensibilities have not always included his current penchant for orderly communication. When he ascended to the NHL as an eighteen-year-old in 1959, he immediately became the most lawless and penalized centerman in the game and remained so for some five years. "He was the worst little cuss that ever was," notes his former teammate Bobby Hull.

Stan says, "At my size—160 pounds—a lot of people didn't expect me to be around long. I once said to Ted Lindsay, who was with the Hawks when I joined them and who was just a little bigger than me, 'How did you ever last so long?' And he said, 'I hit them before they hit me. If you do that, you've got the element of surprise on your side.' So I took his advice. I figured if I was going to stick around, I had to show them I could handle myself."

Hall of Fame defenseman Bill Gadsby recalls Stan as "a miserable little pain in the butt. . . . He'd cross-check you; he'd spear you in the belly. You'd be going around the back of the net, and he'd spear you in the calf—down you'd go. I used to watch the better players, pick out their bad habits, and do my best to exploit those habits. Stan had a very bad habit of passing to the left side and then looking to see if it was a good pass. If you came from his blind side, while his head was turned, you could really crank him a good one. I nailed him dozens of times, but I've got to give him credit, he always got back up. I remember hitting him hard during the playoffs one year and telling him, 'Boy, one of these times you're not going to get up.' And he said, 'Ah, get lost, you old man, that was no bodycheck at all.' I'd hit him some nights and he'd have to crawl to the bench. But he'd always be back for the next shift. He had a lot of guts."

Stan's indifference to the rulebook was often matched by his indifference toward his fans. "He and I were always arguing about the way he treated these people," says Bobby Hull. "I'd tell him he should pay a little more attention to them. He'd say, 'Why should I? I don't owe them anything.' I used to tell him, 'Stan, the people you ignore on your way up are the same people you'll be passing on the way back down. When you're finished, you can take one step out of the limelight or you can take a whole big drop.' Oh, he was bad—cocky. I think actually he had a bit of a complex, coming from Czechoslovakia when he was very young, fighting his way, thinking he had to fight his way up the ladder. I'm sure he was called a DP more times than he was called Stan. We'd argue and argue, and finally he'd say, 'Ah, I'm a better player than you are anyway.' And I'd say, 'Yeah, you're a

"Did you get the number of that truck, kid?"

better player, but that doesn't make you any less of a prick.' And he wouldn't know what to say.

"I'd come out after a game, and people would be after me, 'Where's Stan? Where's Mikita?' And I'd cover for him—I'd say he had to go home quickly or something. Then I'd get fed up with this, and I'd tell him to wise up, I was sick of making excuses for him. He'd smarten up for a while, then he'd go back to his old ways, and I'd have to beat on him again. . . . As far as actual hockey was concerned, he used to tell me, 'If I were you, Bob, I'd spear this guy and hack that guy.'"

Stan's first encounter with Gordie Howe epitomized his attitude toward opposition players. And theirs toward him. "I'd always heard of Mr. Howe," he says, "and one night I decided to take a run at him. Unfortunately, my stick came up a little higher than it should have, and I cut him under the eye for five or six stitches. He went in to get sewn up and came back with a little mouse below his eye. The next time he skated by me he said, 'It's a long season, kid.' Anyway, I didn't think much about it; I probably laughed at him and went about my business.

"Nothing happened the next five or six games. Then one night we were playing in Detroit, and we were both turning in the Red Wings' end of the rink. The last thing I remember was him going by me. When I woke up a few minutes later, flat out on the ice, there was Gordie looking down at me. He was a little concerned—concerned that he hadn't killed me, maybe—and he said quietly, 'Did you get the number of that truck, kid?'

"They carried me back to the bench, and Dennis Dejordy, our second goalie, told me that as Gordie had skated by me he'd slipped his right hand up under his armpit, pulled his fist out of his glove, and given me a quick pop flush on the chin. Dennis was probably the only person in the arena who'd seen it. A minute later, Gordie skated by the bench and said, 'We're even, Stan.' And from that point on we left one another alone."

In 1966, Stan made radical changes to his game. "He was taking an awful beating from guys who'd go back at him," says Bill Gadsby. "I guess it was getting pretty hard to take, and he decided to clean up his act."

While not denying that he was being worn down physically, Stan outlines other motives for the transformation. "One morning I came home from a road game, and my daughter Meg, who was two at the time, said, 'Daddy, I watched you play last night.' And I said, 'What did you think?' And she said, 'Oh, Daddy, you were so good. But sometimes when the whistle blew and all the players went one way, you had to go all the way across the ice by yourself.' I said, 'I was going to the penalty box.' And she said, 'But, Daddy, you were there for such a long time.' I thought, What kind of an impression is this for a little girl to have of her father? I thought, I'm going to have to make some changes. At about the same time, I started looking at my penalties and realized that a lot of them were cheap and unnecessary—holding, hooking, tripping, that sort of thing. And I was getting a lot of misconducts, too, for yapping at the referees. The first thing I decided to do was keep my mouth shut. Second, I was going to cut down on the cheap penalties."

The following season, 1967, Stan won not only the Art Ross Trophy for leading the NHL in scoring and the Hart Trophy as the league's most valuable player, but the Lady Byng Trophy for sportsmanship and gentlemanly play. He repeated the three-prize coup the following year.

One thing about the Mikita style did not change. From the time Stan entered the league in 1959, he had about him an exacting, sometimes inane sense of the theater of what he was doing. "We were in the entertainment business, and sometimes you had to be a bit of a showman," he says. "Sometimes nobody caught your act except your wife or your teammates."

Sometimes the entire arena caught it, as they did at the Montreal Forum on November 4, 1962, when Stan gave his most memorable performance. "I'd gotten into a little scrap with Claude Larose," he says. "And when we got into the penalty box, we looked at one another, and he said, 'You no-good DP!' And I said, 'You no-good pea soup!' And we just started swinging again. When we sat down, the crowd started getting on me, really getting on me. In Montreal, they always called me '*Le Petit Diable,*' the Little Devil. They'd say 'Shoo, Mikita, shoo!' Anyway, I turned around to acknowledge them, kind of stood up and bowed, and their noise grew, one section, then another. I thought they sounded pretty good; they were like an orchestra. So I stood up on the bench, facing them, and started conducting. The noise really swelled now. The whole building. So I stood right up on the boards to conduct my orchestra.

"Another night a guy took a dive on me, the ref called a penalty, and, in fun as I went to serve it, I took a dive of my own and slid on my belly over to the box."

*   *   *   *   *

Unlike some players, whose careers have left them with prolonged grudges against their former employers, Stan holds no significant resentment against the Blackhawks. In fact, he can name only two disillusioning incidents from his twenty-two years in the organization. "One thing I didn't like was the way Billy Reay, our coach, got fired in 1977. Management slipped a letter under the door of his office and another under his door at home. Unfortunately, he was on the road at the time, so his wife got the letter at home. She heard it arrive at three or four in the morning.

"And I didn't like it when Bob Pulford took over as general manager and wanted me to take a big cut in pay. I'll admit that by the late 1970s my skills weren't what they had been, but I was still playing thirty minutes a game." In time, Pulford backed off, and Stan played his last two seasons at a salary commensurate with his achievements and experience.

"When I left hockey, our income dropped quite drastically," he says. "But our expenses were still the same. So we had to curb a few things. For instance, we sold three condos we had in Florida. We'd been using one ourselves and renting out the other two. . . . Today, I've still got to work to meet expenses, but we did put away enough of our hockey money to be fairly comfortable financially."

Finances aside, retirement for Stan was by no means what he and Jill might have imagined or hoped for. "There was no real transition for

"When he played hockey he never brought his occupation into the house."

him," says Jill. "He just went from one thing he loved, hockey, to another thing he loved, golf. Unbeknownst to us, the golf would become a hundred times harder on us than hockey had ever been."

Stan's baptism into the golf business had come a year before his retirement, when he was invited to work with the golf pro at a new course owned by Kemper Sports, an affiliate of the Kemper Insurance Company. The course, in Long Grove, Illinois, is a forty-five-minute drive from the Mikitas' home in Oak Brook.

"My first summer there," says Stan, "I really just followed the pro around for a couple of months, trying to get some idea of whether I'd like the work. The next spring, after my last season with the Hawks, the management of Kemper Sports invited me to go full-time, and I did. I was basically assistant club pro, a kind of general manager of the place."

Even today, there is an almost palpable anxiety in Jill's voice as she recalls Stan's years with Kemper. "He had a tremendous amount of responsibility—everything from the restaurant to the people on the tees to the locker rooms to public relations, greeting everybody as they came in. He knew everybody's name, and this is a public course, pay-as-you-play. He'd leave here at five in the morning, get to the course at six, and maybe come home at ten or eleven at night. When he played hockey he never brought his occupation into the house. When he was a golf pro, he got to the point where he was so edgy, so totally exhausted with the job, that we'd hear him come in, and we'd scatter. We'd pretend we were sleeping. We didn't want to talk about it with him, because as soon as he started talking, all his built-up anxiety spilled out on us. This got worse as he went along—the last two years, '85 and '86, were the worst.

"I finally said to Stan, 'I've paid my dues with hockey, I've been alone a lot, and that was fine; I knew when we married that I'd be spending time on my own. But this is ridiculous!' In reality, though, it wasn't so much being alone that I resented; it was the way Stan was being abused. The pressure on him was so intense that he was treating the golf course as if he owned it. If there were twenty divots out of a fairway, and the golfers who'd caused them had moved on to the next hole, he'd go out there and tell them to go back and replace them or get off the golf course. Now, these are things that a golf pro shouldn't have to worry about."

By the summer of 1986, the pot was about to boil over, and Stan realized that he had to make a decision on his future, and make it soon. "My whole personality was being warped," he says. "I'm not saying the pressure on me was all external—some of it I put on myself. I did want the job to go smoothly, wanted the place to look nice. But the effort I was putting in was just affecting our lives way too much."

Stan's abrupt resignation that August was a well-noted event in Chicago. Not only was Stan himself still newsworthy as a Hall of Fame Blackhawk, but the golf course, too, had gained a popular reputation in the area. In fact, at the time of the resignation, the course was hosting the Illinois PGA tournament, the first PGA event for which Stan was an eligible player. "Things had become intolerable for me by this time," he says. "There were the workload problems as well as personality conflicts at the club. After my first day of play in the tournament, I told the boss that if he didn't do something by the time I left the course the next day, I'd be gone. The next day when I came in from the last green, I asked if there were any messages for me. When I was told there weren't, I said, 'Fine,' and I went in and started clearing out my office. There were newspaper reporters covering the tournament, and when they saw what I was doing, they said, 'What's going on?' I told them, 'No comment.'

"The next day I see in the paper, 'MIKITA RESIGNS.' The reporters had gone to the fellow who was running Kemper Sports—I'd rather not mention his name—and had asked about my leaving the club. He was quoted as saying that I'd left because I had 'personal problems.' Well, you know what the implications of that are—am I a drug user? an alcoholic? do I beat my wife and kids? is a divorce imminent? Nothing was specified. It was all open to speculation. I demanded a retraction."

Jill Mikita, who describes herself as "ruthless—like a lioness" when it comes to protecting the privacy and dignity of her family, was as upset as anyone over the incident. "It left us so vulnerable!" she exclaims. "In the meantime, this same gentleman we're talking about called here and said, 'Jill, this is so-and-so. Is Stan available?' For years, I've known when Stan wants to talk to somebody and when he doesn't, and I just said,

'No, he's not.' And he said, 'Well, I just want you to know that I didn't say what the papers said I did—I was misquoted.'"

A retraction appeared the following day, but Stan has never accepted the stated rationale for it. "The papers said they'd misquoted the guy, but they hadn't. He'd said what he was reported to have said. The papers were simply put under pressure to retract. I've seen the guy since then. I nodded my head to him, hello."

The months that followed were not easy for the Mikitas. "We were just floating, no direction," says Jill. "Stan had no idea what he was going to do, or even what he might like to do. Our finances were okay for a while, but not exactly great, with two kids in college."

Stan was forty-five years old and, by his own assessment, "had no real qualifications. I knew how to play hockey, and I knew a little bit about the golf business. But I was so turned off by golf I didn't want anything to do with it. A number of my friends in pro golf phoned and offered me jobs teaching and so on, and I'll never forget them for it. But there was just no way. I mean, I still loved playing the game, but I did not want to have to make a living at it. And I couldn't exactly make a hockey comeback."

One thing did go in Stan's favor during the few months following his resignation—Kemper Sports decided to pay his salary from August to November. Stan contends that the decision was based on guilt over the statements that had appeared in the press. "I was never really paid all that well for golf anyway," he confides. "I was barely covering expenses."

By early autumn, the Mikita family had begun to feel unforeseen effects from Stan's career inactivity. "He'd never been around that much for the kids, but now he started to play serious father," explains Jill. "It was difficult for the kids—in fact, it made them kind of resentful. Suddenly, here was Stan asking them where they were going, what time they were going to be home, this sort of thing. Our oldest boy, Scott, would come home from college, and he wasn't accustomed to this. See, I'd always taken care of discipline, and the kids were used to me. I'm not saying Stan was wrong in taking up this responsibility. It just came along a little too late to be effective. But it was certainly part of our growing process."

As the weeks passed, Stan began talking to business friends, attempting to get some idea of what they thought his strengths might be if he went into business. "And I'd get the typical answers," says Stan, "that all I had to do was make up my mind, that I could do whatever I wanted, and so on, which didn't help much. I didn't want to get into something and go belly up because I didn't know what I was doing.

"One day I was talking to a friend, and the idea of a car dealership came up. It seemed like a good possibility, so we pursued it for a few months. But the more I thought about it, the more I saw potential problems. For example, I really don't delegate authority very well. I'd discovered this in the golf business, where I was always doing things myself instead of getting others to do them. I wanted things done right. But I realized that in the car business, if somebody who worked for me didn't put a muffler on properly, and a customer complained, I wouldn't be able to fix that muffler myself. At least in golf, I knew how to put things right if they screwed up. . . . What's more, the dealership would have been an hour's drive from here—that's a long way."

Jill was perhaps more convinced than Stan that the car business would be a disaster. "I'd always felt that our first obligation at that point was to finish educating our children. And I've always figured I could go to work if necessary—it wouldn't faze me in the least. So I wasn't thinking so much about finances. I just felt that a car dealership would be no better than golf in terms of the pressure it put on Stan. I could see the sixteen-hour days again, and I just shuddered."

In the end it was neither cars nor golf balls nor hockey pucks but the petro-alchemic miracle of the twentieth century that renewed Stan's career ambitions. He describes his re-entry into the job market:

"We were in Florida that Christmas—we had a little place outside Tampa—and Glen Skov, a former teammate of mine, was down there. He'd been in the plastics business for twenty-five years, and he'd quit his job at about the same time I'd quit golf. One day we were having a beer, and we kind of looked at one another, and he said, 'What are you going to do?' And I said, 'What are you going to do?' And he said, 'I'm going to rep for a plastics coloring company in the Chicago area.' Up to that point, he'd managed a similar company's production plant. He said, 'I'm thinking of getting a partner and representing four or five lines—colorings and plastics.' Glen didn't want to work particularly long hours,

> **"Every day I learn something new. Going from golf to this was like coming out into the daylight."**

and I know I didn't. So when we got back home, I let the car thing go, called Glen, and we had lunch. He explained what the business was, and I said, 'I've never been in sales.' He said, 'Don't worry, I'll teach you. You can follow me around for a while.' I said, 'I don't know the first thing about plastics either.' He said, 'You don't have to. You don't tell the customer what he wants; he tells you. You write it down and go to the supplier and say, "Here's what the guy wants—how much is it going to cost?" We don't sell an end product. We sell bulk plastic and we sell the coloring chips that go into it.'"

Stan spent the better part of two years learning the ins and outs of the plastics business so that, eventually, he could hold forth in an industrial dialect replete with the mysteries of "sheet extrusion," "blow molding," and "profile extrusion."

It is something of an irony that, in a field as dynamic as plastics—in a century of computers and spaceships—Stan's fortunes, for several years during the early and mid-nineties, rested with the humble outhouse. "One of our biggest customers was a port-a-potty maker, a john maker—outdoor craphouses," he smiles. "We represented the sheet extruder who made the plastic for the roof and sides of these things. And we represented the color maker—you can't have a transparent craphouse."

During the mid-1990s, Stan took his company, Mikita Enterprises, into a less graphic but so far more profitable direction: industrial packaging, which he now provides to a number of Chicago-area businesses and corporations. He says, "Every day I learn something new. Going from golf to this was like coming out into the daylight."

Jill, too, is happy, because Stan is happy. She says, "I enjoy seeing him doing something he likes. At the beginning he was less sure of himself. But Stan is bright, and he enjoys people. He's in the place he ought to be. And I'm having a ball just acting as his secretary—mostly just answering the phone and doing some typing."

Jill is also pleased that, after twenty-five years of spending more time on her own than she might have cared to, Stan's endeavors are providing plenty of time for togetherness. "Only very rarely does he have to be at a certain place at a certain time," she says. "We have a lot more time for things like the theater—we love going to the theater. Stan really enjoys the lighter stuff. He says that Shakespeare's a bit obscure for him, yet when our son Scott was in college, we attended one of his Shakespeare classes, and it was absolutely fascinating to both of us. We go to the opera and the art galleries. We simply enjoy the arts. When we were in Amsterdam a few years ago, we spent hours and hours walking through the art museums."

Stan admits that during his playing days he didn't have time for the arts. "My whole life was consumed by hockey and other sports. So this has been quite a turnaround for me."

The fact that Stan works at home has undoubtedly aided his contribution to family unity. He is as honest as a Quaker and willingly confesses that he can't afford a separate office at this point. Then again, he hardly needs one. He has a spacious bivouac in the front corner of the house that many executives would kill for: big window, big hardwood desk, plush carpet and furniture. On the walls, among the framed photos, magazine covers, and memorabilia, there are dozens of citations— "for dedication," "for tireless service," "for outstanding work," "for exceptional leadership" (among other things, Stan has operated a hockey school for the hearing-impaired for the past sixteen years). One commendation is signed by the late U.S. Senator Everett Dirksen, "with best wishes to a champion." On the end wall hangs a handsome oil painting of Stan in his red Blackhawks jersey. Replicas of the Hart Trophy, Lady Byng Trophy, Art Ross Trophy, and Stanley Cup sit on a nearby shelf.

On the wall opposite Stan's desk hangs a framed newspaper report about the night in 1980 when the Blackhawks retired Stan's number (he was the first player in the history of the team to be so honored). The account quotes the closing lines of his speech that night: "I have one more duty, and that comes from the heart. I'd like to pay tribute to someone who besides giving me love and affection gave me the greatest commodity in life. He took me out of a communist country and gave me something I think we're all striving for. He gave me freedom. I'd like to pay tribute to the greatest guy I know—my pop.

It is a long trip from Sokolce, Czechoslovakia, to Oak Brook, Illinois, but Stan has not forgotten the stops along the way.

*   *   *   *   *

Epilogue

Anyone who saw Stan Mikita during the early weeks of the new millennium would probably not have recognized the man who was as familiar to hockey fans during the 1960s and '70s as are, say, Eric Lindros or Jarimir Jagr today. His head was bald, he had a sutured incision over his left eye, and his voice was as rough as a piece of Number Five sandpaper. He had lost nearly twenty pounds from a frame already considered slight by hockey standards and had been in and out of doctor's offices for the better part of ten months.

Word in Chicago was that *Le Petit Diable* was in overtime—was perhaps, in fact, on his last shift.

For a man in such condition, Stan was in remarkably bright spirits. "Don't worry about Stan Mikita," he told reporters at New Year's, 2000. "People are supposed to be happy around the holidays!"

The chain of events that had led to Stan's wasted condition began in March 1999, in Puerto Rico, where he and Jill were playing golf. During the course of their holiday, Stan developed an incessant skin itch. His voice was already just an echo of its former clarity, and by the time he got home he had lost eleven pounds.

Months of tests ruled out cancer, tropical viruses, and other infectious diseases. However, an MIR scan during the early fall turned up an aneurysm in a brain artery above and behind his left eye. Doctors believed the problem was genetic, not a result of hockey, and on December 15, Stan's friend, Chicago neurosurgeon Dr. Robert Beatty, operated to correct the damaged artery, which carries blood to a part of the brain that controls speech and the right arm. "Basically, what we do in such cases," said Beatty, "is put a kind of clothes pin at the neck of the aneurysm and then make our repairs."

Stan is now sixty years old, and while much has changed for both him and Jill in recent months, much has remained the same. Stan continues to work at home, and golf and bridge are still mainstays of the Mikitas' lives. When Stan was informed that he had an aneurysm and would need brain surgery, he headed not for bed or for the TV armchair but for the golf course, where he played almost every day for a month as he waited his turn in the operating room. "We couldn't

"Don't worry about Stan Mikita."

get him to come in," said Dr. Beatty. It was only when Jill put her foot down that he began taking life a little easier.

Another constant in the Mikitas' lives—perhaps more helpful in the healing process—is Stan's longstanding sense of humor. "You can tell he's getting better," his daughter Jane said in January. "He's really starting to irritate us again." With his medical problems, which include recent eye surgery, he has more material than ever to joke about. "My insurance company's been real proud of me," he deadpans. And his return to workouts at the local gym brought forth the comment that, despite his lack of hair, voice, and strength, he's determined to keep exercising in case the Blackhawks (NHL bottomfeeders) spot him and want him to suit up.

Stan gets out to three or four Blackhawk games a year, and is still heavily involved in charity work, particularly with the American Hearing Impaired Hockey Association, for whom he runs the annual hockey program that he started during the 1970s. "It's gonna be great this year," a friend joked recently. "The kids can't hear, and Stan can't talk."

A while back, Stan was recruited for a bit part in a Wayne's World movie by Canadian actor Mike Myers, a passionate hockey fan, who decided one of the scenes in the movie would take place in a fictitious restaurant called Stan Mikita's Doughnuts. At an event promoting the movie, Stan was approached by a pair of boys who requested an autograph. "It gave me a bit of an ego boost," says Stan. "I said, 'Geez, fellas, you guys remember me from the Chicago Blackhawks?' They looked at me and said, 'What's the Chicago Blackhawks?'"

"And that was that," says Stan. "I signed as a budding movie star." The one-time hockey ace pauses briefly and adds, "By the way, if you hear of any producers who need a bald, underweight, sixty-year-old leading man, with a scar over his eye, let me know, will ya? I should have the part sewn up!"

CHAPTER

8

Eric Nesterenko

Free of the Burden of Gravity

I traveled to Vail, Colorado, for a three-day visit with Eric Nesterenko, who has lived in Vail since 1980. Toward the end of my stay, Eric and I took a late-evening stroll through the narrow, car-free streets of this exotic resort community in the Rocky Mountains. Snow was falling and beyond the streetlights the surrounding peaks and ski runs were lost in darkness.

We walked up into the heart of Vail Village, walked back down, and stopped on a bridge that crosses Gore Creek. As we stood looking into the water, Eric said, "I've lived a very simple life, and I've probably succeeded somewhat on my own terms. Some people might consider me a failure, and that's their prerogative. But I spent fifteen years living the bourgeois life, and then I didn't want to do it any more, so I bailed out. As a consequence I've gone through periods where I didn't have any money. But I've found if you don't own anything and you're not addicted to anything (I gave my family everything I had), you don't really need any money. I'm pretty well educated and fairly worldly, so something always comes up. There's always a way to get along financially. Of course, most people aren't interested in that. They're interested in acquiring things, owning things, taking care of things, and as a result they need a lot of money. I've tried never to trade on my career as a hockey player. It never interested me. I don't know if it's admirable, and I don't care if other guys do it. It's just that if you do it, you imprison yourself in the past. I prefer the present. I get the odd offer to go sign hockey cards somewhere, but not very often because nobody knows where I am. I do it for the money if I can, but it's a very hollow role, an empty way to live."

*   *   *   *   *

There is a conspicuous diversity to Eric Nesterenko's curriculum vitae. As a career map, it suggests a man of renegade imagination, a man who, somewhere on the road to somewhere, hung a right-angled turn and accelerated not just off the pavement but across the shoulder, the ditch, the right-of-way, and off on his own through the wilderness. He has been a disk jockey, a stockbroker, and the caretaker of an estate in Aspen, Colorado. He has been a high school hockey coach and an Air Canada travel broker, selling what he calls "northern hunting and fishing packages to Americans."

"One of my crazier jobs," he says, "was laying decals on tractor trailers one summer in Texas. The trucks would come in, and I'd take off the old decal design and put new ones on. I'd work round the clock on the weekend and had the rest of the week free." At one point, the job required Eric to place decals on six thousand metal signs, four by six feet, for "some sort of cattlemen's association," a job that was expected to take months of manual labor and was contracted as such. "But I found an old press in the plant," he says, "and did it ten times faster than they expected. I made pisspots of money, because they still had to pay me what we agreed on."

Eric made more money yet when, for two six-month periods during the early eighties, he worked for an American company named Federal Electric on the Arctic DEW Line. "As a kid," he muses, "I used to dream about the Arctic—vivid, primal dreams, with great expanses of ice and water and tundra. Then I got this chance to go up there as a utility operator, driving a loader and a diesel Cat. My job was clearing snow and transporting fuel oil from storage tanks by the ocean to various radar sites. It was light all the time, and at night I'd go out walking on my own—for miles! I'd see peregrines, caribou, giant Arctic hare. The caribou would come up and stare at me—they'd never seen a human being. It's a crazy bunch of people that work the Arctic: misfits, dropouts from regular life. I guess I'm the type."

Eric has been a freelance writer, a university professor, and a construction worker. By his own admission, he has also been an alcoholic, an amphetamine popper, and a beneficiary of the psychiatrist's couch. Although it will never appear on his c.v., he is one of a small number of people to have been present in the courtroom for the 1969 trial of the Chicago Seven anti-war demonstrators.

He is the subject not only of a novel entitled *The Drubbing of Nesterenko* but of a chapter in Studs Terkel's bestselling book, *Working*, about the work lives of Americans.

Today, in his late sixties, Eric is a ski instructor in Vail, where he works approximately a hundred days a year, earning a set fee of some $400 a day for teaching groups of up to seven skiers, or sometimes individuals. He skis an additional eighty days for pleasure, traveling as far as Oregon and Whistler, B.C., to indulge his love of the sport. When he talks about skiing, he does so with rhapsodic intensity, ascending at times into something close to free-form poetry: "The speed and the tremendous sensation of motion, way out there on the edge of control, are extraordinarily exciting," he says. "One of the thrills of skiing is going back to the rich feelings you had as a kid. There's a joy and an openness to it. This area really has some terrain and some of the best powder snow anywhere. I'm up early when it's coming down, a little kid looking out the window—I've got butterflies. I like going out when it's really storming, and there's nobody on the mountain. Your normal tourist doesn't ski much in the snowstorms. But the hard-cores are out there. You let go; you invent a whole new version of yourself, a better version, free of the burden of gravity. I think human beings are meant to be in motion. Dancing. I go with my son into the back areas. I've seen him pop an eighty-foot cliff out there. On a big powder day, I'll go off a fifteen-footer—land in something soft, so it doesn't matter if you fall. We walk in. There's always the danger of avalanche, which adds a dimension. You end up on the highway somewhere, hitchhiking. Somebody stops, curious about what these guys are doing out there."

Eric is best-known, of course, as an NHL hockey player, a gracefully loping defensive specialist whose pro career began in 1951 with the Toronto Maple Leafs and ended twenty-one years later with the Chicago Blackhawks.

> **"I could just never see why playing hockey should rob you of your right to an education."**

In hockey, as elsewhere, he was a radical, a skeptic, a spit in the eye of conformity. Even under the absurdly submissive code that governed the conduct of players in the old six-team NHL, he found ways of expressing not only his contempt for owners and management but also his personal preferences for living. When he joined the Blackhawks in 1956, for example, he insisted that he be allowed to attend university full-time in Toronto, joining the Blackhawks for games only. The team bent its standards to accommodate him. The following season, he attended the University of Western Ontario, in London, flying to Blackhawk games a few hours before faceoff and returning immediately afterwards. "The management didn't like it one bit," he says. "They tried to tell me the players didn't either, that they'd never accept me, but it was nonsense. I did take some ragging, but I held my own on the ice, and that's what mattered to the guys. I could just never see why playing hockey should rob you of your right to an education."

Inspired by the late Lloyd Percival, Toronto's celebrated fitness pioneer, Eric espoused equally unorthodox ideas about nutrition and conditioning. During the early fifties, when pro hockey players routinely—ritualistically—gobbled a pound or more of rare beef within a few hours of game time ("most of them dismissed salads and vegetables as 'rabbit food,'" says Eric); he turned largely to carbohydrates, fruits, whole grains . . . and rabbit food. "I still ate a little meat," he allows, "but before a game I'd have pasta, a salad, a couple of baked potatoes, the sort of things all the players eat nowadays. And I ate yogurt—a Toronto newspaper once referred to me as 'the yogurt kid.'"

Percival also introduced Eric to aerobic training, mostly in the form of running, as a method of getting and staying fit. "I'd go forty, fifty miles a week," he recalls. "In those days it was unheard of. The guys 'played' themselves into shape."

During the early sixties, some twenty years ahead of his time, Eric discovered that, under certain circumstances, even walking was an effective approach to high-level fitness, not to mention mental equanimity.

"I've always had a very strong identification with mountains," he says, "and as I got into mid-career—I was in Chicago by this time—I started taking a couple of weeks before training camp every year and going up into northern Wyoming, the Wind River area, big-time mountains, and hiking hundreds of miles with a seventy-five-pound pack on my back. I'd lose eight or ten pounds, and of course at ten thousand feet the heart and lungs get working pretty efficiently."

His attachment to the area deepened to the point where, during the seventies and eighties, he would make the trek not so much for physical as for spiritual and psychological conditioning. "I really believe human beings need a lot of silence," he says. "We spend half our lives surrounded by electronic distractions and entertainments—television, radio, recordings. They create a reality, a very superficial one, that doesn't demand any effort, so that you end up getting lost in them, with no real sense of time or focus. Out there in the back country, by yourself, you're really forced to deal with who and what you are; you have to create your own reality, in a sense create yourself. And as you do that, things take on a magical quality. When I'm out there, I always have extraordinary dreams."

Even today, Eric heads for the Wyoming mountains when the spirit moves him. "I spent twenty-five days up there this year," he notes. "Two trips. I go with an old buddy from the sixties, Billy Stevenson, who used to play football with the Calgary Stampeders. I always come back energized."

*   *   *   *   *

On my first full day in Vail, I met Eric for lunch and for a lengthy afternoon of conversation, followed by a two-hour drive up and down the Vail Valley in his black four-by-four pick-up. He is a big man, with long arms and legs, and when I walked into the lobby of the hotel where we had arranged to rendezvous, he was not so much seated on the low couch as folded onto it, like a collapsible ruler. He was wearing red-framed reading glasses and was so thoroughly absorbed in the *Denver Post* that he didn't acknowledge my approach until I was virtually on top of him. When I said his name, he threw his head back, smiled, and unfolded, throwing out a hand that by rough estimate was twice the size of my own.

As a child and teenager, I had watched Eric play dozens of games on television and had seen him several times in person at Maple Leaf Gardens. But in thirty-odd years my recollections of his presence on the ice had been reduced to a blur. As I followed him from the hotel, however, I experienced a sudden deja vu, an almost cinematic recall of his skating and checking style, summoned uncannily by the shambling slide of his walk, the slouch of his shoulders, the marionette hang of his arms, his head thrown slightly forward. He was a player who, at times, seemed to have no bones.

At the Sweet Basil restaurant, he exchanged greetings with a number of acquaintances, folded himself into a banquette, and ordered expansively. He ate with unselfconscious gusto. He is handsome in a craggy sort of way; the overall appeal of his face is greater than might be expected from the state of its components. His eyes are small, his lips large, and his nose is in a shocking state of disfigurement. It is not so much a nose, in fact, as a twisted ridge of skin and gristle, a mangled caterpillar, appliquéd more or less to the center of his face where a nose ought to be. He has a full head of graying hair, and there is something in the configuration of his mouth and jaw that creates an expression of slight but constant surprise.

We warmed quickly to one another, and in the hours that elapsed between our first appetizer (gingered shrimp and squid) and our fifth or sixth cup of coffee, the conversation ranged across a panoply of subjects that included wealth, poverty, fear, art, mortality, the oppressive politics of the New Right, and the novels of Michigan writer Jim Harrison, whom we both admire. And of course hockey.

But before he got to any of that, he told me about his family; he has a daughter, aged thirty-two, in Chicago, a son, twenty-nine, in San Francisco, and a son, thirty, in Vail, with whom he sometimes skis. He has been divorced from his wife, Barbara McKechnie, for nearly twenty years, and, a year or so ago, split up with Kaye Ferry, a Vail restaurateur with whom he had lived since 1987. He described his wife at various points in our conversation as "an opera lover," "a genuine intellectual," and "one of the most intelligent people" he has ever met. "I used to study her books on human behavior when she was working on her M.A. in social work," he says, "so she's partly responsible for my education, such as it is. Compared to her I'm just a dilettante. . . . We're still good friends." (He is still good friends with Kaye Ferry.) At the moment, he is living at the home of his friend Kevin Cooke, a former tight end with the Oakland Raiders, who now works as a contractor in Vail.

"Most people in Vail don't even know I played."

By his own assessment, Eric seldom talks or even thinks about hockey—"I have no reason to out here. Most people in Vail don't even know I played." Perhaps on that account, there is a freshness about his reflections on his one-time occupation, a sense that they are coming to life like spring bulbs, having gathered energy during a lengthy period of interment. He speaks lyrically and philosophically about the game and possesses a rare ability to conceptualize his impressions of it (and seemingly of anything else that falls into the focus of his intelligence), to see the shape of the tornado where others see only flying trees and rooftops.

And he is honest. Strikingly. He says without a trace of misgiving, for instance, that he played hockey "in constant fear."

"So much so," he says, "that fear became an old friend. It's a tremendous stimulus; you have to court it at the same time as you try to dispel it. Fear of being humiliated, fear of losing, fear of getting hurt. Those are the big three."

He summons the waiter, orders a bowl of fresh raspberries, and says, "Picture it. There are twenty thousand people at the game, and if you act badly or play badly, there's no place to hide. You can't talk it down or bullshit it; it's there for everyone to see. You are what you are. It's a killer. You have to be ready to hold your own. It took everything I had in terms of my physicality and intelligence. Sure, it's a goofy way to live, but there's nothing like it for excitement."

Typically, Eric's methods for dealing with his fear, of transforming and redirecting it into something useful to him, were twenty years ahead of their time and are now commonly applied by sports psychologists. "One of my tricks," he explains, "was simply to let the fear in, imagine the worst thing that could happen to me. Fear doesn't stay around long if you give in to it; it's when you resist it that it stays with you. You let it in, allow it to have its way, and before long it leaves you in what I call a cold calculating rage. Fear and rage are corollaries of one another. So instead of being terrified, you're completely focused and stimulated."

Like all NHL hockey players, Eric had ample reason to fear the worst of his chosen profession. His poetic nature and various unorthodoxies attracted no particular antipathy from rival players, but nor did they provide even a smidgen of dispensation from the commonplace brutalities of NHL life. "A lotta guys gave it to me when I was starting out," he says. "Bert Olmstead gave me a stick in the gut, knocked my wind out, brought me to my knees. He said, 'Welcome to the league, kid.' Ted Lindsay knocked out a couple of my front teeth with his stick and laughed at me. Same with Milt Schmidt. He practically put me through the boards one night and stood there laughing as I staggered up. Mind you, I could get prickly, too. In hockey if somebody sticks you and you don't retaliate in some way, word gets out on you, and you get more trouble down the line. But I never tried to take anybody's head off. If I threw a forearm, I'd aim into the area between the waist and the shoulders. I wasn't looking for enemies."

Eric views his old foes with remarkable detachment, seeming to bear no grudge against even the most virulent of them. If anything, he harbors an inflated respect for many of them, attributing to them a kind of primitive nobility of the sort that is sometimes ascribed to prehistoric tribesmen. "A lot of these guys were very smart, very intuitive," he says. "They didn't have words, but the game is beyond language, so they communicated in older ways, the ways in which hunters and warriors communicate. Some of the best hockey players I knew were great poker players. They had that ability to intuit, even though their lack of language limited their ability to articulate who they were and their feelings about life. I guess if you don't have words, your intelligence is narrowed. But within the range of intelligence required on the ice, there's no politics, no rhetoric, so the guy with words has no advantage. The smartest guys, period, survive."

His respect notwithstanding, Eric is scornful of any societal tendency to make heroes or role models of professional athletes, past or present. "It's bogus!" he says. "They're not heroes at all. There's still the odd one who does the right thing, but most of the ones I've known lead very flawed lives. Some of them are totally screwed up. And the most venerated of them are often the worst. When I played, the relationship between the players and fans was probably a little more honest than it is now. For one thing, we didn't have as much money, so we were more accessible to them. Wealth isolates today's players to the point where their perceived relationship with the public, the implied kinship, is even more hypocritical than it would be otherwise."

Eric harbors particular contempt for NHL owners, characterizing most of those he met over the years as "really nasty, vicious, greedy, self-serving people. You have no idea how we were exploited by them. Completely locked in. If an owner or manager decided he didn't want you—or worse still, didn't like you—you were dead, finished. By the terms of our contracts, we were the property of one team only; we couldn't move unless they wanted to move us—no free agency. They buried some guys so deep, they never surfaced. And we were grossly underpaid, made to feel we were lucky to be playing the game. . . . Of course there were wonderful rewards and compensations for what we did, too. For an adrenaline junkie like myself, the games themselves could be extremely exciting. I remember games with twenty thousand people and the place going crazy with sound and action and color, the enormous energy the crowd produces all coming in on the ice, focusing directly on the players. It's pretty hard to resist that. I remember a game during the semi-finals of the year we won the Stanley Cup in Chicago, in 1961. It was the sixth game against Montreal. They were the big club; they'd won five Cups in a row. We were the Cinderella team. The score was 3–0, for us, with five minutes to play. As a spontaneous gesture, twenty thousand people stood up. I was on the ice. I remember seeing that whole stadium, just solid, row on row, from the balcony to the boxes, standing. These people were turned on by us. We came off the ice three feet in the air."

The emotional transcendence of such moments was something Eric at times achieved quite independently of the fickle attentions of the crowd. "One of the things I really loved about the game," he enthuses, "was the possibility it afforded for what I guess you could call 'peak experience phenomenon.' I probably spent 25 percent of my time on the ice in a kind of elevated state of being. I guess it was a function of the motion and energy and so on. Time would just slow right down for me; I'd feel terrific joy and well-being, totally disappear into the moment; I couldn't seem to get hurt. Sometimes I experience it when I'm skiing or backpacking. I've talked to other players who seem to know what I mean. I guess the better players achieve it more often. The Eastern religions have explored the human capability to get into such states. Meditation can apparently do it, but it was the game that did it for me. In fact, it helped me survive the game. I felt as if I was somebody else, a remarkable feeling. It's one of the things I've always lived for."

Eric muses for a moment and notes rather sullenly that of course the games could go badly, too—and often did. "Sometimes, I could hardly wait for them to end. Then as soon as they were over," he laughs, "I couldn't wait for the next one to begin."

*   *   *   *   *

When we had talked for perhaps two hours, had finished our dessert, and were on our third or fourth cup of coffee, I asked Eric casually if he knew he was the subject of a novel. He is widely read and possesses an unusually diverse curiosity, in particular about matters that concern himself, and I was all but certain he'd be familiar with the book, written by Canadian Hanford Woods and published in Montreal during the early seventies. I was not so certain he would be entirely open to discussing it. Indeed, I had hesitated until that point to bring it up—and even then was doing so in a most tangential way, avoiding the book's title, for instance—because it deals with an extremely unpleasant incident from Eric's past and is somewhat untoward in its presentation of him. The book's title, *The Drubbing of Nesterenko*, did not pass my lips during the entire time I spent with him.

He looked at me with incredulity and said, "Whaddaya mean I'm the subject of a novel?"

"You're a nonfiction character in a fictional book," I said, proceeding to explain as delicately as I possibly could that, basically, the novel was a kind of loss-of-innocence, coming-of-age story set during the mid-sixties, and that its protagonist, a Montreal teenager, a shoplifter, was a passionate fan of the Chicago Blackhawks and, especially, of Eric Nesterenko.

The novel is fine-textured, intelligent, and, in parts, highly poetic. And anyone who has read it will understand my reluctance to elaborate too fully on its contents in front of Eric.

The event around which the book revolves (an actual event transported to a fictional world and worried into metaphor) is an epochally vicious thrashing laid on Eric by the Montreal Canadiens' legendary thumper John Ferguson. For the teenage protagonist, the thrashing is a rage-inducing cataclysm, a mindlessly brutal introduction to the world of experience and cynicism. And when I first made reference to the brutality in front of Eric—the fight as opposed to merely the book—I do not believe I am exaggerating in saying that, for the briefest of moments, he seemed stricken, even panicked, leading me to believe (perhaps falsely) that I had triggered some long unresolved anxiety or rage of his own. As if in a parody of such moments, his hand, containing a coffee cup, stood momentarily paralyzed a few inches in front of his lips.

As he put the cup down, the faintest of inscrutable smiles transformed his face. "That's bizarre," he said quietly. "It's totally bizarre."

The "fight," if it can be called that (in reality it was a mugging), was thought by many, including Hanford Woods, to be a symbolic threshold in the 1965 final between the Canadiens and Blackhawks, a series the Blackhawks were perhaps good enough to have won but ended up losing. Certainly, for the Blackhawks, it must have been a distressing, ill-omened event—likewise to Hawks' fans of the era, most of whom have never forgotten it. "Ferguson's fists hammered at him, hard, even after the annihilation of what became nothing more than butchered meat," writes Woods. "Nesterenko slumped to his knees, his arms dangled at his sides, he was asleep before he hit the ice. On the television his blood was the deepest black."

Eric was helped from the ice with a towel wrapped around his face. "Later," says Woods, "he returned to the game. He skated from the clinic at the south end of the Forum to the Chicago player's bench, skated through the swaggering contempt of the Canadiens on the ice, Ferguson one of them, impatiently circling, his anger unappeasable, those on the bench malevolently alert to the signal defeat of Nesterenko's broken posture; skated through the resignation of his teammates who with eyes lowered were already fixing him as the scapegoat of the defeat inevitably settling upon them; dragged himself listlessly through the gate, took his seat on the bench."

One of the most unsettling things about the incident was the apparent randomness with which Ferguson had inflicted the beating. Although

> ## "Most people made a lot more of the incident than I did."

Ferguson has always maintained that Eric provoked the carnage by "clipping" him on the head, film of the occurrence supports the belief that it sprang from some merciless causal void, unprovoked, at least in any direct sense.

"I read the Montreal papers the next day with an avid loathing," continues Woods. "The columnists probed the wound pitilessly, brought down their verdict: Nesterenko had been guilty of some indefensible incursion into Fergy's domain, he should never have been there, Fergy had acted within his rights. The writers drew strength for the pronouncement from its utter inexplicability. Talk on the streets was only of the fight; the fans vaunted Fergy's prowess as their own. The entire city reveled in their mean, stupid triumph. . . . Let all weak men die and obloquy be heaped upon their bones."

* * * * *

Eric was obviously unable to discuss the book, but he was by no means reluctant to discuss the fight and its ramifications for his career and image. In fact, he did so with surprising candor and, after his initial agitation had subsided (it took all of a few seconds), impressive equanimity.

"Most people made a lot more of the incident than I did," he said. "Some of them even saw it as an indictment of me, gave me a hard time over it, razzed me during games, that sort of thing, and I had to live with that. But really it was no big deal. I got suckered. The guy nailed me. Our line had been shutting down their big line, the Beliveau line, throughout the series. Just before it happened, we'd been scrambling very hard in the corner, and the whistle blew. I stopped, turned around, and skated into his punch. The only reason I know is that I've seen the films of it; at the time I didn't know what happened. Ferguson's a strong guy, and as I went to my knees he got me with a few more pretty heavy punches. I wasn't badly hurt—picked up fifteen stitches in the face. But I played the next game. In fact, we won the next two games in Chicago, so it's nonsense to suggest that the fight ended the series. In the end they beat us because they had a better team, no other reason."

According to Eric, what affected him most about the episode was the realization that his "perceptive skills" were beginning to wane and that he had been unprepared for the ambush. "I was thirty-five years old by this time," he says, "and I wasn't as focused as I had been earlier in my career. I should have been able to see it coming. Given that we were doing a number on the Canadiens and that Ferguson was out there, I should have been aware that he was going to get me one of these times. A big part of intelligence in hockey is preparing for what might happen, and I wasn't prepared, and in the aftermath it scared me. But I'll tell ya, I was a lot more aware after that. I played six more years. Actually, I had five or six more go-rounds with Fergy. But of course I was ready for him; I carried my stick a lot higher around him from that point on. He never really got the better of me again."

If Eric has not entirely forgiven himself for his consequential lapse of awareness, he has apparently forgiven Ferguson for his attack and is at peace with the egregious allowances of the sport that made such an attack possible. "I respect Ferguson," he says with no apparent irony. "The arena is a survival place. I know he had no personal interest in hurting me; he was just knocking me out of the game. It was his way of getting rid of me."

That Eric could, at this point, speak with such control about the mugging and its consequences moved me to wonder aloud why his initial response to my bringing it up had been one of such seeming agitation.

He reflected for a moment, shrugged, and said, "I don't know. Probably on some level there's still a trace of humiliation. I got beaten up pretty badly; at the time I was humiliated. I guess it kinda caught me off guard that it's still around after all these years."

The incident was certainly still around the following season when, as Eric puts it, "every thug on every team" took a run at him. "It went on till Christmas," he says. "The shark mentality—one guy'd taken a bite outta me, they all wanted a bite." After fifteen years in the NHL, Eric was obliged to re-establish what he refers to as "his space."

"If you can't re-establish it," he says, "they can end up intimidating you to the point where you can't function. They wanta see if you can still play; it's part of hockey. But my sensitivity had been entirely re-honed by the incident, so that before every game I'd go to the kid who

I figured might try to stick me and I'd say, 'I know you're coming after me, and if you do I'm going to hit you over the head as hard as I can with my stick.'"

*   *   *   *   *

Eric was born in 1932 in the mining town of Flin Flon, Manitoba, some six hundred kilometers north of Winnipeg. His parents were Ukrainian political refugees who fled to Czechoslovakia after the Russian Revolution and emigrated from there to Canada. His father, a chemist at the mining smelter in Flin Flon, spoke six languages and, for Eric and his sister, was a ready model for the value of education. "We read a lot," says Eric. "I loved school; I was good at it. But I lived for hockey. My dad bought me a pair of skates when I was four or five. That's how I got started. We lived across the street from an outdoor rink in Jubilee Park. I played every day and night after school. Our de facto coaches were the older boys. If they let you join their game that was a thrill. We didn't have any equipment, so the skills were all stick skills—the ability to take the puck away from somebody with a poke check, or to keep it if you were good enough. It was a never-ending game, shifting personnel, sometimes three kids to a team, sometimes fifteen—or a few games going on at once, so that you had to work at avoiding people."

Eric recalls wistfully what he refers to as "the best nights" in Flin Flon. "They were clear, not too cold, maybe ten or fifteen below, with the northern lights and no wind. The ice was hard and fast, and you'd be so engrossed in the game that time would stop. . . . The kids don't play the way we did any more; it's all organized, indoors. They may be stronger and better conditioned, but they don't have the skills because they don't put the hours in."

At the age of eleven, Eric moved with his family to Toronto, where his dad had been offered a better job in industrial chemistry. In his new city, Eric played for top-level peewee and bantam teams. Then as a teenager he was drawn into the feeder system of the Toronto Maple Leafs. "I was a skinny, ratty kid with a terrible case of acne," he told Studs Terkel in 1970. "I moved pretty well, but I never really looked like much."

He looked sufficiently impressive to the Maple Leaf organization that, by 1949, he had been selected to play for the Toronto Marlboroughs, the

Leafs' top junior club. With the Marlies, he scored a goal a game during his final year and was among the top junior players in Canada. When the Montreal Canadiens signed Jean Beliveau to a contract in 1950, Leaf owner Conn Smythe bragged to the press that he had his own emerging

> **"He was an exploitive old son of a bitch. I had no use for him."**

star, a kid named Nesterenko, who would one day make the hockey world forget about Beliveau.

With a year of junior eligibility remaining, Eric was offered a four-year hockey scholarship at the University of Michigan. "Then the Leafs offered me $6,000 under the table to reject the scholarship and turn pro with their farm team in Pittsburgh," he says.

He took the money. But instead of sending him to Pittsburgh for seasoning, the Leafs put their own uniform on him and kept him in Toronto. "The problem was they tied my game down," says Eric. "They wouldn't allow any free-wheeling. No imagination. You had to stick on your wing. Detroit and Montreal were playing much more imaginatively. Toronto had been a great team in the past, but at that point they weren't doing much."

Eric did get a chance to exercise his imagination by moonlighting as a jazz disk jockey at broadcaster Foster Hewitt's radio station in Toronto. But under the Leafs' uninspired regime, he never became the offensive sparkler that Smythe had imagined. "I guess ultimately I disappointed the old man," he says. "But I don't care. He was an exploitive old son of a bitch. I had no use for him.

"Eventually I got into a big fight with the Leafs about how they were playing me. In those days you didn't question management at all, and in 1954 they got rid of me, sold my rights to Chicago."

Thinking his career was over, Eric enrolled in the physical education program at the University of Toronto and went out for the football team; he had been a football star at North Toronto Collegiate. But the Blackhawks, the NHL's perennial bottom-feeders, were determined to sign him, imagining that with his size and skating ability (they may even have recognized his intelligence), he could be converted into a penalty-killing defensive expert who could be deployed against the league's best forwards.

"I made a lot of trips to Toronto that summer," says Tommy Ivan, who at the time was the Blackhawks' general manager. "But I didn't have much luck. There I'd be, as the university's bus carrying the football team to camp pulled away, waving good-bye to Nesterenko, who would be looking out the back window."

Ivan finally bagged his quarry in January, and Eric became the NHL's first, and perhaps last, full-time university student, a distinction he would enjoy for the next year and a half, at which point he became a full-time hockey player.

When he had contract problems in Chicago in 1956, he decamped not to university but for a try-out with the Toronto Argonauts, a professional football team that, after assessing his skills, offered him a contract. Fearing he would abandon them, the Blackhawks stepped forward with an improved contract of their own, which he signed.

*   *   *   *   *

By the late fifties, Eric had not only accepted his defensive role, as he never really had in Toronto, but had also become an exemplar among defensive forwards, potting a sluggish stream of goals (he averaged thirteen or fourteen a season) but for the most part committing himself to preventing them. "I'm a survivor," he says today. "If I was going to stay in the league, that was the way to do it. And I learned to do it pretty well. I had a good reach, I could skate, and I was willing to scruff around in the corners. I wouldn't give up. But, more importantly, I could control the space around me. I always played against the other teams' top lines, and I got to a point where I could often keep a guy in check without even touching him, just by playing the angles and leverage. Mind you, it got harder as I got older and my skills started waning. But by that time a couple of waves of expansion players had come into the league, and that tended to balance things off. A lot of the new players weren't very smart; they were easy to control. They shouldn't even have been there." Eric pauses at this point and his voice broadens with conviction: "Hockey is a very simple game," he says. "You control the space and don't let the other team play. If you have enough skilled forwards to take advantage of the openings, you'll always be competitive."

*   *   *   *   *

When we had finished lunch, we took a spin in Eric's pickup, out I-70 toward Beaver Creek, a glaringly affluent housing and ski development, where until a year ago Eric shared rented accommodation with Kaye Ferry. As we sat at a stoplight in West Vail, I asked him about the roots of his nonconformity.

"I guess I've always marched to my own drummer," he said. "Never cared what others thought. Certainly, my parents were conformists. I just know that by my early teens I'd started realizing I was an individual. I was a very high-level player even as a child, so the coaches let me do pretty much as I pleased. I imagine that reinforced my sense of individualism."

By the late sixties, Eric had begun to pass along his habit of mind to his three children, born in '62, '65, and '66. "Every June," he says, "we'd close shop in Chicago, pack up the van, and go on the road for ten weeks. We'd find places to stay, sometimes on ranches in Wyoming and Montana. We'd car camp and hike and fish. These are things my father had exposed me to in Flin Flon. We did this for five years or so. The kids all remember it, and they've all become back-country types themselves. My son, in particular, is an Indian. He's so at home in the woods and mountains, it's scary."

Chicago, on the other hand, had become a kind of Xanadu for Eric, a pleasure dome of artistic and intellectual stimulation. "I saw a lot of theater in those days," he recalls, "a lot of experimental and esoteric stuff. And Barbara and I would go to the opera. I developed my taste for it through her." The Nesterenkos were also patrons of the Chicago Symphony, and Eric spent numerous hours exploring the Art Institute of Chicago, with its hoardings of work by Picasso, Kandinsky, Gauguin, Chagall, and Van Gogh. In the meantime, he took university literature courses and read authors as diverse as John le Carre, Peter Mathiesson, and Henry David Thoreau. "There used to be a great bookstore in Chicago called Kroch and Brentano's," he says. "I used to like to hang around there—in fact anywhere writers were. I always valued words. It's very difficult to understand anything if you don't have words. . . . When the Blackhawks were in New York to play the Rangers, I'd go to the Lion's Head pub on the edge of the Village, where the writers hung out. I met Norman Mailer there and Jimmy

Breslin. And I knew the newspaper writers. I loved hearing their b.s. They were fun to be around. Some of them were wonderful story-tellers. I guess at some level I was making up for things I'd cut myself off from as a young guy. The game was all-consuming back then; it pretty well had to be if you were going to make it. I know a lot of pro athletes who had the capacity for broader experience, but they wanted to be champions, so they narrowed their focus right down to their sport. It can be pretty dehumanizing. Later, if they didn't have the means or words to deal with things such as art or literature or ideas, they just moved away from them. I didn't want to do that; I was far too curious. That's one of the reasons I lived right on the edge of downtown Chicago—at least until my children were born. Most of the guys lived way out in the far suburbs."

When the Democratic Convention came to Chicago in 1968, Eric was on hand for the now-famous anti-war demonstrations. "I saw the cops beating kids up," he says. "It was extremely depressing." And when the most famous of the demonstrators, the so-called Chicago Seven, were put on trial for sedition the following year, a lawyer friend provided Eric with access to Judge Hoffman's courtroom. "I was fascinated by the free-speech thing," he says. "Like a lot of other people, I'd always assumed free speech was a right in America. But for some, it apparently wasn't. I was amazed at how primitive it all was. Judge Hoffman was a very lim-ited mainstream guy; he had no way of dealing with these people like Jerry Rubin and Abbie Hoffman and Bobby Seale—either judicially or intellectually. They taped Seale's mouth shut so that he wouldn't be able to disrupt the proceedings! As hockey players, we were expected to shut up," he grins, "but they never went so far as to tape our mouths."

* * * * *

By 1970, Eric's hockey skills were, by his own estimate, "in pretty severe decline." So too was his interest in the game. "I should have quit earlier," he says. "I was doing it for the money. I was in pain a lot. I stopped taking risks, reduced my game. I'd get beat. It was awful. Besides that, the kids were getting meaner and tougher. I'd come up against some hard twenty-one-year-old stud who wanted the puck, and I'd be inclined to give it to him. And that's not a good sign for a pro-fessional hockey player."

Eric's physical decline was accompanied by an increasing restlessness with the psychological imperatives imposed by the game. "The role of the professional athlete is one I learned to play pretty well," he says. "Laughing with strangers, signing autographs, shaking hands, accepting people's good wishes, indulging the adulation. It doesn't take much; it has its built-in moves, responses. But it's all quite meaningless in the end, and I got fed up with it. More and more when somebody I didn't know came up to me and said, 'Hello, Eric' I'd be inclined to brush them off. It's exhausting."

> **"When you've done it for twenty years in the NHL, and for fifteen years before that, ordinary life just isn't very exciting by comparison."**

Eric got equally fed up with the restrictions and fatigue of the lengthy road trips. "I'm not wild about living in hotels, plane travel, having to spend time in a room, sometimes a whole day, waiting for a game. I didn't mind killing time when I was younger, but I grew to resent it. I didn't want to kill time—I wanted to do something with it."

Yet like most professional athletes, Eric harbored a fear of relinquishing what he refers to as "the thrill of the game," the drama and motion, the adrenaline high, of which he speaks with such eloquence. "When you've done it for twenty years in the NHL, and for fifteen years before that," he says, "ordinary life just isn't very exciting by comparison. It's a very rare athlete who finds another all-encompassing action to sustain him when he quits." During the early and mid-sixties, Eric had tried off-season work both as a travel-package salesman and as a stockbroker and had found both jobs stiflingly unappealing.

When he was invited to become playing coach of a team in Lausanne, Switzerland, a few months after his retirement in 1972, he leapt at the opportunity, packing up the family and taking off for Europe. "It was great," says Eric. "The hockey life was relatively relaxed; we had all that exposure to another culture, learned some French, and I was introduced to skiing."

At the end of the year, however, his wife, Barbara, was offered what Eric describes as "a really good job" back in Evanston, Illinois, and the family came home.

For Eric, it was the beginning of a five- or six-year period of restless emotional transience and, at times, outright dissipation. Within a year of returning home, he had separated from Barbara and taken an apartment of his own in Evanston, where he could be close to his children. "Barb and I had had some wonderful times," he allows. "But it wasn't working at that point, and we couldn't see any way of keeping it together."

Eric played briefly for the Chicago Cougars of the WHA, then in 1975 took a job coaching semi-pro hockey in Trail, B.C. Although the position itself was ultimately of little consequence to him, it afforded him an opportunity to ski in the Rockies and to work part-time on the ski patrol at Rossland. "It was kind of a threshold year for me," he says. "Skiing was the first thing I'd done that gave me anywhere near the thrill that hockey had given me. And it put a notion in my head that just maybe I could eventually make some sort of a life out of it."

He returned to Evanston and attempted unsuccessfully to put his marriage back together. "About this time," he says, "I got in with a really goofy bunch of people—people in the media and advertising. They were very heavy drinkers, into drugs and so on. It was the seventies— even forty- and fifty-year-olds were playing some heavy-duty games. Basically, I was drunk for three years, during and after my break-up. Alcoholic. I'd drink beer and wine, occasional hard stuff. Chicago's a twenty-four-hour town, and I'd go two or three days straight, putting back a couple of drinks an hour. I was strong then. I'd toss back some amphetamines and keep going. I wasn't into drugs, I just wanted to stay awake. I put on fifty pounds. Needless to say, I didn't have a job at that point. Couldn't keep one."

Inclusion in Studs Terkel's bestselling book in 1971 had raised Eric's profile somewhat and thrown light on his poetic sensibilities, and at the height of his alcoholic binge, a Toronto publisher, Fitzhenry and Whiteside, suggested he write an autobiography. They sent him an advance of $5,000. "I got thirty thousand words into it, all the stuff about growing up in Canada," he says, "and I bogged down—didn't send them anything for months. It's a miracle I got as far into the book as I did, the way I was living. . . . It was practically a cliche: the bad winters, dreams of success, and so on. I really had no idea that writing was so hard. Anyway, I never finished it. They ended up publishing what I wrote as a kids' book."

When, in Eric's words, he was "close to bottoming out," he was offered a position coaching the hockey team at New Trier West High School in Chicago's wealthy north-shore suburbs. For a man of Eric's intellect and athletic experience, such a job could hardly have been seen as a significant challenge. He took it anyway, unaware that it would be an important catalyst in his rehabilitation.

"I had twelve rich kids on the team," he says. "Some of them were into drugs and booze. They'd played hockey since they were little, but they'd never won anything, never been properly coached. My only rule was: Show up for practices straight and sober."

Not surprisingly, Eric's coaching reflected the studied defensive tactics that he had employed so effectively as a player. "I took the emphasis off scoring goals and put it onto preventing them," he says. "We had no complicated plays, no break-out patterns or anything like that. Everything very simple. It took me a third of the season to convince them that this was a way to win, but once I did, we ended up so clean in our own end that teams just couldn't set up against us."

In that orderly manner, Eric guided the team to the state high school championship.

"But really," he says, "the kids gave me a lot more than I gave them." Most importantly, he explains, they triggered a baleful realization that if he was going to be around them and be respected by them, he could not, in his words, be "a fat drunk."

He weaned himself gradually from the bottle and lost weight. He began to see a psychiatrist. "I told him my problems," says Eric, "and over the course of a year, he persuaded me that I had to quit lying to myself—that I was just going to fool myself if I settled into some normal middle-management job, or, worse, took the typical path of the ex-professional athlete, trading off my past as some sort of sales or public-relations-type person. A lot of players have done that and made the transition very comfortably. But, intuitively, I was resisting it, which was probably responsible for the heavy drinking. In the end, the guy told me, 'Look, you've obviously got to find another life for yourself, something that turns you on. What do you like to do?'"

Eric notes that, for one thing, he knew he'd be best off with physical work, preferably something outdoors. "I've always loved the physicality, the sensuality of life," he says, "particularly in my interactions with the landscape and elements." He knew, too, that sooner or later he would have to leave Chicago. "If I'd stayed," he explains, "I'd have been an ex-Blackhawk forever, perpetually recognized and defined in that role. I don't have any need to be acknowledged by people I don't know. The people who know me in Vail know me for who I am here, not as a hockey player."

Gradually, it became clear to him that skiing would make a healthy focus for his future, though at that stage he had no idea how he would go about making a living at it, if at all. Given his love of mountains, Colorado seemed an ideal destination, particularly in its proximity to his beloved Wyoming. "So, in 1978," he says, "when my older kids had reached university, I came out here and started life as a ski bum."

He went first to Aspen, where (ever a man of his roots) he started an adult recreational hockey program. "I had a job as a caretaker on a wealthy Texan's estate," he says. "But we had a disagreement, and he fired me, so I went over to Summit County." There, for a lark, he attended a three-day trial for jobs in a local ski school. "I never figured they'd hire me," he laughs. "I just wanted to enjoy some free skiing. But they ended up giving me a job that I kept for a couple of years, before moving on to Vail."

*   *   *   *   *

For a man who has chosen the present as his psychophilosophic domain, Vail is perhaps the perfect earthly locale; it has no history. On the other hand, it is a somewhat unlikely location for someone who has forsworn luxury and affluence. For it is not so much a town as an indulgence on a grand scale, an almost unseemly aggregation of wealth. "We're not rich," Eric says of his fellow ski instructors and joyriders (some of whom are forty years his junior), "but we live off the rich."

Vail was founded in 1962 and first came to the attention of the mass of North Americans when President Gerald Ford began taking well-publicized winter vacations there during the early seventies (he is reported to have been given a luxurious chalet by the town as a public-relations gesture). But the place did not hit its stride as a resort until roughly 1980, when, as Eric puts it, "the building boom started," and what was essentially a pleasant winter hideaway exploded into one of the largest and most lavish ski resorts anywhere.

"We're not rich, but we live off the rich."

The town and its contiguous real estate developments stretch for some twenty miles along I-70, 120 miles west of Denver, in the trough of what is frequently referred to as "Happy Valley." Vail's year-round population of approximately eight thousand is swollen by five thousand seasonal employees in winter and, on some days, up to fifty thousand skiers. "The amazing thing," says Eric, "is that, even with that influx, the town works." As well it might. Its sole reason for existing is, and has always been, skiing; millions upon millions of dollars have been spent converting Vail Mountain into more than a hundred ski runs serviced by twenty-five lifts and an army of attendants and instructors.

At one remove from those attendants is a second army of hoteliers, restaurateurs, and high-end retailers of skiwear, furs, and exotic bric-a-brac. (Provided one has the money, it is easier to buy a fur coat or a $2,000 skiing outfit in Vail than to track down a loaf of bread or a quart of milk.) "When I need everyday clothes, that sort of thing," says Eric, "I'll drive in to Denver."

Many of the town's seventy-five hotels bear the trappings of Tyrolean lodges, while the restaurants (there are a hundred or more) are festooned with ersatz remembrances of the Alps. An inordinate proportion of the town's dwellings are multimillion-dollar chalets; and, for the most part, the people who occupy them are short-term outpatients from the high-life of cities such as New York, Chicago, Los Angeles, Dallas, and San Francisco. The local TV channel is little more than an ongoing "infomercial" for ski-wear, real estate, dining, and fashion. (A televised advertisement for a Vail plastic surgeon contends that "a well-constructed face" [i.e., reconstructed] is a "work of fine art.")

Vail has no poverty, no racism, and no serious crime. Seen otherwise, the insidious racism of economic exclusion has kept African Americans away, and the crimes on which many of the town's fortunes are found-ed—the graft and exploitation and environmental plundering—were committed somewhere else. The social problems, for a change, are those of the rich, not the poor. "We've had a few Wall Street criminals build out here," said Eric as we drove through Beaver Creek just west of Vail. "See that house over there? It was built by Mexican gangsters. They sold it for $7 million, twenty-five thousand square feet. Jack Nicklaus has a place here. We get a lot of actors and entertainers."

On a symbolic level, it hardly seems surprising that many people, on visiting Vail for the first time, suffer intense lightheadedness and nausea—and, often, difficulty in breathing—brought on by an inability to adjust rapidly enough to the altitude, with its low levels of available oxygen.

Beyond any cynicism that might be inspired by Vail and its ethos, it is an extraordinarily beautiful place. The peaks of its namesake mountain rise to nineteen thousand feet, and the glistening ski trails descend off the slopes like mile-long streamers at some magnificent winter Saturnalia. At night, it is alive with what its promotional pamphlet refers to as "a hundred thousand glittering lights." "In winter," says Eric, "it's just magical. I probably tend to take the beauty for granted. But when I'm away I miss it; there's a hole in my life."

After fourteen years in Vail, Eric is a well-known figure about town. During the time I spent with him, he was greeted warmly everywhere we went—by restaurant and hotel people, by shop owners, and by other ski instructors and patrol members. He is connected to them in a multiplicity of ways: sends his ski students to a particular ski shop and in return is given preferential treatment as a customer; frequents this restaurant, that cafe, this bookstore; visits the library for its periodicals, the post office for his NHL pension checks. His posture is somewhat droopy, and as he strides through the "Tyrolean" heart of the commu-nity, dressed in his Wolverine shoes and brown leather jacket, his aura is that of a slightly impatient curmudgeon, skeptical of the glitz but so well acquainted with it that, for the most part, he barely seems to notice. His low-key antipathy toward Vail's obvious materialism and socially privileged smugness is implicit in his democratic spirit and lean preferences for living, but otherwise it tends to be obscured by his out-spoken affection for the local skiing and topography. For the most part, he seems to like the town just as it is. He clearly takes pleasure in its better restaurants and hotels—a throwback to what he calls "the big fat times" he had as an NHL hockey player. To be sure, Vail is a long way from the workaday grind that he loathes.

It is perhaps an indication of Eric's true valences with the town that his friends tend to be other free spirits like himself, often other "ski bums," rather than members of the local power elite or bulwarks of the social register. He is so poorly connected in any conventional sense that, during the mid-eighties, when he founded a hockey team—high-level amateurs that drew sell-out crowds to exhibition games at the local arena—he was snubbed by the town's administration when he went to them asking for support. "I was providing an obviously popular entertainment in a community that exists for such things," he says. "I was working hard at it, and I thought they could at least provide me with some money to help support myself—God knows they've got lots of it. But they wouldn't, so I stopped doing it."

On another occasion he suggested to a Vail lawyer prominent in the local minor-hockey program that, for a fraction of the typical lawyer's hourly fee, he would coach the boys in proper hockey techniques, make winners of them as he had done with the boys at New Trier West. "I never heard from the guy," laughs Eric.

Vail gets an astounding thirty feet of snow a year, and in some years as much as forty feet. The first serious snowfalls come in early November, and by the end of the month, Eric is spending as many as thirty hours a week on the mountain. "Early in the season I teach three or four week-long classes," he says. "Then I have my own clientele, often people who've skied with me before, mid-level skiers who don't so much want help as they want a kind of athletic confidant, a decent skier with whom they can share their experiences on the mountain and perhaps move into some new territory where they're not quite sure of themselves. It's pretty lighthearted, a lot of fun. And I'm connecting with them in a nice way, at times a very immediate way, because one of the things I have to help them face is their physical fear. I try to show them ways of dealing with it and still take some risk. I'm on a pretty intimate level with these people right away. A lot of them don't even know I was in the NHL for twenty-one years. And that's good, because my old life is a distraction. They just see an older guy who tends to go for it, and I tend to pull them along. It's not the greatest job in terms of saving the world or creating anything, but I'm not doing anybody any harm, and I guess I help people live in the moment and forget their problems."

Eric's best days on the slopes are those in which he can cut loose, "re-create" himself, as he puts it, sometimes with his son, sometimes with an adventurous client. Sometimes by himself. "On a good powder day," he says, "you give yourself up to the motion and speed; and for that brief time on the mountain you're in the wonderful state of being free of your own mortality."

In lesser moments, Eric admits to being increasingly aware of his mortality. "I think about it a lot," he says. "I feel I have to if I'm going to come to terms with it."

He is reminded of it by, among other things, the arthritis in his back and limbs. "I live a lot with Advil," he says. "I can't bend my wrist because the cartilage is all worn out from decades of handling the puck. The knees are sore. The joints work, but they ache. I've gotta stay active, or I'm afraid everything'll seize up."

During the summer, Eric golfs, hikes, and fishes. One summer, he skied in Australia. Since moving to Colorado, he has augmented his winter income with a variety of summer jobs that include his two sessions in the Arctic during the early eighties and his time in Texas applying decals to trucks. He played the role of a coach in a hockey film called *Youngblood.*

Recently, Eric worked as a carpenter's assistant for his friend Kevin Cooke, in whose home he lives. "I hated it," he says. "I only did it because he's my friend and because he asked me to. Half days for a couple of months, that was it."

In Eric's domain, play has always been a far more important consideration than work. And he has well-developed thoughts on the subject, many of them formulated more than a decade ago, when he was invited to the University of Guelph for a term, to lecture on the psychology, philosophy, and sociology of play. "What a lot of people don't seem to realize," he says, "is that play—and by extension finding new forms of play—is almost as important for adults as for kids. Higher animals and human beings really can't live without it. If we could renew and reinvent ourselves through our work, that'd be terrific. But most people can't, because most work is more about conformity, obeying the law, coloring within the lines, than using the imagination. Too many forms of kids' play these days fall into that category, too—too much of it is overly structured. I'm told the outdoor rinks are empty. . . . I've been lucky, or at least persistent; for the most part, I've been able to 'play' at making a living, as I do when I ski."

The last time Eric played hockey was in 1993, in a tournament of NHL old-timers, staged in the Canadian Maritimes. "There were five of us over fifty," he says (Eric was over

> **"I guess it'd be nice to be recognized by my peers, but it's so far removed from my life now, it doesn't make much difference; I don't really give a damn."**

sixty): "Billy Harris, Alex Delvecchio, myself, and a couple of guys from the Bruins. That's where I realized it was completely and utterly over for me. I really didn't belong."

It can't be said, however, that "it is completely and utterly over" for Eric's fans. Every year for the past two decades, a long-suffering follower of the Blackhawks, a Chicago resident, has petitioned the Hockey Hall of Fame in Toronto, pleading the case not only for Eric's unique talents but for his nomination and election to hockey's permanent shrine.

The petitioning is almost certainly in vain. Hanford Woods described Eric's career as "a minor legend of uncelebrated works." And minor it may be. But it is a legend nonetheless—one far more resonant than those of many of the game's Paul Bunyans.

"I've heard about the petitions," smiles Eric. "Apparently I was nominated one time but didn't get in. I guess it'd be nice to be recognized by my peers, but it's so far removed from my life now, it doesn't make much difference; I don't really give a damn."

As Eric and I walked through Vail, on the last night of my visit, he said: "I don't think many people would term my life a success—no wife, no money; I don't own or run anything. I could have handled my money and my personal situation a little better. But, ya know, I've made the choices I wanted to make. It's cost me, sure, but it's also allowed me to go in search of meaningful things. I'm still trying to discover who I am,

WHEN THE FINAL BUZZER SOUNDS

why I'm doing what I'm doing. I seem to be following some inner voice."

As for the future, Eric is planning "a low-key, contemplative life," with lots of reading. "I hope to stay healthy," he says.

He also plans to spend a summer or two in Alaska. "I was up there a couple of years ago," he says, "and I had a very strong feeling of subliminal connection to the place. And I like northern British Columbia. I'd like to float some of the great rivers that are up there. If I can't get anybody to go with me, I'll go alone."

Some three decades ago, during the last days of his career with the Blackhawks, Eric described to a writer how one day he had been driving along the shore of Lake Michigan in Chicago when he spotted a vast expanse of natural ice. "It was a clear, crisp afternoon," he said. "And damnit if I didn't pull over and put on my skates. I carry a pair in the car. I took off my camel-hair coat; I was just in a suit jacket; nobody was there. The wind was blowing from the north. With the wind behind you, you can wheel and dive and turn; you can lay yourself into impossible angles that you never could walking or running. You lay yourself at a forty-five-degree angle, your elbow virtually touching the ice as you're in a turn. I flew. I was free as a bird. Really happy. That goes back to when I was a kid. You're breaking the bounds of gravity. I have a feeling that's the innate desire of man."

It is a feeling that dies hard. And, at times, lives hard. "Now I satisfy it mostly on skis," says Eric.

But on the off-chance that ice and wind and innate desire should ever reconvene in quite the way they did that day in Chicago, Eric will, like the Boy Scouts, be prepared. For in the small back seat of his pick-up, he carries a pair of aging skates.

"Oh, those," he says when asked about them. "They're always there. You never know . . ."

He stops short of finishing the thought, but the gist of the message is clear.

You never know when you might feel an urge to break the bounds of gravity.

*   *   *   *   *

Epilogue

During the months that followed the writing of this profile, Eric broke not just the bounds of gravity, with his continued skiing, but the (relative) bounds of poverty, when the NHL pension settlement put nearly two hundred thousand dollars in his bank account.

Today, he is as much a part of the Vail ski scene as ever, getting out into fresh powder as often as possible, taking to the back country on occasion, and continuing to hire out as a private guide for affluent skiers from across North America. He has also become an occasional correspondent to a variety of skiing magazines, at times a feature subject, as well as a kind of private assessment bureau for everything from goggles to skis to particular resorts and mountainsides.

He is as plainspoken as ever . . . and as testy. When a pair of wealthy idlers hired him, sight unseen, for a day of skiing last winter, they complained to the resort management after meeting him that they didn't want "some old guy" leading them around. "The assumption was that, because I have grey hair, I wouldn't be able to do much for them," said Eric. "But the management sided with me, and I deliberately kicked the shit out of them all day. They couldn't even come close to keeping up."

Eric's democratic spirit is equally unblunted, especially where the decidedly advantaged are concerned. "Even the rich," he said recently, "are usually pretty decent people. It's just that the economic and social margin-dwellers tend to be more interesting."

Eric used some of his pension windfall to fund his planned canoe adventures on the rivers of Alaska and northern British Columbia. Last summer he spent six weeks in the wilderness with people he describes as "old wilderness friends."

"I enjoy the company," he said. "On the other hand I can be just about as happy on my own."

He remains as remote as ever from his past as an NHL hockey player but is reminded of it occasionally by a journalist's question, or by the stiffness in his joints . . . or the awareness, say, that Studs Terkel's famous essay about him has found its way onto the English syllabus at Missouri Western State College.

Eric still carries his skates in his vehicle and is still an extreme long-shot for induction into the Hockey Hall of Fame.

"It'd be nice to think I'm a little closer to figuring out some things about my life," he reflected recently. "Like who I am—and why. But probably I'm not. I've certainly learned what I can—as much by doing as by thinking and reading. It's important to me that I've lived as I want to live. And maybe that's enough—to just go, to live now, and to make meaning of that. That's why I keep skiing and canoeing—because they transcend the bullshit; they're beyond the trap.

"Or at least help you forget the trap exists."

9

Maurice Richard

In the Mood

(Editor's note: On May 27, 2000, while this book was being assembled for publication, Maurice Richard passed away in Montreal. Except for the epilogue at the end of the chapter, the text remains unaltered.)

Some facts about the Rocket:

■ He has a recurring dream that, after nearly forty years of retirement, he has renewed his contract with the Canadiens and has returned to play in the NHL. His opponents are contemporary players such as Jarimir Jagr, Eric Lindros, and Mark Messier. He can still maneuver. He can still put the puck in the net. He re-establishes all his old records.

■ He rises daily at 7:30 or 8:00 A.M. and, though he is not a heavy drinker, begins the day with two ounces of Dekuyper's gin, mixed with grapefruit juice and Vichy water. He sips it as he reads the newspaper.

■ He does not enjoy reading about himself—has never looked closely at the encyclopedic scrapbooks his wife Lucille kept on him for nearly half a century.

■ Despite having spent months cooperating on the writing of his biography, *L'Idol d'un Peuple*, published in 1976, his sole payment for his time and the rights to his story was one free copy of the book.

■ Every year, he gives away approximately twenty thousand photos of himself, each one autographed. Some are supplied to him by Grecian Formula hair coloring for men, which for years he used and endorsed, some by Molson Breweries, for whom he does public relations work, and some by S. Albert Fuels in Montreal, which he has represented since his playing days. He insists that he was never a good hockey player, that he was just a guy who worked hard at the game he loved.

*　　*　　*　　*　　*

It happened at the Montreal Forum during the seventh game of the 1952 semifinals between the Canadiens and the Boston Bruins. The Rocket was given a savage bodycheck by Boston defenseman Leo Labine and for several minutes lay on the ice unconscious, blood pouring from a bone-deep wound in his forehead. There was fear that his neck had been broken, and it was some time before he was removed from the ice and his forehead stitched shut.

During the third period of the game, still dizzy and barely able to stand, the Rocket insisted on returning to the Canadiens' bench. There he sat gazing silently across the ice and occasionally up at the clock. He inquired twice about the time remaining in the game, and when his teammate Elmer Lach told him four minutes, he turned to his coach Dick Irvin and told him he was ready to play. Irvin hesitated briefly, perhaps pondering consequences, and sent his injured star over the boards. The score was tied 1–1.

What followed was a now-legendary eruption of strength, talent, and obsessive will. The Rocket picked up the puck in his own end of the rink and headed up ice in a kind of personal variation on the heat-seeking missile—past the Bruins' forechecking wingers, past their centerman, around one of their defensemen, and deep into the right-side corner of the rink. Still in manic mode, he surged out toward the front of the net, eluding Boston's other defenseman and coming into the range of goaltender Sugar Jim Henry. In the words of the late sports writer Andy O'Brien, "There was a flurry of sticks, Henry dove, Richard pulled the puck back and blasted the netting."

There is a somewhat gothic photo of the Rocket shaking hands with Sugar Jim following the game. The Rocket is staring as if out of a coma at the smaller goalie. His forehead is bandaged; blood still streams down his face. Sugar Jim is half bowed as if to say: "You win, Mr. Richard, you win."

When Canadiens' president Senator Donat Raymond entered the team dressing room and shook hands with the Rocket after the game, the famous right-winger began to sob, then went into fitful convulsions that were only stilled when the team doctor injected him with a sedative. In the course of his long rush up the ice, he had had several opportunities to pass the puck; and it was not known until later that he had held onto it only because his vision had been too blurry to pick out a teammate to whom he could pass.

Maurice Richard is thought by many to be the most spirited professional that hockey has ever known—and the game's finest goal scorer. In an era when scoring twenty goals was considered a mark of excellence, he several times scored more than twice that many and, once, during the 1944–45 season, scored fifty goals in fifty games, a record that stood for thirty-seven years. But it wasn't just the number of goals that the Rocket scored; it was the way he scored them. Hall of Fame goaltender Frank Brimsek once said, "He could shoot from any angle. You could play him for a shot to the upper corner and he'd wheel around and fire a backhander to the near, lower part of the net." Another Hall of Fame goaltender, Glen Hall, said of the Rocket, "When he skated in on the net, his eyes would shine like a pair of searchlights. It was awesome to see him coming at you."

To be sure, it was the Rocket's eyes that signaled the spirit within. Even in publicity shots his eyes revealed an intense inner passion—"the Rocket's Red Glare," it has been called. During the early 1950s, American novelist William Faulkner, on a special assignment for *Sports Illustrated* magazine, went to Madison Square Garden to watch a game between the New York Rangers and the Canadiens. A short time later, he wrote that one player, Richard, had stood out beyond the others with a "passionate, glittering, fatal, alien quality of snakes."

*   *   *   *   *

"No doubt, I was a fiery hockey player," the Rocket submits today. "I'm still fiery when I play sports. Golf, for instance. I used to be pretty good,

"I never mellowed, even in the end."

but now I hate playing because I don't play enough to stay in practice, and I get mad when I make bad shots. Same in tennis—I hate to lose. I want to win. Even when I go fishing I like to catch more fish than anybody else. I don't get mad if I don't—not anymore—I just like to be on top. It comes naturally to me."

During his playing days, the Rocket's intensity frequently got him into more trouble than he could comfortably bail himself out of. "One night when we were playing Detroit I got into an argument with Ted Lindsay," he says. "We started swinging at one another, then Sid Abel came in, and I fought him, too. I tried to get up and fight again, and Gordie Howe started swinging at me. I took a good beating there."

The Rocket readily acknowledges that his temper was "too fast," that he did not have the necessary self-control to turn his back on provocation. "If I took a bad bodycheck, I had to retaliate, had to go after the guy right away—I never waited so much as a minute. And I never mellowed, even in the end."

The Rocket has not fully mellowed to this day. "When I go to a game now, I don't get excited unless it gets rough. I like the big bodychecks. When I see a dirty check against one of the Canadiens I wish I could be out there, especially if somebody I know well gets hit. . . . One night years ago a Maple Leaf defenseman, Kent Douglas, hit Bobby Rousseau over the head with his stick. I was sitting just above the passageway the players go through on their way to the dressing room at the Forum. When Douglas passed underneath I tried to hit him on the head with my fist. But I missed him."

It is a conspicuous paradox of the Rocket's genius that his worst sins and greatest achievements as a hockey player arose out of the same volcanic intensity at the core of his personality. When he talks about that intensity, however, it's as if he were speaking not so much of an internal force as of a powerful and unpredictable foreign energy that regularly settled on him for better or worse. "When it was going in my favor I was on top of the world! I was a winner!" he says. "When it went in the other direction . . . well . . . let's say I did some bad things. It hurt my career."

The career damage was never greater than in 1956 when, in a late-season game against the Bruins, the Rocket committed the ultimate hockey malfeasance of striking an official. The incident began when Bruin defenseman Hal Layco raised his stick and cut the Rocket over the eye. "I went after him, took a swing at him, then one of the linesmen grabbed me from behind and held me so I couldn't move." For several seconds Layco rained knuckles on his defenseless opponent's shoulders and skull. "I turned my head twice and told the linesman to let go of me, so I'd have a chance. The third time I turned, I took a poke at him. I knew I was in trouble."

Two days later, the president of the NHL, Clarence Campbell, countered with one of the severest punishments ever meted out by a league executive: suspension for the remainder of the season and for the entire postseason playoffs. The Canadiens were as good as finished. "They could have suspended me for ten, fifteen games the next season. I would have accepted that. But not the playoffs! We were in first place! Oh, I was mad."

Canadiens supporters were equally incensed by Campbell's decree. When the team returned to the Montreal Forum for its final game of the season, Campbell, who regularly attended the Canadiens' games, entered the arena and took his seat, ignoring a sustained assault of insults, boos, and projectiles. He had been warned by both the police and the mayor not to attend the game. At the end of the first period, with Detroit leading 3–0, a fan threw a smoke bomb that landed within yards of Campbell's feet. The game was canceled immediately and awarded to Detroit.

"I wasn't sitting with Maurice," recalled the Rocket's wife, Lucille, when I chatted with her a year or so before her death in 1995. "I was behind the other team's bench, where I'd been sitting every game for fifteen years. Maurice was beside the goal judge, right near Mr. Campbell.

"When they threw the bomb, Maurice went into [physiotherapist] Bill Head's room. A minute later, someone came up to me and said, 'Come, Lucille—join Maurice!' Clarence Campbell came in there, too. We stayed a good hour until things had calmed down."

As the well-guarded threesome huddled in the bowels of the Forum, thousands of angry fans raged down St. Catherines Street, throwing rocks, breaking store windows, creating terrible chaos, and destroying whatever lay in their path.

"We didn't win the Stanley Cup that year, and I didn't get my play-off money," says the Rocket. "But during my suspension I got so many invitations to attend banquets, referee games, and so on, I ended up putting more money in the bank than I would have if I'd been in uniform. Back then I got paid $150, $200 for an appearance."

The Rocket is convinced that, to this day, many people have not forgiven him for his intense, confrontational style of play. "Even people in Quebec!" he exclaims. "When I take the Metro to the Forum, there's always somebody staring at me. I say 'Hello!' and if they don't answer, I say, 'Hello, sir! I said hello to you!' Maybe they're just shy, but maybe they don't like me from my hockey days—how do I know? I'm very sensitive about it. If somebody writes something bad about me, it gets me right in the heart. And I'll tell you, a lot of writers have said terrible things. It's been hard on Lucille and the kids over the years."

Whatever discomfort the Rocket feels in looking back is by no means limited to the barbs and accusations of others. Twenty-nine years after his retirement, he is still bothered by what he has always seen as deficiencies in his style of play. For a man of extreme pride, the great goal-scorer is remarkably self-effacing about his talents. "Everybody always wanted to compare me to Gordie Howe," he explains, "but I was never a natural hockey player like Gordie. He was stronger, more fluid, better with the puck. I used to say to him, 'Gordie, you're much better than I am, but you don't have the drive to win games like I do.' I always had a big heart for scoring—oh, I loved scoring goals. But I had to work hard for them. I wasn't a good skater. I played right wing for one reason only—because I could turn better from the right, and it was easier for me to cut to the net from that side. A really good player can cut from both sides. See, I shoot from the left side; I should have played the left wing instead of the right, but I wasn't any good over there. Even from the right, I could usually only get around the defenseman by holding his arm or body to keep him away from me . . . I was just a guy who tried hard—all the time."

Game films from his career—even films in which he was clearly the star of the show—do little to raise the Rocket's opinion of his game.

"When I see myself, I'd love to be able to say, 'Gee, I looked nice when I skated or scored!' But I honestly can't say it; I never did like my style. The one thing I could do was put the puck in the net. I was the best scorer, not the best player."

Asked who he considered better, the Rocket names several of his former teammates, none of whom had nearly his impact on the game. For one, he considers his brother Henri

"Most players in my day made the same play every time. So the goalies knew what to expect. I tried to keep them guessing."

a more accomplished all-around player than himself. "I played with Henri and Dickie Moore my last five years with the Canadiens—both of them were better than I was. Henri could make a beautiful pass. It made hockey a pleasure."

The Rocket's love of scoring was surpassed only by his love of scoring in the third period when a game was on the line. "My secret was that I always tried to keep enough strength for the end of the game. Conserve my energy. Sometimes you work too hard at the beginning, and at the end you're too tired; you don't feel like doing anything. Scoring in the first period was okay, but I preferred to score game winners."

The Rocket can name only one other tactical "secret" of his success: "When I had a breakaway I never used a shot or move that I'd used before. Always showed something different. Shot a little different. Faked a little different. Most players in my day made the same play every time. So the goalies knew what to expect. I tried to keep them guessing."

*   *   *   *   *

More than half a decade has passed since I spent an evening with the Richards' in their limestone bungalow in north Montreal—a home to which they moved shortly before the "Richard Riot" of 1956, and in which the Rocket lives today. Immediately across the street flows La Riviere des Prairies, the "back river" as Maurice calls it, the north boundary of Montreal Island. Maurice knows the river well, having swum and fished in it as a boy. "Every morning I used to get up early, and, before I went to school, I'd go and set a line. I'd catch eels, suckers, pickerel—I'd lift the line before I went home at night. My mother liked that."

The interior of the seventy-five-year-old home is a richly endowed museum—verging on a temple—to the Rocket's career. It houses a dozen or more paintings of him in uniform—some exact likenesses, some folky and naive. It also houses trophies and knick-knacks and mementos—on the mantel, on shelves, in a display case in the basement rec room. Some of the trophies go back to the Rocket's teenage days; others are the fanciful inventions of local clubs and charity organizations (to "Hockey's Man of the Age," to "Le Champion d'Histoire d'Hockey"). Others still are esteemed awards such as the Lou Marsh Trophy, presented to the Rocket in 1957 when he was chosen Canada's Athlete of the Year. In the living room, behind the Rocket's television chair, stands a six-foot marble goddess, a lamp, presented to him in 1954 by L'Ordre des Fils d'Italie du Canada. By another chair stands a lamp made of wrought iron and featuring tiny iron hockey sticks and an iron "500" welded into its shade. The unusual creation is a sentimental favorite of the Rocket's, handmade for him after his five hundredth goal by the students of the technical high school where he attended classes as a teenager. An enormous family photo hangs above the fireplace—Maurice, Lucille, their seven children, and seven grandchildren.

Lucille was old-fashioned in that she devoted her life to raising her family and to the support of her husband's career. During the Rocket's eighteen years with the Canadiens, she missed just two of his nearly six hundred home games at the Montreal Forum. Even her summer holidays were spent accompanying him to the outposts of rural Quebec where, night after night during the 1950s, he refereed professional wrestling matches, attracting more applause and attention than the wrestlers themselves.

"I went along because it gave me time with Maurice," she once said.

The Rocket says, "Everybody used to think Lucille was alone a lot during my career. But, really, I was away more after I retired than when I was playing. I refereed old-timers games all over the country—dozens of them. During my playing days, I'd go to practice in the morning, and I'd be away on the weekends. But overall I was probably at home more than if I'd been working in a plant or for a company."

Lucille's immense contribution to the Rocket's career began during the 1930s when, as a teenager, she was heavily and happily involved in the typically male domain of competitive hockey. "My brother ran a hockey team," she told me. "Maurice played for him. I never missed a game."

Although Lucille's brother was nominally in charge of the team, it was Lucille's mother who more often than not ran the show. "She was always telling the players what to do," recalls the Rocket, "phoning them up to make sure they were out for games and practice, that sort of thing."

Lucille, too, did her share of phoning and enterprising. "She used to have the players to their house after the games," says the Rocket. "We'd have soft drinks, chips, peanuts. She'd have her girlfriends over, and we used to dance until four or five in the morning. She taught me the tango—we were always playing 'In the Mood.'"

At the time, Maurice was suiting up not just for Lucille's brother's team but for four or five other Montreal hockey clubs—so many that, in order to maintain his eligibility on certain rosters, he had to disguise his identity. "He was Maurice Richard on some teams," Lucille said, "Maurice Rochon on others. Oh, he was good. Everybody wanted him. He used to score six, seven goals a game."

Even so, neither Lucille nor Maurice ever imagined that he would one day play professional hockey, much less become the sport's biggest attraction. "My Junior team was the Verdun Maple Leafs, sponsored by the Canadiens," says the Rocket. "It was exciting being part of the organization, but back then the NHL was just a dream. No one I knew ever got close."

When the Rocket graduated from Junior hockey, he played eleven games for the Canadiens' Senior A team, then broke his ankle, snuffing any last hope he might have had for a pro career. Or so it seemed.

"While he was hurt he came to stay at our place for a few days," Lucille recalled. "He used to stay there because he and my brother were such close friends. One day he said to my mother, 'I'm lonesome this afternoon—I'd like to see a movie. Can I take Lucille?' I loved movies, so I went with him. We saw *Garden of Allah* at the Stella Theater—Charles Boyer and Marlene Dietrich. It was our first date. I was sixteen."

The following year, Lucille and Maurice were engaged, and a year after that they were married. The same year, 1942, Maurice made his debut with the Montreal Canadiens. He says, "I'd followed them on radio since I was twelve or thirteen—Howie Morenz, Aurel Joliat, Pep Lepin, Toe Blake. But as a kid I could never go to the Forum—that was for people with money."

As rare as it might seem for a boy who had grown up in Montreal and had played four years in the Canadiens' organization, the Rocket had never seen the team play until he skated onto the ice in the club's famous red, white, and blue jersey.

It was during his second year with Les Glorieux that the young star earned the monicker that would become the most famous in the history of the sport. "One of our lines back then was Ray Getliffe, Murph Chamberlain, and Phil Watson," he recalls. "I scored so many goals against them in training camp that year that one of them started calling me 'Rocket'; then they all did. The press picked it up, and that was that."

By the mid-1950s the name was known wherever hockey was played throughout the world. It's fame was strikingly revealed when the Rocket attended the 1957 world hockey championship in Prague, Czechoslovakia. At the time, Czechoslovakian newspapers carried no news of the NHL, and television was practically nonexistent in the country. Yet when Maurice entered the Prague arena for the tournament's first game, some twenty thousand fans rose to their feet and, as if greeting a national hero, began screaming, *"Rock-et . . . Rock-et . . . Rock-et!"*

The Rocket speculates that the Czechs knew about him through occasional newsreels that might have reached the country. Certainly the newsreels of 1957 were replete with his achievements; it was earlier that year that he scored his five hundredth big-league goal, a nearly unaccountable total in the defense-minded NHL of the day.

"I always enjoyed that kind of attention; I liked the limelight," declares the Rocket without a trace of self-consciousness. "I liked meeting people and signing autographs. I often say today that if a time comes when nobody recognizes me, I won't go out anymore. But everywhere I go they still know me, even the kids eight, nine, ten years old. It surprises me. I quit twenty-nine years ago. But they've read the stories, seen the books, seen the films. In fact, they come to me for autographs more than

"A lot of the things that happened to me in hockey I don't even remember. I don't know how my goals went in unless I watch them on film."

to the guys who quit ten years ago. Even the press still talks about me. Every time a record is broken, they talk about the Rocket. It makes me happy. Hockey is my life—always will be."

For a man who has enjoyed his fame so thoroughly, the Rocket's recollections of the events and achievements that inspired that fame are at times curiously minimal, if not absent altogether. "Some people like to tell stories, but I'm not one of them," he says with a shrug. "A lot of the things that happened to me in hockey I don't even remember. I don't know how my goals went in unless I watch them on film."

His protestations notwithstanding, the Rocket creates the impression that he has not so much forgotten his stories as simply never formulated them in any tellable way. He never had to; his stories were always told for him—by fans, by television announcers, by writers. It was enough for the Rocket to live the stories. It was up to others to put them into words.

When the recollections are available to him, their focus is often not quite what you might expect. Asked, for instance, to name his finest memory of eighteen years with the Canadiens, the Rocket settles not on a Stanley Cup victory or an epochal goal but on a regular-season game during the early 1950s when he scored five goals against the Detroit Red Wings (it was by no means the only time he scored five goals in a game). And it is not so much the goals themselves that excite the Rocket's memory as the context in which they were scored. This time there is a story. "The night before, Lucille and the kids and I had moved from Desirables to Papineau Street. It took us most of the night, and once we got there we just put mattresses on the floor and dropped. I hardly got any sleep at all—an hour or two. When I went to the team meeting that morning, I told the coach, Dick Irvin, that I didn't think I could play—too tired. I said, 'Use somebody else.' He used me anyway, and every puck I shot that night went in. Five goals, three assists."

The Rocket's most disquieting recollections are of the months immediately before and after his retirement in 1960. On the surface the retirement was a simple and understandable development. "When I turned pro in 1942," says the Rocket, "I weighed 160 pounds. But every season I put on two, three pounds, so that by 1960 my playing weight was about 210. It affected my play. My reflexes weren't the same—too slow. I couldn't get out of the way of the bodychecks anymore. During each of my last three seasons, I had bad injuries. In 1957, I had a cut tendon in the back of my ankle—I missed twenty-five games. The next year I had a broken cheekbone, the next a broken ankle. I hadn't had a serious injury in fourteen years until then. . . . Two or three times during my last five years I went on diets—salad, vegetables, not too much dessert, not too many beers. And I lost eleven, twelve, thirteen pounds. But then I always ended up feeling worse than when I started. Too weak. No strength. So I'd let my weight rise again, even though I knew I was too heavy. The problem was that I always tried to lose weight quickly just before the season. I should have lost it over two or three months during the summers. Then I would have had time to build my strength at a lower weight. But I used to go out too much in the summertime—I had all kinds of invitations to dinners, barbecues, cocktail parties. And I loved eating."

During the summer of 1960, Frank Selke, Sr., then general manager of the Canadiens, told the Rocket that if he were willing to retire he would be given a job in public relations with the team and would be paid his regular salary for three years. "He told me to think about it," says the Rocket, "and I thought about it all summer. Talked to my wife, talked to my kids. I knew that after all my injuries I'd have to lose at least twenty to twenty-five pounds to play again. Going to training camp at 210 was no good. But I went at that weight anyway, and I knew after a week that I couldn't keep going. My kids didn't want me to quit, but Lucille wouldn't say one way or the other."

In early September of that year, a few weeks before the start of the season, the Rocket deserted the Canadiens' training camp and made a public announcement that his playing career was over.

It is clear, however, that the Rocket was never entirely at peace with the decision. "I wasn't ready to retire in 1960," he reveals. "I would have loved to keep going and probably should have tried harder."

There is a suggestion that Mr. Selke's offer of a job may have been accompanied by a subtle twist of the arm—in fact, may have been more along the lines of an offer that his onetime star couldn't refuse. But on this issue, the occasionally outspoken Rocket is an almost perfect diplomat—perhaps out of self-preservation. He has seen it before, one day's unconsidered comment reincarnated as the next day's hysterical newspaper story. After nearly thirty years of retirement, the Rocket's remarks still have headline potential in Montreal's racier tabloids. So he protects himself and those he chooses to protect. Asked point blank if he feels Frank Selke, Sr., persuaded him unfairly into retirement, he smiles faintly and says, "I could tell you what Mr. Selke said or thought—he's dead now—but his son is still alive. All I'll say is that I think I could have played two or three more years."

Whatever the case, when the Rocket signed his retirement papers he signed away his right to play for any other NHL team, perpetuating a form of indenture with which he had grown severely disenchanted during the final years of his career. "We were like slaves," he says, "both to our team and to the league. In Montreal, we used to ask for a $2,000 raise every year we won the Stanley Cup. They'd give us half—$1,000. If we didn't like what we got, there was nothing we could do, nowhere we could go. It was either sign or go home. Today, the players have more freedom. Not that I wanted to play anywhere else than Montreal— I just feel they should have paid us properly. I heard a rumor in the fifties that Connie Smythe in Toronto was willing to buy me from the Canadiens for $100,000 and pay me $100,000 a year, but I don't have proof of that."

In 1967, seven years after his retirement, the Rocket was asked by Sid Solomon, owner of the St. Louis Blues, an expansion team, to return to the NHL as a part-time player. It was assumed that his presence alone would be motivational to the talent-thin Blues. "But I didn't feel like it. I wasn't in good shape. I didn't want to make a fool of myself playing with the pros. Doug Harvey went to St. Louis, but he was a different kind of player than I was—slow motion. Everything was easy for him. My game was a lot faster."

The Rocket's term as a public relations representative for the Canadiens was a four-year exercise in frustration. "I was always thinking that I could still be playing," he admits. "I wanted to be on the ice. Instead, I was spending all my time at banquets, carnivals, hockey tournaments, charity functions, that sort of thing," says the Rocket. "It went on year-round—six or seven days a week. All over Canada. Sometimes in the States, too. I was booked solid two or three months in advance. I had no time at all for myself or for Lucille and the kids. It was way too much."

Two years passed before the Rocket protested openly to Frank Selke, Sr., making it clear that he needed a day or two to himself from time to time. Selke agreed to a lighter schedule and promised not to lower the Rocket's salary. A year later, however, for no stated reason, his pay was summarily chopped in half. "I continued on through that year," says the Rocket, "but I didn't do nearly as much. Then I quit altogether. I was upset. I told Selke, too. I said, 'Keep the job for yourself.' And I went home. It was the happiest moment of my whole retirement—telling them I wanted to be free to do what I wanted."

The Rocket takes pains to point out that, after years of coolness between himself and the Canadiens, he is again on good terms with the organization—in fact, he has been for some time. The evidence is in a long-term promotional contract he holds with the team's owner, Molson Breweries, which he has represented since 1981. "I do what I can for them," he says, "and they treat me very well." It is all but forgotten that, while playing for the Molson-owned club during the 1950s, the Rocket did promotional work for his employer's arch rival, Dow Breweries. "I was with them for ten years," he says. "Molson's never said a thing. They were always good that way. Even when I spoke out against them, they said nothing. Same with the club—I often criticized them, certain players or the coach. I had a newspaper column in *Dimanche Matin* back then; I used to write about them. They never commented. Maybe they thought my criticism was fair. I thought it was fair."

Within months of leaving his public relations job with the Canadiens in 1964, the Rocket bought a run-down tavern on Montreal's St. Laurent Boulevard, refurbished it, and named it Tavern Number Nine, in honor of his old number. "I had a big sign outside saying '544 goals!' I'd go to the place every day for three or four hours. What I didn't like was that once I got in there I could never get out. There was always somebody asking me to sit at a table and drink beer and talk hockey. Besides, I used to get thieves in there, Mafia types. It wasn't that they gave me a hard time—in fact, they helped me at times; there was always somebody trying to collect 'protection,' and these guys would tell me, 'Don't pay anybody anything; don't worry about it.' Even so, I didn't care to have them around."

The Rocket sold the tavern after three years, for twice what he'd paid for it. Within months, he turned his attention (and his cash) to an old love, fishing, sinking his profits from the tavern into the purchase of General Fishing Lines, a small company, which he operated out of his home for twenty-three years. He says, "I used to buy line from a big company in the U.S.—fly line, monofilament, different test weights—and package it under my own trademark, 'Clipper.' I'd travel the province, distributing it to sporting goods stores. But I had to quit in 1988, because all the big companies were undercutting my prices. With the cost of travel, it was too hard to compete."

There is something touching, almost poignant, about the basement room in the Richard home where, on hundreds of winter nights during the 1970s and '80s, the Rocket would sit gluing metallic labels onto spools of fish line and stacking them in cupboards for the spring and summer. His plywood work table still occupies the middle of the floor, and the shelves are still stocked with a varied inventory of spinning line that will never be sold. Each spool bears a circular label that features a stylized trout and a microscopic rendering of the famous signature, 'Maurice Richard.'

Among the Rocket's other ventures of the 1960s and 1970s were a variety of advertising contracts for products as varied as Chrysler cars, Vitalis hair tonic, and Salada tea. None of his endorsements, however, had as much exposure or staying power as his good-humored television advertisements for Grecian Formula hair dye. The Rocket used the product

"I don't have to work. I do it because I like it."

before he began endorsing it and used it well into the 1990s. "Not the liquid but the cream," he emphasizes, "and always with a little water. But not too much water, or the grey wouldn't disappear. When I started using it, it didn't work, because I was swimming in my pool every day. But when the summer was over, and I stopped swimming, I saw a big change. . . . Even today, kids all over the country tease me about the ad: 'The wife likes it!' 'Two minutes for looking so good!'"

The Rocket did the ads for a dozen years, earning as much as $14,000 a year from them, plus residuals. "So they must have worked," he says. He has also done more than forty years of promotional work for S. Albert Fuels in Montreal, and since his playing days has written a weekly newspaper column. "I started with *Dimanche Matin*," he says. "They helped me do the writing. But they went out of business during the 1980s, so now I'm with *La Presse*. I take notes during the week on whatever I'm thinking about—baseball, hockey, any sport at all—and I do my column for Sunday."

By his own assessment, the Rocket has always been comfortable financially. "Only once did I lose money. I had a two-year contract to promote natural gas, and I took the money and invested it in a store that sold gas appliances and equipment. But the gas company was giving the same stuff away free, so we didn't sell much." Otherwise, the Rocket has put his money into bonds, certificates, blue-chip investments that pay steady dividends. "I don't have to work," he admits. "I do it because I like it."

Until the early 1990s, the Rocket especially enjoyed lacing on the blades and taking to the ice with a gang of former NHL stars for whom he would referee games. The drafty arenas and overheated dressing rooms of the old-timers circuit were a long way from the big time, and traveling by bus had its discomforts, but in his late sixties and early seventies, the Rocket asked no more from hockey. As it was, he was probably the only referee in the history of the game to get louder and longer applause than the players themselves. "I played myself till I was fifty-seven, fifty-eight," he says, "but I sometimes went too hard trying to check somebody, or I'd make too big an effort to put the puck in the net. I'd get dizzy. I didn't want to risk a heart attack, so I started refereeing. At the peak, I was reffing fifty, sixty games a year, sometimes six or seven nights in a row."

During the summer months, the Rocket does what he has always liked doing during the warm weather—fishing. "We have a place in St. Michel des Saints—a cabin in a fishing camp. We go up every summer. I go mostly for trout—sometimes walleye or salmon."

For years, when the Rocket went fishing, Lucille would make the rounds of her sons' and daughters' homes—a few days here, a few there. Or else her sons and daughters and their families would come home to her—especially in summer, to use the pool.

"And Lucille and I always did a lot of traveling together," says the Rocket. "Lucille loved it—especially Florida. We went every winter."

But despite Lucille's preferences for the Sunshine State, Florida wasn't always ideal for the Rocket. "There are a lot of Canadians down there," he says, "and they've always come up to me on the beach, always taking pictures, asking for autographs—one comes along, tells his friends, then they all come. When we'd go someplace to eat, we couldn't even get through our meal. I'm not saying I don't like the attention, but I like to eat, too."

As he and Lucille aged, the Rocket developed a preference for European vacations, on which he was less likely to be put upon by hockey fans. "Our nicest trip was to Italy in 1987," he says. "We started in Rome and went everywhere by car—Capri, the Adriatic, then to France, Nice, St. Tropez. On most of our trips to Europe we didn't even reserve hotels. We'd just stop where we liked. We felt free."

On the night of my visit with the Richards, Lucille reflected for a moment on her travels with the Rocket, then, as if some resonant chord had been touched within her, said, "We've had a very good life. We've been married forty-seven years. Not many couples are as happy as we've been." She looked at the Rocket and added, "Hockey has been good to us."

The Rocket declared that it could have been better.

"He was born thirty years too early," said Lucille. "But it was good anyway."

Again the Rocket declared that things weren't what they might have been—especially the money.

"Maurice made plenty," she said softly. "But then again, we needed it with seven kids. It cost a lot. Today, people have two kids, that's it. But we're happy with what we've got. Very happy."

"Yes, yes, we're very happy," nodded the Rocket, at which point he paused for a second and added perfunctorily, "I don't know what we'd do about it if we weren't."

*   *   *   *   *

Epilogue

In early 1995, Lucille Richard suffered a fatal relapse of the cancer that had plagued her for the better part of a decade (but had gone unacknowledged during my visit with the Richards at their home on "the back river").

In the wake of Lucille's death, the Rocket's own health declined; he lost weight, grew withdrawn—which many assumed was the result of emotional strain. "He could see Lucille's death coming," his friend and former teammate, Ken Reardon, said at the time, "but still it hit him hard."

The Rocket's physical lapse, however, was by no means entirely psychosomatic. During a Florida vacation in February 1998, he checked into a south Florida hospital with abdominal pain, was examined, and told he should return to Canada immediately. Forty-eight hours later, in Montreal, he was diagnosed with an inoperable tumor of the abdomen.

For several days, the news sparked foreboding stories in both the cultural and sports sections of North American newspapers: his condition was irreversible; he had been sent home to die. In rural Quebec a network of radio stations begged listeners to pray for the suffering hero, and for nearly a week, the obituary mill hummed in anticipation of the worst.

But on the night of Saturday, March 8, the media frenzy slowed when the Rocket appeared unexpectedly at the Molson Centre in Montreal for a game between the Canadiens and the Buffalo Sabres. He was frail and subdued, and he departed the arena after the first period. But he was on his feet—he was out and about and was clearly not at death's door.

During the weeks that followed, the Rocket endured powerful doses of chemotherapy (no one ever doubted his fortitude). His strength improved. He gained weight. He resumed driving and writing his weekly column for *Le Journal* in Montreal. He was seen in public. His cancer was under control.

But the hockey world had been alerted to the fragility of a man once considered all but invincible. And the following spring, acting on that alert, Ronald Cory, the outgoing president of the Canadiens, persuaded the NHL to pay timely tribute to the Rocket's accomplishments by creating the Maurice Richard Trophy, to be presented yearly to the league's leading goal scorer in regular season play.

In June 1999, the Rocket himself presented the award for the first time to Finnish-born sniper Teemu Selanne. Sports columnists seized the opportunity to enumerate Richard's own glories and passions.

Eight months later, at the 2000 All-Star celebrations in Toronto, the Rocket was feted among other aging stars who had played in the first All-Star game at Maple Leaf Gardens, in October 1947. On cue, his photo appeared on the front pages of newspapers across the country, and, again, sports writers were moved to elaborate on his legend. Canada Post issued a stamp bearing his likeness.

For the Rocket and his fans, however, no tribute would surpass that paid him at the closing ceremonies for the Montreal Forum, on March 11, 1996. As the Canadien captains of the past were introduced, each received a minute or more of appreciative applause. But when the Rocket's name was announced and the spotlight fell on him at center ice, the crowd responded not so much with applause as with a kind of tribal roar that evolved through several stages of volume and veneration to become after several minutes an unequivocal tide of affection that did not subside for nearly fifteen minutes as the Rocket stood weeping and waving—the entire scene captured live on national television.

In the media the next day, the Rocket was hailed as a political and cultural icon, a modern symbol of the French struggle against English domination in Canada, the latter embodied by the heavy-handed NHL administration of the Rocket's day. "He carried the flag for an entire population," wrote Montreal sports writer Red Fisher. "And that was pretty heavy."

But the more expansive the rhetoric, the less the Rocket seemed to believe it. Asked, days later, about his investiture in the cultural and political pantheon, he responded quietly, "I did what I did because I loved the game of hockey, I loved winning, and I loved scoring goals. They can say what they want about politics. For myself, I was just a hockey player . . . like the others, except I scored more goals, had a little more fire.

"When I crossed the blueline, believe me, I wasn't thinking about Quebec—I was thinking about putting the puck in the net."

In mid-May of 2000, the Rocket's illness was again news. His cancer had invaded his abdominal organs, and some reports, including one from his agent Jean Roy, placed him in the hospital in a coma. Other reports described him as being past the worst and again on the mend.

Then on Saturday, May 27, came the news—in reality, a flood of news from every media source—that the man whose rage had incited riots, whose skills and determination had inflamed an entire culture, had died at 5:40 in the afternoon in Montreal.

At first the Rocket's family was determined to forestall any excesses of public demonstration that might accompany his wake. The funeral, they said, would be quiet and dignified and would remain in their control. But within a day, they had succumbed to requests from the Canadiens that the fans have a last chance to pay their respects. So, for two days, the Rocket's body lay in state at the blue line of the Molson Centre as tens of thousands of mourners, including celebrities and government officials, filed past.

On Wednesday, May 31, the Rocket's funeral procession inched through the downtown streets past hundreds of thousand of fans, many of them weeping or waving Quebec flags. The state funeral, a lengthy and tearful tribute held in Notre Dame Cathedral in Old Montreal, was attended by professional hockey players from all over the world, as well as by dozens of politicians, celebrities, and public eminences. The funeral, one of the largest in Canadian history, was broadcast live on eleven Quebec television channels and was watched nationally on CBC and CTV by more than ten million viewers.

In all, it was a grand and impassioned farewell to the modest son of a Montreal machinist. In his closing remarks, Montreal's Archbishop, Jean-Claude Cardinal Turcotte, drew attention not only to the Rocket's humility but also to his love of fishing. The Rocket, he said, would be in good company in heaven, among the apostles whose fishing endeavors are noted in the Bible. He then wished the Rocket good luck in his transit, and good fishing in the hereafter.